Complete Boot Up

Complete Boot Up

The Daily Telegraph

EVERYTHING YOU NEED TO KNOW

TO GET THE BEST OUT OF YOUR PC

Rick Maybury

TEXERE

New York • London

Copyright © 2003 Rick Maybury

This edition published in 2003 by

TEXERE Publishing Limited
71–77 Leadenhall Street
London EC3A 3DE

Tel: +44 (0)20 7204 3644
Fax: +44 (0)20 7208 6701
www.etexere.co.uk

A subsidiary of

TEXERE LLC
55 East 52nd Street
New York, NY 10055

Tel: +1 (212) 317 5511
Fax: +1 (212) 317 5178
www.etexere.com

TEXERE books may be purchased for educational, business, or sales
promotional use. For more information please write to the Special
Markets Department at the TEXERE London address.

Designed and project managed by Macfarlane Production Services,
Markyate, Hertfordshire, England (e-mail: macfarl@aol.com).

A CIP catalogue record for this book is available from the British
Library.

ISBN 1-58799-160-8

Printed and bound in Great Britain by Mackays of Chatham plc,
Chatham, Kent.

This book is printed on paper responsibly manufactured from
sustainable forestry, in which at least two trees are planted for each
one used for paper production.

Thanks once again to Jane, Katie and Alex for their patience and help.

Contents

Introduction

It's easy to be intimidated by computers, after all, a personal computer or PC is probably the most technically sophisticated and complex device you will ever own or use but don't let that put you off. The computer industry has worked long and hard to make them easier to use and to a large extent they've succeeded – age, intelligence, race and physical ability are no impediments to using one – but ironically as personal computers have evolved they have actually become more impersonal.

One of the consequences of making computers 'user-friendly' has been to corral owners into narrower ways of thinking and working. This can be incredibly frustrating when, for example, you want to do something that you're fairly sure your PC is capable of but the instruction manuals and program Help files either treat you like an idiot or are completely impenetrable. This book aims to be an antidote to the computer industry's apparent intention simultaneously to dumb down and blind us with science, and hopefully help you to take control of your PC, rather than the other way around…

Complete Boot Up draws together articles from the popular weekly practical computing columns – 'Boot Camp' and 'Faqs! Facts! Fax' – published in *The Daily Telegraph* technology section since 1996, and extensively updated chapters from the first three highly successful books in the Boot Up series.

The book is divided into five self-contained parts and it covers a lot of ground, including buying your first PC, putting your word processor to good use, email and the Internet, digital cameras and scanners, upgrades and how to revive a dead PC but don't worry, computers are nowhere near as scary as they appear when you know something about what makes them tick, and for those of a curious disposition there's plenty of behind-the-scenes info, tips and tricks to try out.

The point is the more you know about what computers can do and how they do it the more you'll get out of owning one. *Complete Boot Up* is not aimed at any particular interest group or ability level, I hope that both

novices and old hands alike will find it useful and wherever possible it has
been written in more or less plain English. In fact the only things you will
need to get something out of this book are an open attitude to new
possibilities, a desire to make your computer do as it's told and when it
misbehaves – as it will – to have a go at diagnosing the fault, and possibly
even fixing it!

I should explain that this book is entirely devoted to computers using the
Microsoft Windows operating system, including the most recent XP
versions. This should not be regarded as an endorsement of Microsoft, or
indeed a criticism of any other type of computer, just recognition of the fact
that over 90% of the world's personal computers use Windows, and
nothing's perfect…

Part I

THE BASICS

CHAPTER 1 **Buying and getting to know your PC**

You've decided to buy a PC, but where do you start?
Let's begin with the basics and a few home truths...

Frustration is something PC owners quickly become accustomed to, and that's long before the inevitable software crashes or inexplicable error messages appear on the screen. Within weeks of buying a new PC you can be fairly sure you'll see the same, or a similarly specified, model selling for significantly less than you paid for it, and within a few years it will be practically worthless. The point is, there's never a right time to buy a PC; if you want one buy it now but resign yourself to the fact that it will be effectively obsolete before you get it home and out of the box.

That might sound a bit bleak, but it's not meant to be. The modern PC is an amazing bargain, how many other products double in performance and halve in price every two or three years? Even though most PCs are effectively outmoded before they reach the end of the production line, you can expect to get at least four or five years of service out of an up-to-date model; in any case most PCs can be upgraded to extend their lives and adapt to newly developed software or peripherals, so what should you be looking for?

For the sake of simplicity we'll be focusing on desktop computers using the Windows family of operating systems, currently used on over 90% of the world's PCs. There are alternative operating systems, including the Macintosh OS and Linux to name just two and there is much to commend them, but Windows PCs still represent the best value and provide the greatest flexibility for the vast majority of home and business users.

Buying a PC is actually very easy and these days your choice will be largely determined by what you intend to do with it. Broadly speaking the options are between a basic 'workstation', a general-purpose 'multimedia' model or high-end 'graphics and gaming' machines.

Workstation PCs are configured for straightforward tasks like word and number crunching (word processing, spreadsheets, accounts, etc.) and

Internet and network applications. They're usually quite cheap and fine for office work but for home use you'll want something with a bit more oomph. That's where the multimedia PC comes in, they have faster processors, more memory and lots more storage space for all of the documents, picture and music files and the thousand and one other things that will end up on your computer. High-end graphics machines are geared towards generating richly detailed still and video images and this depends on having the fastest processors, even more memory, lots of storage space and exotic video processing facilities that can be expensive but if you want to play the latest games or edit movies shot on a digital camcorder this is the kind of PC you should be aiming for.

PC performance, and hence the cost, is mostly determined by three components; they are the central processor unit (CPU), the amount of random access memory (RAM), and the size of the PC's hard disk drive (HDD).

The simplest and most consistent measurement of processor performance is speed or how quickly it carries out calculations and this is usually denoted in cycles per second or 'hertz'. However, since PCs carry out hundreds or even thousands of millions of calculations per second speed is measured in 'megahertz' or MHz and 'gigahertz' or GHz. (A gigahertz is a thousand megahertz, thus 1000MHz = 1GHz.)

There is constant competition between the leading chip manufacturers to produce the fastest and most powerful chips and until the late 1990s every new generation of processor chips spawned new software applications, designed to take advantage of the increased performance. However, the good news is that for the past few years developments in hardware have outpaced the software industry's ability to keep up and it's no longer absolutely necessary to buy the fastest and most powerful machines to run the latest applications.

The CPU is the single most expensive component in a PC and the one that drops in value the quickest, so bearing in mind that for the vast majority of users speed is not the necessity it once used to be, there is a very good argument for being one small step behind the leading edge. You can make significant savings, without compromising utility by getting the processor that was the 'fastest and most powerful' three or even six months ago.

Computer memory used to be eye-wateringly expensive, prices still fluctuate widely but these days it adds comparatively little to the overall price and there is no excuse for a PC not to come with several hundred megabytes of RAM. Windows and most popular applications work quite happily with between 256Mb and 512Mb of RAM, but like most things concerned with PCs, you can never have enough because you're never quite sure what's coming next.

Hard disk drive capacity used to be a major limiting factor and many otherwise perfectly serviceable PCs used to grind to a halt for lack of storage space. Disk drive capacity should no longer be an issue; nevertheless newcomers can still end up running out of disk space early on, especially if they develop an interest in video editing so go for the biggest option available as, like memory, it adds comparatively little to the final price.

Now we come to the ancillaries. Almost all new PCs come with a basic 15-inch CRT (cathode ray tube) monitor. A 17-inch screen is better, and usually adds little to the package price, though be aware that they take up quite a bit more desk space. If you can afford it, or desk space is at a premium, it's well worth upgrading to a flat screen LCD monitor. Apart from taking up less room, consuming less power and emitting no harmful radiation – good enough reasons in their own right – they are better for prolonged use as they do not generate any kind of flicker. The only downside is a very small reduction in image quality, though it is largely irrelevant for word processing and web surfing, etc., and it becomes significant only on sophisticated graphics, video and gaming applications.

CD-ROM drives are a standard fitment on all PCs but more companies are now providing a CD-writer and DVD-ROM drives (sometimes combined in one drive) as well, or instead of CD-ROM. A CD-writer is perfect for making backups of your valuable or irreplaceable data (documents, accounts and so on) and let you create your own audio CDs. Some software is now supplied in the DVD (Digital Versatile Disk) format – a DVD can hold more than ten times as much data as a CD-ROM – however most people use them to play DVD video disks, so you can watch the latest movies on your PC screen. Some PCs and laptops have video output connections, so they can be linked to your TV, though with home DVD players now so cheap it's hardly worth the bother. Incidentally, all CD-writers and DVD drives can read CD-ROM disks, so there's no need to worry about compatibility with older programs and data disks.

Built-in modems are more or less standard and these operate at the 56,000 (56K) bits per second (bps) standard. These are fine for occasional emailing and web surfing but if you want to spend more than a few hours on line each week it is likely that you will want to upgrade to a high-speed 'broadband' connection and this is something we'll be looking at later on in Chapter 10.

All PCs come with a keyboard and mouse but the quality of the standard offerings varies enormously. It is worth trying to negotiate an upgrade to better made products or ergonomic alternatives, particularly if you are going to be doing a lot of typing or have any type of disability in your fingers or wrists that could be aggravated by cheap input and pointing devices. Always try before you buy. An 'optical' mouse is highly recommended, this has no moving parts on the underside that on a normal mouse rapidly becomes clogged resulting in erratic movement of the on-screen pointer.

You can expect a new PC to come with the Windows operating system pre-loaded. This is likely to be the latest 'XP' version, though a lot of companies are still supplying Windows 98 (SE or ME versions) which some users prefer. Generally speaking Windows XP is the best bet if you are starting from scratch with a new multimedia machine. It is less prone to crash, has a number of future-proofing features and improved trouble-shooting facilities, though some older programs and peripherals may not work properly or at all, so check first with the dealer if you plan to use any 'legacy' software or hardware with your new machine.

PCs are pretty reliable these days, most of the trouble is caused by software; even so they are incredibly complicated and you can expect to suffer a few teething troubles. Make sure the supplier or dealer offers a free telephone support service at the very least, and carefully check the conditions of the warranty. Finally, ask the salesperson to explain the ins and outs of their on-site or return-to-base servicing facilities, and if you decide to place an order, insist on a written copy of all of the details, and a firm delivery date. If possible pay by credit card as this will give you the most protection, should anything go wrong.

THE INS AND OUTS

You've unpacked your shiny new multimedia computer, what now? Unlike most other electronic devices and appliances, PCs retain an air of mystery. The functions of the monitor, keyboard, mouse and loudspeakers are all fairly obvious, but the big cream-coloured box or 'system unit' – which they all plug in to – gives little away. It's not necessary to understand how a PC works in order to use one, but it helps to know a bit about what's inside. Sooner or later you will want to remove the lid, to carry out an upgrade, add extra functionality, or try to find out why it has stopped working.

The heart of any PC is the motherboard. This is a large printed circuit board, mounted on the side or the bottom of the case. It contains the central processor unit (CPU), which is usually the biggest component on the board though more often than not you can't see it because a finned metal heat sink and cooling fan has been attached to it to stop it overheating. The CPU does all the hard work and calculations. First-generation CPUs used to have a simple number designation – 80086, 80286, 80386, 80486 – which was quite helpful for determining performance but nowadays chipmakers give them names like Pentium, Duron, Athlon and Celeron which doesn't tell you much at all, so you have to rely on the speed rating.

Other areas of interest include the rows of memory sockets; some or all of them will be populated with memory boards. These are small strips of circuit boards, a couple of centimetres wide, with RAM chips on one or both sides. They come in several different type sizes and capacities, which we'll look at in more detail in Chapter 5. Motherboards often have a number of 'daughter-boards' that plug into rows of sockets or 'expansion slots'. These may include the graphics card, that processes the video output for the monitor, a sound card, connected to the speakers and the modem though these functions are often incorporated into the motherboard on a lot of recent PCs, especially workstation and budget multi-media models.

Most PCs have three disk drives, which are normally mounted close to the front of the case. Windows assigns each of them an identification letter, A, C, D, E and so on (missing letter B: is a throwback to the olden days and a now obsolete type of floppy disk drive using 5.25-inch disks). Drive letter A: is allocated to the 3.5-inch floppy disk drive; several recent PCs have no floppy drive at all and this trend is likely to continue. The C: drive is the main hard disk drive and this is where all of your computer's operating systems and application software are stored. Some large C: drives are sub-divided or 'partitioned' and the partitions are designated drive letters D: and E: and so on. On PCs with an unpartitioned C: drive the CD-ROM (or DVD or CD Writer) is allocated drive letter D: (or E: or F: if the C: drive is partitioned). Drive letters are also assigned to 'removable' storage media, such as memory cards used in digital cameras

A couple of other items to look out for are a metal box with a built-in cooling fan; this is the mains power supply module and most PCs have an internal speaker that bleeps when you switch on or 'boot up'. One or two bleeps usually mean all's well; if you hear any more then it may indicate there's a problem. For a more detailed explanation of what happens when you switch your PC on, and more importantly, what to do when things go wrong see Chapters 15 and 16.

On the back of a PC you will find a rash of plugs and sockets but don't worry, they're mostly non-interchangeable and there's little chance you'll get the important ones mixed up. There are normally two small round sockets for the mouse and keyboard; the latter is often colour-coded purple, though this is by no means an official standard so check the labelling carefully. Most PCs have at least one serial 'COM' (communications) port; they're rectangular-shaped sockets with 9 or 25 pins. Com ports are little used nowadays, though you may need one if you have an older modem or digital camera. Another socket gradually falling into disuse is the 'parallel' printer port, which the PC designates LPT 1. The other rectangular socket, with 25 pins, used with printers is also used for some older peripheral devices like scanners and external disk drives.

Most recent peripherals (printers, scanners, web cams, personal music players, digital cameras, etc.) now use a USB (Universal Serial Bus) connection, which is small and rectangular in shape. The majority of PCs have at least two USB sockets on the back and a growing number of manufacturers are now fitting them to the front of their machines, but more can be added in the form of 'hubs', which plug into a spare USB socket and work like multi-socket mains adaptors. USB, unlike the other connector types can be 'hot plugged' – i.e., plugged and unplugged without switching the PC off.

The monitor plugs into a 15-pin socket on the motherboard or on the back of a graphics card. There should also be a row of three jack sockets, for the loudspeakers/audio output, microphone and audio input and again check the labelling as it's easy to get them mixed up. Many PCs also have a 15-pin rectangular socket which may be variously labelled as a 'midi' or 'games controller' port (used for joysticks and music keyboards). There should also be a socket for a telephone cable, you may see a larger telephone-type socket, that's for a network connection and on advanced multi-media machines, a FireWire connector (it looks like a mini USB socket) which is used to connect the PC to a digital camcorder.

A DATE WITH THE DESKTOP

If you have recently come face to face with Windows for the first time, you may not believe it, but computers used to be really difficult to use. When the first office computers appeared in the late 1970s operators required extensive training in order to use them. Programs, such as word processors were controlled using text 'commands', entered via the keyboard or the 'Function' keys along the top edge of the keyboard.

That's all history now (though the Function keys remain...). Modern PCs use a graphical user interface or GUI (pronounced 'gooey') with little pictures or icons, which are basically signposts or 'shortcuts' that tell the computer where to find a program. These are displayed on a virtual on-screen 'desktop' that represents the various functions and programs available on the PC. Most actions are controlled from simple menus, activated by a pointer that moves under instruction from the mouse. To make things happen the user simply 'points' at the icon or menu item and confirms the action by 'clicking' a button on the mouse. The first GUIs were used by Apple Macintosh in the early 1980s, and for several years Macs were sought after because they were so easy to use. Microsoft developed the first version of their 'Windows' operating system in 1984. It wasn't a great success and serious PC users continued to use DOS programs, whilst those looking for an easier solution bought Macs. Then, in 1990 Microsoft released version 3 of Windows. It was a major advance on previous operating systems, and it gave the PC market an enormous boost.

Windows 95, launched in 1995 was the operating system's first major revision and it formed the template – in appearance at least – for all subsequent revisions. Windows 98, 98SE and Windows ME (known generically as Windows 9x) were incremental updates of the original Windows 95 but Windows XP, launched in 2001, marked another major milestone in PC development but only under the skin. Windows XP is based on Windows 2000, which in turn was developed from Windows NT (New Technology) operating systems, which were created for 'critical' professional commercial and industrial applications where stability and reliability were deemed more important than the latest flashy graphics and compatibility with the widest possible range of software applications and peripherals.

Microsoft wisely decided to keep many of the most fundamental changes in XP hidden from view and anyone accustomed to the look and feel of Windows 9x should have no difficulty upgrading to XP and most of what follows applies to all versions of Windows from 95 onwards.

The opening display on a Windows PC, otherwise known as the 'desktop' is a well-chosen metaphor. On a new PC the first thing you see – after it has finished booting up – is an almost empty workspace with just a handful of icons. Remember this well, it quickly fills up as you load new software and

The Windows XP desktop, soon it will begin to look like a real desktop as it becomes cluttered and disorganised.

create files. Soon it will start to look like a real office desk, cluttered and covered with things that you don't use or no longer need.

If you are new to computing get to know your desktop and the various icons that you'll find in the sub-menus when you click the Start button. In particular you should become familiar with My Computer and Windows Explorer, which are both ways of looking at all of the hardware and software on your PC. There you will find all of the disk drives, and if you click on them, all of the programs, folders and files they contain will be displayed. If you want to keep a running check on how much disk space you have left simply right-click on the disk drive icon in My Computer and select properties and you will be presented with a pie chart representing disk usage.

You should also have a look at Control Panel (Click the Start button then Settings) or click Start then Control Panel if you have Windows XP. Control Panel contains lots of utilities that let you change the way your PC operates.

A good way of getting used to the way Windows works and for personalising your computer is to click on the Display icon in Control Panel, then select in turn the Background, Appearance and Screen Saver tabs. There you will find an assortment of colour schemes for the various desktop displays and a selection of screensavers; don't be afraid to change a few things, like background colours and wallpaper, you can't break anything and it's a good way of getting to know your computer.

Q&A Real world problems

Build or buy?

Q I am student at University and would like to buy a PC with multimedia capability. I was thinking of buying the components and building it myself but as far as I could see this wouldn't save me a lot of money. The University computer lab technician – a very wise man – says that you can save up to 40%?

A That kind of saving might just have been possible a few years ago, but not any more. Companies putting together PCs have tremendous buying power, and there's intense competition, so high street prices are very low. You might be able to save a few pounds, building a machine from off-the-shelf components – even at current retail prices – but you couldn't match the kind of package deals, that include warranties and support and often several hundred pounds worth of software, or peripherals, like printers and digital cameras.

That's not to say building a PC isn't a worthwhile exercise. It is, particularly if you can scavenge some parts to keep the cost down. Cases and power supplies, keyboards, mice and monitors can usually be safely recycled. It's not difficult and you get the exact specification that you require. It can be very rewarding, especially if it works first time; if it doesn't, you'll get a crash course in PC fault-finding...

Head start

Q Can I plug headphones into my PC, instead of speakers, so I can play games without disturbing others?

A   You can, though be very careful with the volume setting as on some models it can exceed the power handling capabilities of the headphones. You can also plug headphones into most CD-ROM drives, so you can listen to audio CDs.

CHAPTER 2

Looking after your files

The first thing you are going to want to do with your new PC is load some software but if you want to keep your computer running smoothly there's a few things you should know...

Imagine a large, well-used filing cabinet in a busy office. It starts out all clean and shiny, and empty. Gradually it fills up; at first it is fairly well ordered, with all the folders neatly arranged, but as time goes by files are removed and not always put back in their right place. Soon there's a build up of clutter, parts of files go missing, the office idiot gets them mixed up and it takes longer and longer to find what you're looking for. Does that sound familiar?

The hard disk drive in your PC is a lot like a filing cabinet; in order to keep it working smoothly it needs to be tidied up every so often. As you install and later remove software odd bits get left behind and the file structure becomes disorganised, slowing down the time it takes for your PC to retrieve data from the disk drive. One way to avoid this happening is to load only programs that you're sure you will use; after a few months most PCs have dozens of unused programs that not only waste disk space but may interfere with other programs loaded at a later date.

These days most programs are very easy to install and the process is largely automatic, however it pays to observe a few simple rules. Always exit all running programs before installing any new software and after each installation exit Windows and re-boot, even if the program doesn't ask you to do so, and only install one program at a time.

Sooner or later you will want to uninstall some programs, to free up disk space or simply to tidy up your filing system, again following a few simple guidelines will help prevent problems later on. Never, repeat, never remove programs by deleting file folders using Windows Explorer as this can have disastrous consequences! In addition to creating a program folder most programs store lots of additional files in folders within Windows, they change start-up and system files and make changes to the Windows Registry (an important collection of files that regulates and controls your computer, see Chapter 18). Simply removing the program folder leaves all the extra files behind and these may confuse Windows, telling the computer to look for programs that no longer exist, making Windows crash, or do all kinds of horrible things and display worrying warning messages.

Almost all Windows programs have their own uninstaller utility, which safely removes the program and all of its components. A shortcut to the uninstaller can usually be found on the list in Add/Remove Programs in Control panel, occasionally the uninstaller can only be accessed from the program's own folder and a few applications have the uninstaller on the installation disk.

Some uninstaller programs require you to shut down and re-boot the PC, to remove any remaining program fragments, this is a good idea in any case as it allows Windows to refresh and backup its system files.

Whilst this strategy works perfectly well with the vast majority of the software you will install on your PC a few programs do not have their own installers and these can be difficult to remove safely; however you can avoid problems by loading an 'uninstaller' program on your PC like Clean Sweep, WinDelete or Uninstaller. They work best if they're installed early on, as soon as possible after you've bought a new computer. They monitor each new item of software as it is installed, noting where files are stored, so they can be safely removed. Most uninstallers make compressed backups of all the files deleted, so if a problem arises they can be re-installed.

No matter how careful you are, over time the process of installing and uninstalling software will eventually disrupt your PC's filing system, causing it to become 'fragmented'. Windows includes a couple of simple utilities that can help to restore order and even speed up operation if it starts to become sluggish. The two utilities in question are called Scandisk and Defrag. Scandisk checks the structure of the filing system and if it finds problems, will automatically effect repairs. Defrag reorganises the files on the disk, putting the most frequently used ones into more accessible locations and making the most efficient use of the space available. Opinions vary as to how often they should be used; very heavily used machines with a high turnover of software may benefit from weekly defrag sessions but for most users once every month or two is usually more than enough.

Before you run defrag it's important to do a spot of housekeeping. Shut down all running programs, then click on the Recycle Bin icon to make sure there's nothing you want to keep (if so right-click on the item and select

Restore), otherwise select 'Empty Recycle Bin' on the File menu. Next, if you've been doing a lot of web surfing, empty your web browser's cache (storage space for web pages you've viewed). Open Internet Explorer and select Internet Options on the Tools menu select the General tab, click Delete Files then OK and exit Internet Explorer. It is important that no other programs are running and this includes Screensavers, which will interfere with Defrag. To do that right click anywhere on the desktop to bring up the Display dialogue window, select the Screensaver tab and 'None' on the list.

If this is the first time you've carried out this kind of maintenance and your PC is more than a few months old run the Scandisk utility first which can be found by clicking Start > Programs > Accessories > System Tools. Unless you have been experiencing problems select the Standard Test, and make sure the item 'Automatically Fix Errors' has been checked. All being well the test should only take a couple of minutes. In the unlikely event that any problems do arise refer to the troubleshooting section (Chapters 15 to 17).

Now you are ready to defrag. Depending on which version of Windows you are using there can be two or three different versions of Defrag; the best one can be found alongside Scandisk in System Tools in the Accessories folder. This one has the option to optimise your hard disk's file structure by grouping the most frequently used programs together (when Defrag opens click the Settings button and check the item 'Rearrange files so my programs start faster'). On some versions of Windows Defrag might report that you don't need to defragment now but if the value shown is more than 8%, say, then it is still worth doing.

If you like, click on the Show Details button, and watch Defrag go to work. You will actually see blocks of data being moved from around the disk to the file areas of the front of the drive. It's quite entertaining for the first few minutes, if you've got nothing better to do, though again it can take a while to complete the job.

If you find that Defrag repeatedly 'hangs' (and you've switched off the screensaver and all running programs) then try this. Insert your Windows 98 CD-ROM, if it starts automatically click on 'Browse This CD', otherwise use Windows Explorer to open the disk and work your way to the Tools and Mtsutil folders, right-click on Defrag.inf and select Install. Exit and re-boot, Defrag will run and give your PC's filing system a really comprehensive once-over.

Windows 9x Disk Defragmenter, the coloured squares represent blocks of data, Defrag helps to make your disk drive run more smoothly by optimising your computer's filing system.

Q&A Real world problems

Lost in space

Q   I wanted to clear out some redundant files to make more room on my laptop. The most regularly used programs are Word, WinFax Pro, and Netscape. In my DOS directory I have a growing list of files with extensions .tmp. Most use 0 bytes, about every fifth one has 1,506 bytes, and a few have serious numbers between 15k and 250k. Any advice about what they might be and whether I can safely dump them?

A   They are temporary files, created by the PC and its software for the short-term storage of data. Normally they're automatically deleted when you close Windows, but they can be left behind if the PC or the application locks up, or isn't closed down properly. Any file ending with .tmp or .swp (swapfile) and starting with the tilde sign (~) can be safely deleted. You may also find a lot of leftover temporary files stored in a directory called 'Temp', which is normally inside the Windows folder. Whenever you delete a file or application it's a good idea to wait a day or two, before you empty the recycle bin, to make sure your PC is still working normally. Whilst deleted files are still in the bin they can still be restored.

Missing links

Q   What are DLL files? I currently have 1296 of them on my laptop, what do they do?

A   DLL stands for Dynamic Link Library. They're a family of files that contain programming code, bitmap images, icons and other resources that can be shared by one or more applications. Some of them can be quite large and it's not unusual for a PC to end up with lots of duplicate and redundant DLLs, left behind by deleted programs; it is possible that some of the 1300 odd files on your machine are wasting valuable hard disk space. However, mess with DLLs at your peril! Do not be tempted to erase any of them without first making sure they're not being used. The only safe way to do that is with a disk cleaner program.

CHAPTER 3 **Protecting your data**

If the worst should happen – and it will – and all the priceless files on your hard disk are wiped, you'll wish you had a proper backup system. Don't wait for disaster to strike, here's what to do...

Whether you are new to computing or an old hand ask yourself this, how would you cope if the hard disk drive in your PC suffered a catastrophic failure or a virus scrambled all the data? A lot of PC owners gamble that it won't happen to them, but what if it does, have you worked out how much you stand to lose? A faulty disk drive can be replaced, and you should have original copies of all the programs on your machine, but every letter, document, database or file you've ever created or downloaded from the Internet could be lost forever. If you use your PC for business, organise your personal finances, or those of a club or society, the consequences could be serious!

Thankfully hard disk crashes are quite rare these days; nevertheless, there's still plenty of other ways for data to be lost, from tinkering tots to power surges. You may have been lucky so far but you really must get into the habit of copying or backing up essential data, so that if the worst should happen, you can get your system up and running again, or transfer the data to another PC. The trouble is few PC users take the threat of disaster seriously, until it is too late!

As an interim measure you can keep relatively small files like text documents on one or more floppy disks but if you want to do the job properly you have to consider some form of mass storage device. There are plenty of alternatives, ranging from tape cassettes, secondary fixed and removable drives and CD-writers. High-capacity magnetic disk drives like Iomega Zip and Jaz are still quite popular, and they are comparatively cheap and easy to use but they're only useful for transferring data if the drive can be moved to another machine, or another machine with a suitable drive. They work in exactly the same way as a standard floppy drive, except the disks – they look like fat floppies – have a capacity of between 100 megabytes and 2-gigabytes (or up to twice as much when the data is compressed).

Most backup drives are quite easy to fit and external models are the easiest. Once installed, Windows treats them as another disk drive, automatically assigning them a drive letter and files can be saved or copied to disk in exactly the same way as a normal floppy and as an added bonus they read and write data between 5 and 20 times faster.

Magnetic tape drives – internal and external types are available in a range of capacities, suitable for backing up a complete hard disk drive, and they are relatively cheap. Tape drives used to be very popular but the problem with tape is that it's quite slow and a major backup can take several hours, they're not terribly reliable either and unless you get into the habit of routinely verifying the data you might find that when the time comes the data is corrupted or unreadable.

Fixed or removable hard disk drives are another inexpensive solution and with the right software you can create a complete 'image' of your main C drive, so if the main disk fails you can easily switch over to the backup drive. However, if the second drive is permanently installed inside the PC it is vulnerable to the same kind of threat as the main drive (i.e., fire, theft, etc.), so for a serious backup solution the drive should be removable and preferably stored 'off site' in a safe and secure location.

By far the best and simplest solution is a CD-writer and details of how to fit one can be found in Chapter 5. CD-writers use recordable CD-ROMs with a capacity of up to 650 megabytes. CD recorders can read normal CD-ROMs and audio CDs as well, so they can replace the original drive fitted to your PC. There are two types of disk: Blank CD-R disks are very cheap (just a few pence when purchased in bulk) but they can only be used once; CD-RW disks can be re-written, though normally you can't change files by simply writing over them, and it may involve re-writing the whole disk.

DVD-RAM drives are another possibility and disks (rewritable and record once) can hold several gigabytes of data. However, drives and disks are still relatively expensive and they're less convenient than CD-ROM for transferring data as not all PCs have DVD-ROM drives.

Whatever system you use it's important to adopt a strategy or routine and stick to it. That means making regular backups. There's nothing to stop you copying files and folders manually but it can be quite tedious; fortunately there's a good selection of backup software on the market and Windows 9x has a built-in backup utility (My Computer > right click drive C: > Properties > Tools), though it's not especially CD-R/RW friendly.

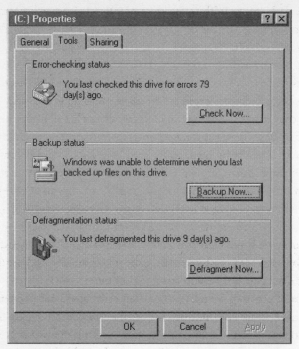

Windows 9x Backup utility, a simple way to preserve your valuable data.

A lot of tape and disk systems come with their own backup utilities that can be programmed to do it for you automatically at a particular time. This doesn't have to interfere with your normal work, it can be done in the 'background' whilst you're engaged on another task; the computer makes use of the gaps and pauses that occur during normal operation. Most types of software can be set to backup incrementally, which saves time as it copies only files or folders that have changed since the last backup.

If you are creating a lot of frequently changing files, that could mean backing them up at least once or twice a day. It's no good keeping the tapes or disks in the machine; they must be stored separately. If your data is particularly vulnerable you should think about making multiple copies, and keeping at least one of them off-site, in a secure location.

VIRUSES AND WORMS

Conspiracy theorists have a field day after every PC and email virus outbreak. Everyone from anti-virus software manufacturers drumming up business to the FBI and dark forces within the music industry have been blamed for spreading them. But wherever they come from the bottom line is that your PC is under attack! The main target for viruses is Outlook and Outlook Express email programs. In adding extra functionality to these programs Microsoft has inadvertently created a number of security loopholes that virus writers have been quick to exploit. However, providing you take sensible precautions, the chances of being infected are relatively small.

We'll look in this chapter at some simple commonsense measures you can take to protect your PC and the data stored on it. Most viruses contain clearly identifiable code patterns or 'signatures' that anti-virus software can be programmed to recognise. If you haven't got a virus 'scanner' on your PC you are just asking for trouble – get one now, and make sure you regularly backup all non-replaceable data. The effectiveness of anti-virus programs depends entirely on how often you update the software. It's no good hoping that the freebie anti-virus software that came with your PC will protect you; it was out of date long before you got the computer home!

An estimated 500 new viruses are created each week and as events have shown they can spread like wildfire. In 1999 the 'ILOVEYOU' or 'Love Bug' virus infected several million PCs and systems around the world in a matter of hours; anti-virus software companies respond quickly but it can still take them several days to come up with countermeasures and make them available to users.

The damage caused by viruses varies enormously and the good news is that most are relatively harmless or benign. If you receive a lot of email you may have one or two infecting your machine without you knowing it, even if you follow the very sensible advice about not opening unsolicited email attachments. Email viruses, more correctly known as 'worms', can get into your machine just by opening a message and this can be a very serious problem. If you are still using an older version of Outlook Express (v. 4 or 5) you should download the self-installing security patch which can be found at: http://www.microsoft.com/technet/security/bulletin/ms99-032.asp or upgrade Internet Explorer (v6 or later) which includes a more secure version of Outlook Express, this can also be downloaded from free the Microsoft website http://www.microsoft.com/windows/ie/downloads/ie6/default.asp, and is regularly included on computer magazine CD-ROM cover mount disks.

These measures will protect you against the many variations of the 'BubbleBoy' Worm, which was released in 2000 and continues to proliferate under a variety of different names. These worms, known generically as 'mass mailers' rarely damage files but they are self-replicating and will attach themselves to emails sent by you to others.

The trouble is that most worms can be sent to you quite innocently inside an email from someone you know and trust. Simply reading the message activates the worm and the first you know about it is a stream of angry email from contacts in your address book! One way to prevent the work activating is to close the Preview window in Outlook Express, which automatically opens an email; this can be disabled by clicking Layout on the View menu and unchecking the item 'Show Preview Pane'.

Another worthwhile precaution is for Windows 95 and 98 users (the loophole has been removed from Windows ME onwards) to disable the Visual Basic Script feature. It's unlikely to cause any problems if you're using a stand-alone machine running standard office-type applications. The procedure is very simple. In Windows 98 open Control Panel (Start > Settings) double-click on the Add/Remove Programs icon and select the Windows Setup tab. Double click on Accessories and scroll down the list to Windows Scripting Host, deselect the check box and click OK. In Windows 95 open My Computer, go to the View menu, select Options and the File Types tab. Scroll down the list to find 'VBScript Script File', click Remove and in the confirmation dialogue box that appears select Yes. For more information on current virus infestations have a look at:

http://www.symantec.com/avcenter/index.html

Beware of hoaxes; a number of email messages have been circulating warning the recipient to delete certain files on their PC as they contain viruses. The messages are often passed on by concerned friends and colleagues and usually sound very plausible. In almost all cases they are hoaxes and you should never delete files on your PC without first verifying that they are unsafe. If in doubt check your virus scanner manufacturer's web-site or enter the name of the allegedly dangerous file into a search engine like Google (www.google.co.uk), which should quickly check its authenticity.

TROJANS

Viruses and worms are bad enough but here's something else for you to worry about the next time you're on-line. When you are connected to the Internet it is possible for others to gain access to your PC, read files, scan your address book, see which sites you've been visiting, steal passwords, download files and viruses onto your machine, even wipe your disk, and you won't know a thing about it!

Fortunately for most users the risk of it happening on a short-duration Internet and emailing session is quite small; nevertheless the possibility exists, and with the growing popularity of 'always-on' and broadband connections this kind of snooping can be a real threat.

This is how it works. Typically a program called a 'Trojan', which gets onto the PC as an email attachment or is deliberately planted by someone with access to the machine, opens an unauthorised 'backdoor' into the computer's hard disk. Once there it remains hidden but will activate whenever you go on-line, and provide anyone with the necessary 'Client' program full remote access to your machine.

If you connect to the Internet by a normal 'dial-up' telephone line connection you are protected to some extent by the fact that your PC is relatively anonymous. When you go on-line most Internet Service Providers (ISPs) assign a 'dynamic IP' address to your PC that changes every time you log on. This makes it difficult, but not impossible, for anyone to deliberately target your computer. Some Client programs randomly trawl through IP addresses for infected PCs but some Trojans automatically report back to the sender your current IP address as soon as you go on-line.

Unlike a conventional virus or worm Trojans are not necessarily destructive, which makes them hard to detect. Most of the top virus scanners – if regularly updated – will find the commonest Trojans, which for the record have names or go under file and program aliases like Back Orifice, Netbus, Buddylist, Deep-Throat, Girlfriend and Winsaver.

In addition to all of the usual commonsense precautions, including not opening suspicious and unexpected email attachments, you should install software that prevents anyone from remotely accessing your PC. This type of program is commonly called a 'Firewall', and there are plenty of commercial programs available but there are also some excellent 'freeware' programs that can be downloaded from the Internet. The better known are ZoneAlarm (www.zonelabs.com) and Agnitum Outpost (www.agnitum.com/products/outpost).

Both programs are very easy to set up and use and can be set to start automatically when you boot your PC. They operate in the background, monitoring programs that you have given permission to connect to the Internet; if a program unexpectedly tries to open a connection without your

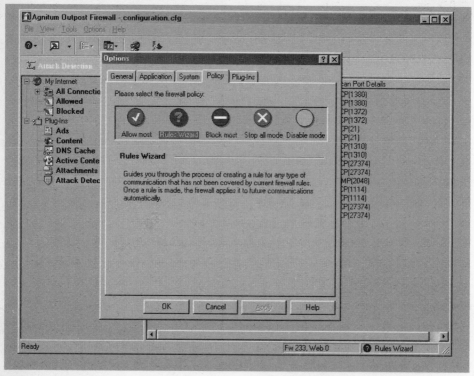

Outpost, an advanced Firewall program that can protect your PC against hackers and malicious 'spyware' programs.

say so you will be warned. ZoneAlarm also checks incoming email for 'Love Bug' type worms and it will alert you when any attempt is made to gain access to your PC. What surprises a lot of users is how frequently this happens; you might get two or three warnings in a half-hour session. Usually most alerts are entirely innocent and are often nothing more sinister than delayed Internet site responses, if you're tired of waiting for a page to download, or sites calling the previous user of your current IP address.

If you want to give yourself a really nasty shock there's an excellent Internet site that automatically tests the integrity of your machine and its defences – or lack of them. With your permission it simulates the kind of surreptitious backdoor snooping an intruder might use to gain access to your system. The utility is called Shields Up! It's free to use and it can be found at: http://grc.com/. If that doesn't convince you of the need for a Firewall on your PC, nothing will!

Q&A Real world problems

A plage on your PC

Q   I recently had to kill a virus caught by Norton Anti-Virus software. Now when I start up the PC (Windows 98) I get error messages about a file called 'Inetd.exe'. I have tried to find the missing file in my Windows disk without success. These messages are very annoying! Any ideas?

A   You have been infected by a nasty little email worm called Plage. Amongst other things it modifies the Windows system file win.ini, which it appears your anti-virus software may have missed. Full instructions on how to manually delete this intruder can be found at:

   http://www.fireantivirus.com/virusinfo/library/plage.htm

Over protected?

Q   I have seen contradictory advice about installing anti-virus programs. Some 'experts' say that one should only ever have one program installed, because they will interfere with each other. Others say that to be really safe – as no one manufacturer can give 100% protection – one should and can install a proprietary retail product (e.g., McAfee or Norton) and also download and install a 'free' one such as AVG alongside it. Who is right?

A   Whilst it's true that you can't have too much protection there are many cases of programs clashing where the signature files used to identify viruses in one program have been identified as a threat by another. The vast majority of viruses nowadays come attached to emails and are fairly easy to identify so stick to just one program, keep it religiously updated and take all sensible precautions by not opening any attached files, unless you are 100% sure of their provenance, and only then when they've been run through the virus checker.

CHAPTER 4   # Routine maintenance

A few minutes spent on preventative maintenance now could save you from a potentially disastrous failure in the future.

In addition to processing words and crunching numbers your desktop PC does a pretty good impression of a vacuum cleaner and rubbish bin. Cooling fans inside the power supply module, and attached to the main processor chip, suck air in through and around the disk-drives, loudspeaker grilles and gaps in the cabinet. After just a few weeks use everything inside the case is coated with a thin layer of dust particles and airborne contaminants. It gets everywhere and could eventually cause your PC to operate erratically, or worse!

Dust and pollutants can interfere with the pickup heads and other moving parts inside the floppy disk and CD and DVD drives. Intermittent contacts may develop on switches, plugs, sockets, expansion cards plugged into the motherboard; even the microchips can be affected. The biggest accumulation of dust is in and around the main cooling fan and in extreme cases it can cause the power supply to fail by blocking the path of cooling air to critical components.

The keyboard uses gravity to collect your detritus. A noxious mixture, made up of biscuit crumbs, cigarette ash (even if you don't smoke), nail clippings, hairs, tea and coffee spillage finds its way past the keys and into the inside of the keyboard case. The keys themselves also suffer a build up of sticky surface grime made up of skin oil, sweat, makeup and other substances. Most PC users seem to favour leaving it, until it gets full up, the keys stop moving or it starts to smell.

Then there's the mouse. They're especially good at keeping the mouse pad clean, hoovering up crumbs, dirt, hairs and liquid spills. Debris is transferred from the ball underneath onto the rollers that move optical or mechanical switches. After a while pointer movement becomes jerky, or stops altogether. It's worth mucking out your system at least once a year, more often if you work in a particularly dusty or smoky atmosphere, or if you regularly eat lunch at your desk.

There's really only one way to clean out the system unit, and that's to take off the lid. It's not difficult or dangerous but don't try it unless you are reasonably confident of your abilities. Before you reach for the screwdriver you must disconnect your PC from the mains and once the case is open do not touch anything! To be on the safe side you should touch the case metalwork at frequent intervals when the lid is off, this will dissipate any static charges that may have built up on your body or clothing.

Do not be tempted to suck out the dust using the hose on your vacuum cleaner, that's just asking for trouble as you might dislodge cables plugs or expansion cards. Instead, get hold of a can of compressed air/gas – the sort used to clean cameras – and blow the dust out of the case. So-called 'air dusters' are also better at getting into nooks and crannies. Most of them have extension tubes, so you can also blast dust out of the power supply and off of the cooling fan blades. Don't poke the tube inside the disk drive slot – you could damage the delicate innards; use proper disk-drive cleaning kits, available from your local computer store.

This step is optional and for advanced users only! Before you put the lid back on, and after taking anti-static precautions give the plugs and sockets going to the motherboards and disk drives a gentle push, to make sure they're properly seated. All of the components inside a PC are subjected to repeated heating and cooling cycles as the machine is switched on and off, and this can lead to an effect known as 'contact creep' whereby plugs and microchips gradually work their way loose from their sockets. When you have finished replace the lid, switch on and make sure everything is working properly.

Back now to the outside. It's worth treating the floppy and CD/DVD drive to a run through with disk cleaning kits; always buy good quality items from reputable suppliers and always follow the instructions, especially with 'wet' cleaners that use an alcohol cleaning fluid. Allow the fluid plenty of time to evaporate before using the drive.

Give the whole case a wipe over with a lightly moistened cloth and some washing-up liquid to remove the finger marks, especially around the disk slots and switches. While you're at it give the outside of the monitor a wipe over and clean the screen with an anti-static cleaner wipe or a dab of window cleaner liquid on a soft cloth.

Now it's the turn of your desktop crumb-catcher, otherwise known as the keyboard. Flip it upside down and give it a shake to dislodge the bigger bits

Keep your CD-ROM or DVD drive working smoothly by regularly using an optical drive-cleaning kit.

lodged between and behind the keys. You can also try sucking out any remaining debris with the flexible hose attachment on a vacuum cleaner. Incidentally you can get miniature battery powered models for this kind of job but they're not very powerful. You can clean the keys with a lightly moistened cloth and a dab of washing up liquid. If any water drips into the innards – and this applies to any of the parts you are cleaning – it's best not to switch the PC back on but leave the affected component overnight in a warm place.

If there are still bits inside the keyboard the only solution is to take it apart. Disconnect the keyboard from the PC; designs vary but most keyboards are held together by half a dozen (or more), crosshead screws on the underside. Once removed the top and bottom halves should come apart. You may have to prise some small lugs with the tip of a screwdriver but if it doesn't separate easily don't force it! Tip out all of the loose dirt and using a new soft paintbrush remove all the crud from underneath the keys. Reassemble, making sure there are no wires trapped between the case sections.

The best way to clean your mouse is to take it apart. If you don't fancy tinkering around inside it's still worth removing and cleaning the ball, but only when the PC is switched off. The ball is usually held in place by the ring surrounding it. It should drop off when turned a few degrees. Give the ball a wipe over and blow into the hole, to shift any loose dust. Most mice are held together by one or two crosshead screws on the base. Separate the two halves and clean it out using the paintbrush. Handle with care as the rotary sensors may only be clipped lightly into place and could fall out if the circuit board is turned upside down. Check the condition of the rollers that come into contact with the ball. If there's a coating of gunge it can be scraped off with a matchstick. If you want to avoid this kind of unpleasantness in future get an optical mouse, which has no moving parts.

Printers are best dealt with using the air duster; if possible open the top or front so you can get a good shot at the rollers and paper path. On inkjet models avoid blowing near to the ink cartridges, better still take them out first but keep the air jet away from any ink ports or tubes, it can be incredibly messy, and it probably doesn't do it any good either! Wipe the outer casing over and it's done. Scanners don't usually get very dirty, though the glass 'platen' is often dotted with greasy finger marks, so give that the once-over with a glass cleaner or a screen wipe.

Next the monitor. Do not on any account take it apart, this is a no-go area! The high voltages flying around inside CRT-based monitors produce a powerful static electrical charge that works like a magnet on dust and airborne particles. The screen will probably need a thorough clean, especially if there are any smokers nearby as their exhalations leave a particularly sticky residue. Use one of the specially made screen cleaners as these usually contain anti-static agents that slow down the build up of dirt. Remove all of the clutter from the top of the monitor; it might be blocking ventilation holes, which could cause problems. Give the vents a quick blast with your air duster and clean the outside of the case with your damp soapy cloth.

LCD viewing screens are generally a lot easier to deal with, they run fairly cool and do not attract dust to anything like the same extent as CRT monitors so a quick wash and brush up is usually all that's needed.

Finally, if you're feeling diligent, sort out the rat's-nest of cables on the back of your PC. Untangle the leads, unplugging them one at a time if necessary and making sure the retaining screws on the large multi-pin connectors are tightened up. Plugs working loose can cause a lot of problems.

THE POWER TO PROTECT

No matter how carefully you treat your PC it is still at the mercy of outside influences, and ones that you certainly should protect your machine against are power cuts, voltage surges and lightning strikes. Even a brief interruption in the mains supply lasting no more than a split second can be enough to cause the files and data you are working on to be lost, or worse! Important system files can be corrupted and you'll be left with an inoperable PC.

We have become accustomed to a reliable mains supply in the UK. For most of us living in towns and cities blackouts and 'brownouts' have been a comparatively rare occurrence in recent years and this has given us a false sense of security.

Power supply modules inside desktop PCs have improved enormously in the past few years and they can iron out minor variations in mains voltage and even cope with small 'spikes' and surges lasting a few milliseconds but a complete power loss can cause considerable damage. There is only one solution – other than using a battery-powered laptop – and that's a box of tricks called an uninterruptible power supply (UPS).

A UPS connects between the mains socket and your PC. Inside there's a re-chargeable battery, a battery charger and a circuit called an inverter. Its job is to convert the low-voltage DC from the battery into 240 volts AC. When the mains fails the UPS switches automatically to the battery supply, maintaining the supply to the PC. Depending on the size of the battery the backup power supply can last from a few minutes to an hour or more, which should be long enough for you to save files, close programs and carry out a safe shutdown.

Broadly speaking there are two types of UPS, online and standby. Online models operate all of the time by keeping the battery constantly charged and supplying power to the inverter, which powers the PC. In this case the battery acts as a buffer between the PC and the mains, eliminating any irregularities in the mains voltage. Standby models kick in the instant the supply fails, taking between 2 and 10 milliseconds to restore power. The interruption is too brief to upset most modern PCs though it could cause problems on some older models. Incidentally, standby UPS tend to be a little cheaper than online types. Some more recent UPS designs are in effect hybrids, using what's known as a double conversion process, which lightens the load on the battery and provides a constant supply.

Most UPS modules are supplied with operating software that flashes up an on-screen warning when the mains supply fails. Some programs will carry out an automatic save and shut down routine for you, in case you are not there to do it yourself. UPS management programs can also monitor the health of the battery, indicating when it needs replacing (usually every two to three years) and continually check the condition of the mains supply, logging trends and predicting possible failures. Most models now have a 'hot-swap' facility that allows the battery to be exchanged whilst the unit is operating. Additionally, all UPS devices filter and 'condition' the mains voltage, removing potentially harmful spikes and surges, maintaining a steady smooth supply.

It all sounds terribly complicated and expensive but surprisingly it's not. UPS units designed to protect stand-alone Windows desktop PCs cost less than £100, which is a very small sum to pay when you consider how much your data, or even your computer is worth. UPS systems are normally rated by capacity quoted as volt-amperes or VA. The typical range is from 200 to 1500VA. Heavy-duty UPS systems for servers and networks, fed from high-power circuits, go from 2000VA upwards. However, for most home PC users UPS modules in the range 200 to 500VA are usually more than adequate, providing between 5 and 15 minutes worth of power, depending on the PC, size of monitor and any peripherals.

Q&A **Real world problems**

A wee problem

Q After my daughter and her friend had a little accident with a can of 7 Up and my PC keyboard, I decided to buy a cordless and mouseless keyboard. Can you explain to me why my cat has now urinated into two of these keyboards within the space of ten days? Both gave up the ghost, I have now had to resort to a normal keyboard and mouse. Could it be the infra-red system is causing the cat to think it is now the local poo tray?

A Unless your present cat litter tray incorporates some kind of infra-red device it seems more likely the keyboard is emitting an odour that is either attractive or offensive to your cat, which is responding by marking its territory. You could try keeping the cat away from any new objects until they have acquired your smell. Another method is to stroke your cat around the chin area with a piece of cotton cloth then wipe the cloth on the new object, which makes it smell of the cat. You can also get cat-repellent sprays and there is even a PC utility called PawSense, designed to keep cats off computer keyboards. It analyses key-press combinations and timings to determine when a cat climbs onto your keyboard. When a cat is detected, the utility plays a cat-annoying sound to repel the feline. More information is available at: http://www.bitboost.com/pawsense

Grubby cables

Q   The curly lead connecting my keyboard to the PC, and the mouse lead are absolutely filthy. They were probably white once but now they are black with grime. Can they be cleaned, and if so what is the best way?

A   Make sure the PC is switched off and unplugged from the mains then you can clean the wires with a damp cloth and a little washing-up liquid. It will be easier (and safer) to clean the cables after they have been unplugged. Make sure the cables and plugs are thoroughly dry before they are reconnected, leave them overnight if possible.

Safe solution

Q   Is it safe to use cleaner wipes, meant for telephones, on my PC keyboard and mouse? I'm wary of using anything that might contain harmful chemicals that attack plastics.

A   PC peripherals and telephones are made from the same family of plastics so it's very unlikely the wipes would contain any damaging solvents but do check labelling for warnings.

CHAPTER 5   **Simple upgrades**

Your PC can be easily upgraded for improved flexibility and performance, here's how...

First a few words of warning; if electronic gadgets keel over and die if you so much as look at them, or you always seem to have bits left over when you take something apart, please skip this chapter. On the other hand, if you can wire up a three-pin plug or change a fuse without electrocuting yourself, upgrading and adding extra bits to your PC should be a breeze.

The so-called 'open architecture' of the Windows PC means that most machines are basically a collection of standardised modules. They're a bit like grown-up Meccano sets and you can do just about any job, from replacing one of the modules to building a complete PC with nothing more complicated than a cross-head screwdriver, however, there are some basic ground rules.

The most important one is to remember that desktop PCs are mains powered so before you do anything always unplug the PC from the socket. Some experts advocate leaving the mains plug connected but with the socket switched off, so the case remains earthed, however, there is a small chance that the wall socket could be incorrectly wired, in which case there could be live connections inside the PC.

You should take great care when working inside your PC because a static charge can build up on your body or clothes. Static electricity can damage or destroy some sensitive electronic components and there's a fair few of them inside the average PC. The chances of it happening are actually quite small; nevertheless you can minimise the risk by frequently touching or holding onto the case with one hand whenever you open the lid, avoid handling components or modules any more than is strictly necessary and keeping all parts in their anti-static packaging until they are needed.

If you're ultra cautious it's worth using an earth wrist strap. It's basically a wire with a resistive load that connects your body to the case. These are available from most computer parts dealers for a few pounds.

INSTALLING A CD WRITER OR DVD-ROM DRIVE

Whilst a lot of PCs these days come with CD-Writers and DVD-ROM drives already fitted they're still quite rare on basic workstation models, and adding a new drive to an older PC can give it a new lease of life. CD-ROM, CD Writer and DVD-ROM drives all conform to a standard pattern and are designed to fit into a spare 5.25-inch drive bay. Virtually all models also have just three connections, a ribbon cable for the data, a four-pin power plug and the analogue audio output socket (there are at least two styles for the latter, though).

Step one is to identify the vacant drive bay – on most machines there will be a space immediately below or to the side of the existing CD-ROM drive. Incidentally, you should leave this in place unless it is faulty; having two CD-ROM drives is an advantage – you can leave frequently used disks in the tray – and it will allow you copy non-copyright disks and your own data and backup disks.

Next, locate a spare power connector. These are small white four-pin plugs and on most PCs there's usually one or two of them, possibly attached by cable ties to other cables to stop them dangling or getting in the way. Don't worry if you can't see one, you can get 'splitters' from most PC parts dealers that use an existing power connection to one of the other disk drives.

Lastly, locate a spare data connector. There are a couple of possibilities; the flat ribbon cable going to your existing CD-ROM drive may well have a spare connector along its length, otherwise you can use the one that came with your new CD-Writer/DVD-ROM drive. This plugs into a spare 'IDE Drive' socket on the motherboard. You should be able to identify this from the motherboard manual that came with your PC and it will usually be labelled 'IDE 2'. Data cables look symmetrical but note that one side of the plug has a notch and one edge of the ribbon should have a red marker along its length, indicating 'pin 1'. You only need to worry about the audio cable if you want to use the new drive to play audio CDs. In most cases if your original drive is functioning properly and you're happy to continue using it for playing CDs then leave it alone.

Remove the new drive from its protective packaging and check the back panel for the position of the power socket and note the orientation of the data connection (pin 1 is usually labelled). Check also for a small bank of pins marked 'Master' and 'Slave'; most drives are factory set with a small shorting link to the 'Slave' setting, but double check with instructions before proceeding.

With the PC switched off, unplugged from the mains and the lid removed pop out the blanking panel covering the empty drive bay. It's usually easier to do this from inside the case, but before you go poking around don't forget to touch the metalwork first. The next step can be quite fiddly. If at all possible try to fit the data cable – length permitting – to the back of the drive, before you insert the drive into the bay. The plug should fit only one way – don't force it, the pins are easily bent – so check the orientation of the ribbon cable connector and plug first, so you know which way around they should go. Plug in the power lead and carefully align the drive in the bay so you can fix it into place with four screws. Replace the lid and reconnect the PC.

When you boot your PC Windows should automatically detect the new drive and start the hardware installation wizard. If not use the Add/Remove Hardware utility in Control Panel. Follow the instructions and be ready to insert any driver and software disks as requested. Windows will assign the drive a new letter (usually E, if the C: drive isn't partitioned). It will be ready to use straight away; your old CD-ROM drive should continue to operate as normal though the drive letter may have changed. It sounds easy, and it is, but if you have problems the most likely causes are badly/wrongly fitted ribbon cables, you dislodged something or you installed the wrong driver software.

ADDING MORE MEMORY

A memory upgrade is the easiest, quickest and most cost-effective improvement you can make to many older PCs, built a few years ago when memory modules were expensive. The memory in question is known as RAM or Random Access Memory. It's a collection of microchips that the computer uses to temporarily store programs and data that it needs to access quickly and frequently. RAM capacity is measured in megabytes. In theory a Windows 95 or 98 PC will operate with just 8 megabytes and 16Mb is considered the safe minimum but it will be painfully slow. For Windows 98 onwards, and on any machine using memory-hungry applications and peripherals like digital scanners, cameras and graphics programs, a safe minimum is 256Mb, and 512Mb should see most home PCs through to their eventual retirement.

RAM chips are mounted on small strip-like modules that plug into sockets on the large printed circuit board or 'motherboard' inside your PC's system box. The modules are designed to be easy to fit, and impossible (hopefully) to insert the wrong way around. If you're properly prepared the whole job shouldn't take more than fifteen to twenty minutes.

Increasing RAM capacity can make a dramatic difference to the speed of applications; you will experience fewer crashes and it may even extend the useful life of your machine. It is usual to increase PC memory by a factor of 2, 4, 8, 16 and so on, up to the capacity of the motherboard, which is usually mentioned in the manual. If in doubt ask your vendor.

Begin by familiarising yourself with your PC's current memory status; it is essential that you have this information – you cannot proceed without it! You need to know how much RAM your PC has now and what type it is. If

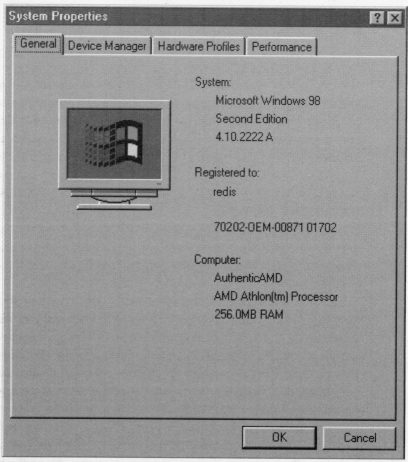

System Properties provides basic information about the configuration of your computer.

you can't remember how many megabytes you have open Control Panel, click on the System icon then select the General tab and it will tell you.

There are lots of different types of RAM module but the most common on recent PCs are 168-pin DIMM (dual in-line memory module) or 184-pin DDR (double data rate) memory modules. Many older PCs use the now obsolete 30-pin SIMM (single in line memory module) modules; these are still available but, in general, memory upgrades on older machines with slower processors are not worth the effort or expense.

In fact there are many more different types and numerous sub-groups and differing operating voltages but the important point is that you must only upgrade or replace with the same type of memory module. Unfortunately it's not always obvious what type of memory you are using but there may be a label inside the system box or you could ask the dealer or vendor.

You need to find out how many free memory slots there are on the motherboard. To do this you have to remove the system box lid or cover and have a look inside. Have a desk lamp or torch handy, so you can see what you are doing. There should be a diagram or photograph of the motherboard in the motherboard manual that accompanied your PC. This will show you where the memory sockets are located. If they are obscured by ribbon cables gently move them out of the way. Make a note of how many memory boards are installed, which sockets are occupied and the orientation of the memory boards. If your PC has 256Mb of RAM and two memory boards, that's 128Mb per board, and so on. Notice how the boards are kept in place, most memory sockets have little spring clips at each end. If it looks as though you are going to have to disturb some cables to get at the sockets make a sketch of where they go, or take some photographs of the innards. Replace the case or lid and check everything is working.

The motherboard manual should also mention memory capacity and the combinations of modules you can use. It varies from make to make but newer machines are usually more flexible. On some older motherboards it may be necessary to upgrade RAM modules in pairs. Be prepared to compromise; you may have to discard some original modules in order to get the capacity you require. You may be able to offset the cost of the upgrade by part-exchanging your old RAM modules.

You should now be in a position to work out the number, type and size of memory modules for the upgrade. Have this information to hand, plus the motherboard manual and the make and model of the computer when you order your memory modules. You may well be asked some additional questions. If you can't supply all the answers or there are any doubts don't guess or take chances, pay to have the upgrade carried out by a qualified engineer.

If everything has gone according to plan you should have in front of you a small plastic bag or box containing the new modules. Don't take them out of their packaging until they're actually needed; the plastic has been specially treated to protect the modules from static electricity, so don't take chances.

Before you start make sure the PC is working properly, shut it down, disconnect from the mains and remove the case or lid from the system box. Ensure there's plenty of light, so you can see what you are doing. Frequently touch or hold the case metalwork when you're working inside the case to get rid of any static build-up. If you have to unplug any cables to gain access make a note of where they go, and any alignment indicators. That's especially important on the ribbon cables that connect the motherboard or expansion cards to the disk drives. One edge of the ribbon cable usually has a red marker or line. Most of the rest of the plugs have notches or lugs, so they fit only one way around.

You will probably have to remove one or more of the incumbent modules, so do that first. Socket designs vary but usually there's a small plastic or metal clip at either end. Using your fingers or the tip of a screwdriver, prise the clips outwards – only a little pressure should be needed – the module should then flip up or tip back at an angle and it can be lifted out. You may find that an adjacent module gets in the way, if so, unclip this first. Avoid touching the contacts and place the module(s) on the anti-static bag or box containing your new modules. Don't get them mixed up.

Touch the case metalwork again and remove the new modules from their packaging, again try not to touch any of the contacts. Inserting the new modules is a reversal of the removal procedure; note the position of any small notches on the contact strip and the socket, so that they line up. Some modules have to go in at an angle, in all cases they should seat easily. If not, re-check the alignment and notches. Now press down or tip the modules up to the vertical position one by one – ensure any pegs on the outside edges of the socket line up with the holes on the board – and you will hear a satisfying click as the clips engage. Check to make sure they're all seated properly. If not, go back and do it again. Reconnect any cables, and double check any other plugs and sockets you may have disturbed.

You can now replace the lid. Reconnect mains plug and switch the PC on. The new memory should be automatically recognised by the motherboard, the first indication that everything has gone according to plan is a new, bigger number on the 'Memory Test' message that appears when the machine first boots up. Some machines may hang at this point and ask you to press a key – usually F1 – to confirm the new settings, others will continue as normal. In the unlikely event that the PC won't boot up, or one of the disk drives doesn't work, the most likely explanation is that one of the ribbon cables has become unseated.

If you heard a series of bleeps when the machine booted up it usually indicates that one of the memory modules is faulty or you have fitted the wrong type. The safest thing to do is to remove the module or modules and contact your supplier; they may be able to talk you through it or determine the correct type of modules from the numbers or markings on your original memory boards.

Assuming everything is okay, you should find that the Windows opening screens appear much quicker – that's another good sign. When Windows has finished loading confirm that the machine recognises the new memory by clicking on System in My Computer, and selecting the Performance tab, where the new RAM capacity will be displayed. Give yourself a pat on the back and see what your newly turbocharged PC can do.

ADDING EXTRA USB SOCKETS

Most PCs built in the last few years have at least two USB sockets, and very useful they are too but on most machines they are quickly used up, usually by a printer and scanner, making it difficult to connect any more peripherals; there's a long list, including digital cameras, web cams, broadband modems, memory card reader and so on.

It's easy to add extra USB sockets using a simple plug-in device called a 'hub', which plugs into one of the existing sockets, however, this only adds to the clutter around the back of most PCs; a far more satisfactory solution is to add an internal hub or expansion card. Cards are available with two, three or four USB sockets and if required extra cards can be added to increase the number still further.

Step 1: make sure your PC has a spare PCI expansion socket on the motherboard, most PCs have at least two but the only way to find out for sure is to unplug the PC from the mains and remove the lid. PCI slots are usually quite easy to identify, on most PCs they are coloured white and they are usually arranged in banks along the back edge of the motherboard. They are usually easy to tell apart from other types of expansion socket. ISA slots (now almost obsolete and not fitted to some motherboards) are a lot longer and usually coloured black. There may also be an AGP socket which is usually on its own and used exclusively by graphics cards.

Step 2: obtain your PCI adaptor card. It's a good idea to get one with at least three or four sockets as they will be quickly used up. They can be obtained from most PC suppliers and mail order specialists advertising in computer magazines. By all means peruse the instructions that come with the card but only for amusement, they're often written in a Pidgin English that makes the average computer manual look a model of clarity.

Step 3: after taking all necessary anti-static precautions and possibly removing any blanking plates covering the vacant PCI slot, you are ready to insert the card. It might be a little tight but never force the card into the socket as you could damage the card, or the motherboard. When you're happy it is correctly seated insert and tighten the retaining screw.

When the PC is switched on Windows should automatically recognise the card and you may be asked to load your installation CD-ROM but from start to finish the whole process should only take a couple of minutes, after which the card is ready to use.

Q&A Real world problems

Drive to distraction

Q   Some time ago a friend installed a couple of memory boards for me to improve the paltry 64Mb bytes that I had at my disposal. All seemed fine but when we started up the PC it informed us that drive A: was not installed. On dismantling the machine we found that the lead to the A Drive had become disconnected, so we reconnected it and screwed everything back in place. However Windows told us that it could not read the floppy, which we had inserted in the drive. Also the little light remains permanently on, even when the drive is empty! We tried another drive from a discarded machine, but got the same result. We asked Windows to recognise new hardware but it informs me there isn't any. Help!

A Check to make sure you haven't inserted the ribbon connector plug the wrong way around – it can easily happen – the connectors are not 'polarised' and can go in either way. However, the more likely explanation is that you've been using the wrong plug on the ribbon cable. The one intended for Drive A: is towards the end of the cable. It's easy to identify, immediately in front of the correct plug, about one-third of the way in from the edge of the ribbon – there should be a group of seven wires, twisted through 180 degrees.

Write to life

Q I have bought a CD-Writer and installed it on top of my existing CD-ROM, the idea being that I would use both and reduce wear and tear on the (expensive) CD-Writer. However, I cannot seem to get any sound from the CD-ROM drive. Can you help? Does using the CD-Writer for bog standard CD-ROM functions reduce its life?

A If you have suddenly lost the ability to play audio CDs on your original CD-ROM drive it is likely that the audio cable was dislodged during installation. It plugs into a small socket on the back of the drive, the other end goes to the sound card or a socket on the motherboard. You will only be able to hear audio CDs on one of the two drives (the one with the audio lead). In general, wear and tear is not an issue with CD-ROM drives and CD Writers; there are only a few moving parts and the disk never comes into contact with the optical read/write head. You needn't worry about shortening its life by using it; other components in your PC will probably fail long before your drive will have a chance to expire.

Part II

PROJECTS

CHAPTER 6   **Word processing projects**

If pressed you could probably come up with several good reasons why you've bought a personal computer – games and the Internet figure prominently on many people's list – but the one application that really makes sense of all that expensive and baffling technology is word processing.

Windows PCs have a very useful built-in word processor program though few users realise they have it, let alone use it. Nowadays most new PCs come with a software suite that includes a powerful word processor like Microsoft Word or Lotus Word Pro. Nevertheless, Windows WordPad is well worth getting to know, it shares many key features with MS Word and other more grown-up word processors. If you haven't yet taken the plunge with Word, or been thoroughly confused by the vast array of complicated looking features, WordPad is a very good place to begin. It can be found by clicking on the Start button, then Programs and Accessories and you'll usually find it towards the bottom of the list.

WordPad has more facilities than most users will ever need for creating everyday documents, like letters, reports or faxes. You could easily use it to write that book you've been planning; in fact it has more features than many top-of-the-line word processors from the late 1980s, and it's a darn sight easier to use.

We'll start with the basics, and look at some more advanced operations later on in this chapter. The biggest advantage a word processor has over a typewriter is the facility to manipulate text before it is committed to paper. In other words, if you make a mistake or change your mind you can easily correct it.

Changing a single word or letter using the backspace key is simple enough but when it comes to editing whole sentences, paragraphs or larger blocks of text the most useful feature is highlight. Highlighting text can seem a bit awkward at first but with practice it soon becomes second nature. Use the mouse to place the cursor in front of the first letter of the word or words you want to work on, click, hold, and carefully move the cursor to the last letter in the block and release the mouse button. If you find the mouse difficult to control with the necessary precision you should try changing the Pointer Speed setting, which you will find in Control Panel (Start > Setting and select the Motion tab).

In WordPad and most variants of Microsoft Word you can highlight a single line, a whole paragraph or the entire document, by putting the mouse pointer into the space before the beginning of a line and clicking the left mouse button once, twice or three times. To remove a highlight, left-click into an empty part of the page area.

Once a word or block of text has been highlighted you can do all kinds of interesting things to it, including moving it around, copying it, altering the font, font size, alignment and changing it to bold, italic or underlined characters. To move text to another part of the document put the pointer into the highlighted area, click and hold the left mouse button, drag the highlight to the new location and release the mouse button. To copy a word or block of text highlight it, click and hold the mouse button, press the Ctrl key (note that the cursor changes to a 'plus' sign) then move the cursor to where you want it to go and release the mouse button. Should you want to repeat a highlighted word or text block more than once, put it into the Clipboard by clicking on the Copy icon on the toolbar, or click on the Copy option in the Edit drop-down menu. You can also use the keyboard shortcut Ctrl + C. Place the cursor where you wish the repeated text to go and click on the Paste icon (it looks like a small clipboard in WordPad and Word) and click the left mouse button or use the shortcut command Ctrl + V. Copy and Paste options can be accessed quickly by pressing the right mouse button.

If you want to erase highlighted text simply press the Delete button or click on the Cut (scissors) icon. Should you change your mind about an action click on the undo icon, it looks like an arrow curving to the left. MS Word also has a re-do feature (an arrow curving to the right) to change it back again.

You can customise your pages and screen presentation. Options include setting page width, paragraph layout, font, font size and zoom settings, which are normally located on the toolbar or listed under menu items, such as Format. Experiment with the various styles and settings on offer.

CUSTOMISING WORD

Microsoft Word is the world's most popular word processor, and it's not difficult to see why. Word is simply the best and since the very earliest versions this sophisticated word processor program has set the standard by which other word processors are measured. If there has to be a criticism it's that it is too powerful and many owners never use more than a small fraction of its many features.

We'll begin with a few tips and tweaks to help you get Word up and running, and tailored to suit your needs. Later on we'll delve a bit deeper into some of the more interesting and useful facilities. There are several different versions of Word but one of the program's strengths is that the overall design, the desktop and main menu functions vary little from version to version. It's also worth pointing out that Word is available as a stand-alone program and as part of the Office suite of programs.

Word is reasonably intuitive and even complete novices are usually able to start writing and printing letters or documents straight away. The first thing most users want to do is customise the blank page that appears when Word starts; this is called the Normal Template. If you don't care for the default typeface or font, and the size of the characters, simply click Format on the menu bar and select Font. Choose your preferred font, size and style – even the colour if you wish – then click on the Default button, and that's what you'll get every time you open Word.

You can have as many, or as few toolbars on show as you like; however most of them just waste valuable screen space, with functions you're unlikely to need more than once in a blue moon. The two most useful ones are Standard and Formatting; they're worth keeping on screen all the time. The Toolbar display option is on the View menu, or put the mouse pointer into a toolbar, right click and the selection menu appears. The Toolbars and Menu bar can be shifted around by pointing at the border, clicking and holding the mouse button and then dragging it to where you want it to go.

The paper-white screen in Word can become quite tiring on the eyes after a while, you can adjust the screen brightness or better still, give it a light grey tint. Go to Windows Control Panel (Start, then Settings), click on the Display icon then select the Appearance tab. Click in the Window Text box and go down to the Colour box, which should show white. Click the down arrow on the box and the Other button. Use the vertical slider next to the multi-colour panel to select a light tint and click OK.

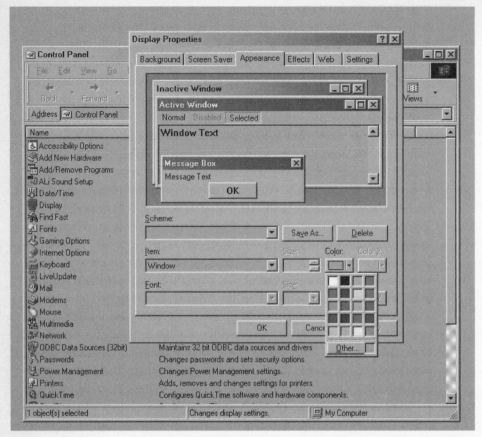

Display Properties in Control Panel lets you apply a light grey tint to your desktop, to make it easier on the eye.

First-time users often get themselves into a tangle when it comes to saving documents, so get organised as soon as possible. By default all of the files you create will be saved in a folder called My Documents, which exists outside Word, on the main C: drive directory tree. The first job is to work out the various types or categories of documents and letters you'll be creating, 'Personal', 'Bank', 'Letters to Bill Gates', that sort of thing. It's a good idea to put the year after each one (and resolve to create a new set of folders every year). Now go to the Start button, then Programs and Windows Explorer and scroll down the list in the left-hand window until you get to My Documents, double click on it and select New from the File Menu and click on the File icon. Create as many folders as you require, re-naming each one as you go. You can instruct Word to automatically use your own file folders by going to Options on the Tools menu, select the File Locations tab and make your changes. Get into the habit of naming and saving a document in the appropriate folder – using the Save As command in the File menu – as soon as you've written the first line or two.

Word can help you with your spelling, highlighting words it doesn't recognise in red and correcting simple mistakes as you type. Word also checks grammar and punctuation; this can be a bit hit and miss but it keeps you on your toes and anything it disagrees with is underlined in green. Going to Options on the Tools menu and selecting the Spelling & Grammar tab enables both facilities. This menu decides how the checks work; there's a more in-depth selection of options under AutoCorrect, also on the Tools menu. Spend some time with these menus, ticking the features you consider worthwhile. Don't rely on AutoCorrect, always run a complete spell check when you've finished a document by placing the cursor at the beginning of the text and clicking the 'ABC' button on the Toolbar.

Word Count is something you'll want to access time and again. You can save time by assigning this and any other frequently used functions a simple keyboard shortcut. Select Customize from the Tools menu, click on the Commands tab and then the Keyboard button. In the left-hand window locate and highlight Tools, and in the right window scroll down the list until you come to Tools Word Count and highlight that. Click a flashing cursor into the 'Press New Shortcut Key' window and choose a simple two-key combination (Ctrl + backslash – next to 'z' on most keyboards – is normally unassigned and simple to do with the left hand) click Assign and it's done. While you're at it have a look through the lists of commands and see if there's anything else you want to have a shortcut to, but not too many or you will have trouble remembering them all.

Be creative with your letters and faxes; there are plenty of embellishments in Word, so get to know them. You'll find a useful assortment of ready-made templates in Style Gallery under the Format menu; these can be applied when you have finished keying in the text. Try adding borders, you will find a good selection of styles on the Format menu, under Borders & Shading. The same menu bar also has options for drop capitals, plus bullet points and paragraph numbering, though it's easier to use the buttons on the Standard toolbar for the latter two features. Don't forget you can add pictures and graphics to your documents. A good way to learn about this feature is to experiment with the Clip Art facility; it's accessed from the Picture option on the Insert menu.

CREATING LABELS

If you write a lot of letters, or you regularly prepare and send out mail-shots then there are some features in Microsoft Word you really should get to know. On the Tools menu there's an item called Envelopes and Labels. The Envelope tab allows you to print directly to envelopes but it can be a fairly tedious business especially if you've got a lot of them, and some printers make heavy weather of it. Select the Label tab for the easier and faster alternative.

Sheets of sticky-back labels are readily available from stationers and they're relatively inexpensive, particularly if you buy the own-label brands. There's a huge range of standard 'Avery' styles plus specialist designs, for floppy disks, videocassettes, name badges and even business cards.

From Envelopes and Labels select the Labels tab and click on the Options button. Scroll down the list until you find the type or style of label you're using; if it's not included you can manually key in the dimensions by clicking New Label. At this point you have several options, you can make a sheet of labels with one address repeated, or create a custom sheet containing your own selection of addresses. In that case check the 'Full Page of the Same Label' option (yes, we know it doesn't make sense) then click on the New Document button. This will bring up a blank sheet of labels, with the outlines marked. Click a cursor into each box and key in the addresses, save and print the sheet as required. It's a good idea to do a test run on an ordinary sheet of paper first, to make sure the text is correctly aligned.

CREATING YOUR OWN STATIONERY

A letterhead or logo can make your correspondence really stand out. A few simple design flourishes can add weight or humour to your message, convey a sense of professionalism, catch the reader's eye and greatly improve the chances of it being read, and you receiving a response.

Of course you could pop down to your local print shop and have them run off a few hundred off-the-shelf letterheads, compliments slips and business cards; or you could mobilise the quite formidable design and printing facilities within your PC, and do the job yourself. Not only will you

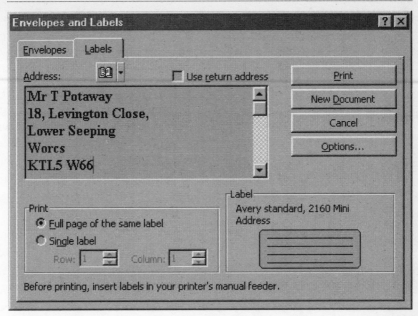

Envelopes and Labels   [?] [X]

Envelopes   Labels

Address: ☐ Use return address   Print

Mr T Potaway
18, Levington Close,
Lower Seeping
Worcs
KTL5 W66

New Document

Cancel

Options...

Print
● Full page of the same label
○ Single label
    Row: 1   Column: 1

Label
Avery standard, 2160 Mini
Address

Before printing, insert labels in your printer's manual feeder.

Bizarrely, Envelopes and Labels in Microsoft Word lets you produce sheets of mixed labels when you check 'Full Page of the Same Label'.

have the satisfaction of creating your own unique personal stationery, it will cost a fraction of what a print shop will charge. There's no need to wait for your order to be fulfilled, you print stationery as you need it and there's little or no waste as you can make instant alterations should your home or business address and contact numbers change.

We'll begin with headed notepaper. If you're using a reasonably up-to-date word processor like Microsoft Word or Lotus Word Pro, then a lot of the hard work has been done for you. In Word go to the File menu, click on New and select the Letters and Faxes tab. There are some really good designs in there, complete with shading and a well chosen blend of typefaces; all you have to do is substitute your name or company name in the text fields. In Word Pro select the New Document item on the File menu and choose one of the preset styles.

Ready-made templates are fine if you're feeling lazy but it's much more satisfying to create a design from scratch, or borrow elements from the templates by copying and pasting them to a blank page. You can also incorporate facilities like automatic date fields using the AutoText and Field options on the Insert menu in Word. Similar features are available in Word

Pro on the Text menu, under Insert Other. Both Word and Word Pro come with extensive clip-art libraries, stuffed full of interesting and useful graphics and logos that can be pasted into your letterhead.

There's nothing to stop you designing your own graphics using the Paint program in Windows or any other paint box program. You can also import images using a scanner or digital camera (see Chapters 13 and 14). Don't be afraid to experiment with typefaces and sizes though avoid using too many different styles on the same page, it can end up looking messy. When your blank letterhead is complete give it a name and save it as a Document Template (*.dot) file in the Letters and Faxes folder in Word; in Word Pro they're saved as SmartMaster files with the extension *.mwp.

Compliments slips can be based on your letterhead. Omit the date line and any other unnecessary elements and key in any additional text you deem necessary. Rearrange the design so that four slips can be printed on a sheet of A4 paper. When you're happy with it use copy and paste to repeat the design. Save it as a document template, run off a few sheets and cut them into strips, so they're ready for use.

Use the best quality paper you can get for headed stationery and comps slips. Make sure you get the right type (i.e., inkjet or laser) for your printer. Inkjet printing on coarse or highly absorbent paper looks dreadful; the ink runs and characters look ragged.

DIY business cards used to be a bit of a problem for PC owners, not because of any deficiency on the part of computers but due to the paper handling characteristics of printers. Nowadays most inkjets and lasers can print on 200 to 250 gsm card, which is well suited to this type of job. Packs of A4 sized card – in various colours – are available at most good stationers. You can also buy sheets of micro-perforated blank business cards from specialist suppliers that are designed to be used with the label-making software in word processors. It's a lot easier than cutting up sheets of card by hand.

In MS Word the label facility is on the Tools menu. It's not especially sophisticated, though it's possible to produce a plain and simple card without too much trouble. Word Pro goes one better with a small selection of business card templates, these can be found in Smart Masters in the New Document menu.

Q&A Real world problems

Customs check

Q   My son has been using Word on our home PC to do his school homework. I noticed him select the assistance of the spell-checker and to my dismay he hit the 'Add' button to save incorrectly spelled words. He now tells me that this is his usual practice. How can I get into the dictionary to correct these additions?

A   User defined spellings in Word are contained in an editable text file called Custom.dic. You can access it from within Word by going to File Open and in the Look In field select Hard Disk C: > Program Files > Common Files > Microsoft Shared > Proof > Custom.dic. Once it's on the screen you can add, delete or change entries before saving the file.

By the numbers

Q   I read somewhere that it was possible to change the format of page numbering in Microsoft Word in order that it would show, for example, 'Page 3 of 10' rather than the single number option currently offered. I am unable to locate the document and cannot for the life of me remember how to do it.

A   Go to View on the menu bar and select Header and Footer then decide whether you want the page number to appear at the top or bottom of the page by clicking a cursor into the dotted Header or Footer box on the page. Next, click the Insert AutoText button on the Header and Footer toolbar, scroll down the list and select the Page X of Y option.

Accursed date

Q   Every time I type the date for a letter in Word (in the form: date, month, year) a rectangle briefly appears reading, for instance '1999-04-01' (it's even done it just now…). Not only does this very irritating item appear but it prints it out of its own accord. How do I rid myself of this accursed thing?

A   It's called an 'AutoComplete Tip', it's another one of those supposedly helpful little features – usually installed by default – that drive some PC users crazy because the means to switch them off is often difficult to find. In this case the option to disable it lives on the Insert menu under AutoText, select AutoText on the submenu that appears, select the AutoText tab and uncheck the box marked 'Show AutoComplete Tip...'

Vulgar type

Q   I have Windows 98 with MS Word. How do I write vulgar fractions, such as 3/16, etc. or any other figure, but written with a horizontal dividing line, with the enumerator above and the dividend below? According to Help I should key in Ctrl \F, but that gets Find.

A   Help isn't very helpful in this case, what it is describing is an equation field code, but it doesn't go into enough detail. There is an easy way however, and that is to go to the Insert drop-down menu and select Field, in the Categories Window click on Equations and Formulas and in the Field Names window highlight EQ. In the Field Code window the letters EQ appear, insert a cursor after the letters and type: '\f(a,b)' (leaving out the inverted commas) where the letters 'a' and 'b' represent the enumerator and dividend respectively, and don't forget the comma. Click OK and the fraction will be inserted into the document. You can reduce the size using the typeface commands on the Formatting toolbar.

Wherefore art thou Euro?

Q   I am informed that somewhere in the oceanic depths of Windows 98 there resides the Euro symbol. Could you please verify what is available in Windows? Also can it be used as a normal font (i.e., change size, boldness, etc.)? Or, if it is available as a download from the Internet, where can it be found?

A   The Euro symbol is included in the 'core' fonts used by Windows 98. The default keyboard shortcuts are Alt Gr + 4 (the right-hand Alt key) and Ctrl + Alt + 4. If you are using a word processor like MS Word, you can also find it in the Symbol table on the Insert menu. It is on the Currency subset under 'Normal Text'. Since the critical core fonts are 'TrueType' you can treat the Euro symbol like any other character and change all or any of its attributes. Users of older versions of Windows can download updated font sets from the Microsoft web site:

http://www.microsoft.com/typography/fontpack/default.htm

Office irritant

Q Recently, I was delighted to discover how to stop automatic date insertion in Word. Now can you tell me how to get rid of that darned Office Assistant who always assumes I need his help to write a letter?

A Click on the Office Assistant icon on the toolbar and then the Options button; on the Options tab uncheck Display Alerts. However, the only way to get rid of it permanently is to uninstall it from Word. You'll need your Office or Word CD-ROM, go to Control Panel and Add/Remove programs, click on Office 97 or Word 97 and then on Add/Remove. This starts the Word uninstall program. Click on Remove Components, then Office Accessories, this leads to a window that displays all of the add-on components. Deselect Office Assistant from the list that appears and click on Continue to remove it. A slightly less drastic solution is to open Windows Explorer/Program Files/Microsoft Office/Office, then right click on the folder named Actors and rename it Dead Actors. In later versions of Word (2000, 2002, etc.) 'Clippit' as he's known to his friends is far more compliant and will not bother you once you've selected Hide the Office Assistant on the Help menu.

Super solution

Q Can you tell me how to get Subscript characters in Word? This is required when writing chemical formula/symbols such as H_2O or CO_2. Is there a reference list of all these various codes?

A Hold down Ctrl and Shift keys then press the = key to toggle superscript on or off. Ctrl+ Caps Lock + = does the same for subscript. Alternatively you can set up buttons on the toolbar. Right click on the toolbar area and, on the menu that opens click Customise. In the Commands section highlight Format and find, in turn, Superscript and Subscript in the list on the right of the window. Left click on each and drag the icon onto the toolbar.

CHAPTER 7 **Design and layout projects**

Word processors aren't just for text; some of them are pretty good with pictures and graphics as well...

Word processor programs like Microsoft Word have a number of powerful presentation tools, which can give your letters, faxes, CVs, reports and newsletters extra visual impact, to make them look as though they were professionally created. The trick is not to try to re-invent the wheel; you can save yourself a lot of time and trouble by using the ready-prepared document and page templates that are included with your word processor. Some of them contain Wizards; they are simple helper programs that enable you to customise the template to your own specifications, so they can be easily reused.

All of the tools can be used retrospectively, which means you can concentrate on keying in the text first, and worry about what the document looks like afterwards. That's important; always check spelling, grammar and anything else that may affect the length of the copy, before you go any further. If you make a lot of changes after the layout has been finished it can easily mess up your design.

Two of the most effective enhancements are to add bullet points, or numbers, to draw the reader's attention to important items. It's incredibly easy, just highlight the block of text you want to emphasise or itemise, click on the appropriate toolbar icon and numbers or bullets will magically appear. It is also easy to enclose a block of text in a frame or border; simply highlight the chunk of copy you want to pick out, select the Tables or Borders icon on the toolbar, specify line width and style then click OK.

One of the most powerful features in Word and Word Pro is the facility to illustrate documents with graphics and pictures. Your word processor almost certainly came with a library of clip-art images. There you will find a good assortment of general-purpose logos and illustrations, but there's nothing to stop you designing your own, or use pictures and images filed on your PC and downloaded from the Internet.

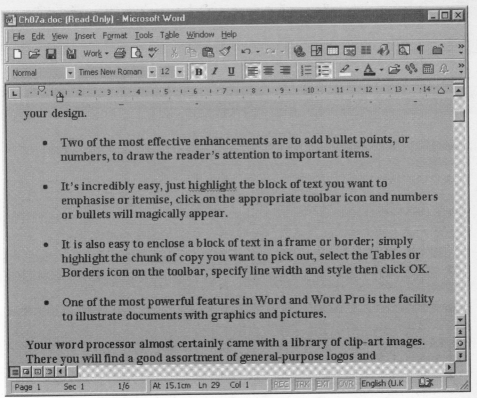

Adding bullet points to a document is a simple way to attract the reader's attention.

There are several ways of importing an image into a document. The exact method varies from one word processor to another, but the basic techniques are usually the same. If you haven't already done so you will need to select the word processor's page layout mode; select a zoom or magnification setting that will allow you to see at least half to two-thirds of the page. If you choose a full-page display, and you're using a small monitor (14 or 15 inches) you won't be able to read the copy or see the images clearly. This will also show you exactly what the finished page will look like when it is printed out.

Using the cursor or mouse pointer decide where you want the illustration to go on the page. In Word images are chosen using the Picture option on the Insert menu. From there you can search through the Clip Art library. Incidentally, additional clip art can be downloaded free from the Microsoft website by clicking on the browser button in the bottom right hand of the dialogue box and there's tons more of it to be found spread around the

Internet. Otherwise you can search for a specific image file, located else-where on your computer, using the familiar directory tree.

When the image has been found click on it and it will be imported into the open word processor document. Initially the picture will be highlighted, so that it can be moved around the page using the mouse pointer and, if necessary, re-sized, by clicking, holding and dragging on one of the squares or 'sizing handles' on the corners and sides of the image.

Alternatively, load the image into the Windows Paint program (Start > Programs > Accessories) or any other graphics software program that you may have. From the Edit menu, copy the image to the Clipboard, then return to the word processor and paste it into the document, from where you can position and re-size it.

Word Processors like Microsoft Word have a powerful text wrapping facility that can run the words around the picture. On earlier versions of Word it is located on the Format menu under the heading Object, though it only appears when an image has been highlighted. Click on the Wrapping tab, and from the selections presented choose how you want the text to surround the picture. On later versions it's on the Drawing Toolbar, if this is not displayed simply right click into an empty area of the toolbar at the top of the page and select Drawing. Text wrapping is actually a lot easier than it sounds; nevertheless, it pays to do a few dry runs, before trying anything too ambitious.

CREATING A NEWSLETTER

Producing a newsletter is easy, the trouble is most word processing and desktop publishing (DTP) programs have far too many options and inevitably some first efforts end up looking like a dog's dinner. So, the first thing to do is open a new page on your word processor, select a big bold typeface and write 'KEEP IT SIMPLE!', print it out and stick it somewhere you can see it.

Word processing programs such as Microsoft Word have everything you need to create a really professional looking newsletter. However, if you're going to be doing a lot of them or want to prepare a succession of longer multi-page documents it is worth investing in some serious (though not necessarily expensive) DTP software, like Adobe Pagemaker, MS Publisher or Serif Page Plus. However, we'll begin with the simplest method, which is to use your word processor to transform ready prepared text, a club or society report for example, into an illustrated newsletter.

For this example we'll be using MS Word, though the basic principles can be applied to most recent WP programs. Start by opening the text file and select the Page or Print Layout option from the View menu; a 75% zoom setting should allow you to see between half and two-thirds of the page on a 14 or 15-inch monitor. You will probably find that 9 or 10-point justified text produces the best-looking results. Next, highlight all the text by putting the mouse pointer into the space to the left of the copy and click the left mouse button three times. Go to the Column icon on the toolbar (or Columns on the Format menu, for a wider choice of styles) and choose a two- or three-column layout from the options presented. Three-column designs look cleaner and allow more flexibility with pictures and illustrations. You will see that the copy flows from one column to the next. If you make changes to column 1, say, then any over or underflow words will be pushed into or drawn back from the next columns, and onto any subsequent pages.

Now create a banner or title by going to the Insert menu and clicking on Text Box. The mouse pointer will change to a pair of crosshairs; position it on the first letter in column one, click and hold the left mouse button and create a rectangular box by dragging the crosshair across the top of the page. The body text will move down the page to make way for the box and a flashing cursor will appear inside the box when you release the mouse button. Type in your banner or title, press return and key in any other information you want to appear at the head of the page, such as a sub-title, the date, volume and issue numbers. Highlight each item and select the appropriate typeface and font size. You will probably have to experiment with the typeface setting and the size of the box, to get everything in.

If you haven't already done so, insert some headlines into the copy, to separate the various items. You can do this by highlighting and enlarging body text, or inserting text boxes. Do not be tempted to use a different typeface for headlines – remember KEEP IT SIMPLE – otherwise it can look messy. To make headlines stand out use bold characters and/or capital letters.

Adding pictures to your page is very straightforward. From the Insert menu click on Picture and select From File or Clipart, the From File option will take you to the directory tree, so you can retrieve an image from another application, such as a graphics program, scanner or digital camera picture library. When you have located the image file click on it, and it will be placed on the page and displace the text. Use the mouse to move it to the correct position, and the sizing handles around the image to fit it into the space. You can use the Crop facility on the Picture sub-menu to trim the image. If you

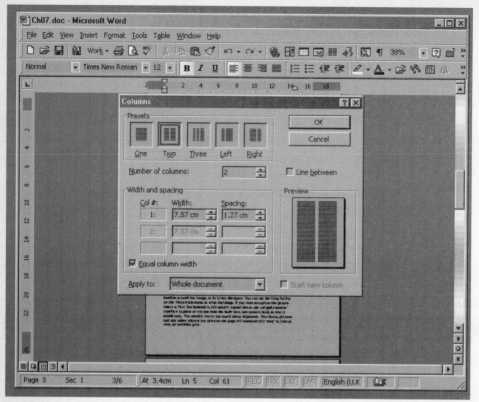

A two- or three-column design will make layout easier and your newsletter look more professional.

want to caption the picture insert a Text Box beneath it; it's usually a good idea to use a slightly smaller typeface (a point or two less than the body text, and make it bold, so that it stands out). You needn't worry too much about alignment. Text boxes, pictures and any other objects you place on the page will automatically 'snap' to line up with an invisible grid.

Sod's law says that there's always too much, or not enough text to fill a page neatly. The former can be solved with some judicious editing, or if you can't bear to cut your masterwork, try reducing the font size by a point, though don't go below 9 points for body copy if you can help it. Filling an empty space is just as easy. Either write some more copy, increase the point size, or better still, create a 'Callout', by inserting a quote or sentence from the text across one or two columns. That's also a good way to draw the reader's attention to a particular point.

Time to add a few finishing touches. Inserting lines between the columns helps break up the page and make it look more interesting. This facility is on the Drawing menu. Position the mouse pointer where you want the line to begin, click and hold the left mouse button and drag the line to where you want it to end. Check the line is straight and release the button. Don't worry if it's too long or short, you can change it by clicking on the sizing box at the end of the line. Create a small text box at the foot of the page and type in a page number, you may want to add the month and year or any other information you feel is relevant. This is a good time to run off a page proof on the printer, read it through, get someone else to double check it for you, correct any mistakes and roll the presses.

DESIGNING YOUR OWN GREETINGS CARD

If you've got a PC and a colour inkjet printer your greetings card problems are solved – make your own! Designing and printing your own cards probably won't save you a huge amount of money, though it will be cheaper than going to a print bureau and DIY cards have a number of advantages over the store-bought variety.

It's personal, people appreciate and remember the thought, and if you're running a business a corporate Christmas card is an excellent opportunity to send greetings to clients and customers with a touch of humour, possibly with a discreet commercial message as well. You print only as many as you need, so there's less waste and if you're not making too many you could personalise each one with the recipient's name or a short note.

Everything you need to create a basic greetings card is included in Windows, though if you want to do a really bang-up job, and make your life easier, one or two extra items of software and hardware might come in useful. Up-to-date word processors, like Microsoft Word or Lotus Word Pro have good page layout facilities and a graphics program, such as PaintShop Pro (available to try before you buy shareware from www.jasc.com and computer magazine cover-mount CD-ROMs) will assist with the artwork. If you have a digital camera, scanner or an Internet connection then you will have much greater choice of imagery to work with. Incidentally, scanners often come with graphics software that includes greetings card templates; you may well find something there that takes your fancy.

Commercial card designer programs are all very well – and there are plenty to choose from – but it's far more satisfying to make use of what you have so we'll look at two very simple techniques using standard Windows software. Which method you choose will depend to a large extent on the capabilities of your printer. Check the manual to find out the maximum weight or thickness of paper it can handle. If you're limited to thinnish paper, between 80–120 gsm, say, then a double-fold A4 sheet (ending up as an A6 size card) is most suitable. If you can print on 200 to 250 gsm card then you can produce a gatefold card, making two A6-sized cards per A4 sheet.

If you have to work with A4 paper then the trick is to place the text message and artwork that will appear inside the card, in the lower right hand quarter of the page. The 'front cover' image or artwork goes in the top right corner. This has to be printed upside down, so that when the page is folded into half, then half again, it will appear on the outside cover – the right way up – and the text will be facing you when it is opened. It sounds more complicated than it is; try it with a sheet of A4 paper, fold it twice, mark the front and inside, open it up again and you'll see how it works.

Begin with the front cover artwork. This can come from a variety of sources; you can create a simple design from scratch using the Paint program in Windows (Start, Accessories). Better still use a scanned picture or digital photo of the family or kids or import some suitable clip art from one of the many sites around the Internet.

To use an Internet image simply right-click on it, choose the Save Picture As option and save it in your document folder. If you are using Paint save it as a bitmap (*.bmp) file in the Save As Type file window. Open the image in Paint (or your preferred paint-box program) and insert any text as required. When you're happy with it, flip or rotate the image (you may have to flip horizontally as well as vertically to make sure text comes out the right way) and save it. Repeat with any other graphics you want on the cover. Now you can paste the artwork into an open document, either by copying it to the clipboard, or using the word processor's Insert Picture option. Position and size the pictures in the top right-hand corner of the page. Insert a text box into the bottom right corner of the page and compose your message. Make a test print, to check alignment and fold lines and amend as necessary.

Printing directly to card requires a slightly different technique. You'll be making two cards at once; moreover the front covers and inside messages are on opposite sides of the paper, so the card has to pass through the printer twice. Once again start with the artwork that's going to appear on the outside. Import it into your open word processor document, this time position it in the top right-hand corner of the page then copy (click to highlight and press Ctrl) and drag or paste a duplicate image immediately underneath, this is easiest in whole page view mode. Next open a second blank page; use the window sizing bars to place it alongside the first, so you can see both pages at once, to check alignment. Create and position a text box in the top right quarter of the page. Write your message, add any artwork then place a copy underneath.

Print the front cover page first (or pages if you're making a lot of cards) then print the inside message by turning the card over, and loading it into the printer upside down. It's a good idea to do a test sheet on ordinary paper first, to make sure everything lines up and comes out the right way around. When they're finished cut, fold and sign.

Q&A Real world problems

Transfer list

Q Help! I want to use my PC to design and print some waterslide transfers using an Epsom printer. This would of course require the appropriate material to print on. Such is either extremely elusive, or simply does not exist.

A A quick search on the Internet revealed a number of sources. It's used in the pottery industry for prototyping designs. Have a word with Tullis Russell Brittains of Stoke-on-Trent; they manufacture A3 and A4 sizes. They can be reached on (01782) 202567 or visit their website at: http://www.brittains.co.uk

Word picture

Q Please help a comparative newcomer to PCs. I have used Microsoft Word to set up and print a personal letterhead and have also printed photographs via my Plustek Optic Pro scanner. However, I can find no instructions on how to transfer a photo, reduced, onto the letterhead. Can you please guide me?

A It's easy; first decide where you want the picture to go by clicking a flashing cursor into the open document. Next, from the Insert menu in Word select Picture and click on the From File option and use the directory tree that appears to locate the image. When you have found it click on the listing once and a preview of the picture will appear in the right-hand window, if it's the one you want click OK, Word will change to the Page Layout view and the picture will be imported into your open Word document. Click onto the image to insert sizing squares, so you can move it around and alter its shape and dimensions.

CHAPTER 8 **Using the Internet**

The Internet is arguably the most important development in communications since the invention of the printing press and several billion pages of information are available to you, at the touch of button, but where do you start?

To use and make the best use of the Internet it helps to know a little bit about how it works, at least the bit that concerns you, the connection between your PC and the vast network of computers and other PC owners around the world. Nowadays connecting to the Internet is almost painless; most PCs are fitted with modems as standard, the devices that convert digital data coming from and flowing into your PC into audible tones that can be sent down an ordinary telephone line. Modems used to be devilishly difficult to set up, as were Internet and email accounts but that too has been made as near idiot-proof as it's possible to get. In most cases it is no more complicated than loading a CD-ROM and answering a few simple questions that pop up on the monitor screen. The most difficult decision most newcomers have to make is to choose between the many Internet Service Providers and the various rates and tariffs, however, things are changing.

Many users are now migrating from traditional 'dial-up' connections to high-speed 'broadband' services. A normal telephone modem can receive data at a theoretical maximum speed of 56 kilobits per second; most broadband services operate at least ten times faster. The Internet comes alive; multimedia-rich web pages with pictures, animation and sounds, etc., generally appear on your PC screen in a fraction of a second, which makes 'surfing' a much more pleasurable and productive experience. Music files that can take half an hour or more to download on a dial-up connection come through in a minute or two, you can watch streamed video and 'webcasts', play games on-line and transfer large files to other PCs in a matter of moments.

Another major plus point is that broadband connections are 'always-on' which means there's no waiting for the modem to dial up and log on, and no call charges, apart from a fixed monthly fee and if you like you can leave your PC connected to the net 24 hours a day. Broadband systems that use existing telephone lines – ADSL or asynchronous digital subscriber line technology as it's known in the trade – also frees up your phone line, which can be used to make and take telephone calls while you are on line.

Under Windows 9x and XP setting up an ADSL connection is no more difficult than plugging in a printer – see also Chapter 10. Once you have established that the service is available from your local exchange and your line has been checked all you have to do is plug in the broadband modem to a spare USB socket, load the installation CD-ROM and enter a few details (provided by your ISP) and you are in business.

Since a broadband connection is always on you will change the way you and others use your PC. Your virus scanner should be updated religiously, you must install some Firewall software on your computer, and if children are going to be allowed to use it, it's wise to install some monitoring software (Net Nanny, Safe Surf, etc.) that will stop them logging on to undesirable sites or chat rooms.

You may want to make some changes to your Internet software so that it connects automatically. To enable this facility, launch either program and the dial-up dialogue box will usually appear, check that the user name and password details are correct and tick the 'Connect Automatically' box. You should set Outlook Express to check for messages every few minutes (1 to 5 minutes), these settings can be found on the Tools menu, under Options (select the General tab).

FIRST STEPS ON USING THE INTERNET

The trouble with the Internet is that it is so big that it can make finding a needle in a haystack look simple! Unless you have the address of a particular website you know has the information you're seeking you will have to call upon the services of a Search Engine. They are the telephone directories, Yellow Pages and guide books to the Internet rolled into one, with a dash of advertising thrown in for good measure – the good news is that most of them are completely free to use.

There are many to choose from, however the faster and more efficient are generally reckoned to be Google (www.google.com), Yahoo (www.yahoo.com), Altavista (www.altavista.com) and Ask Jeeves (www.ask.com). Most search

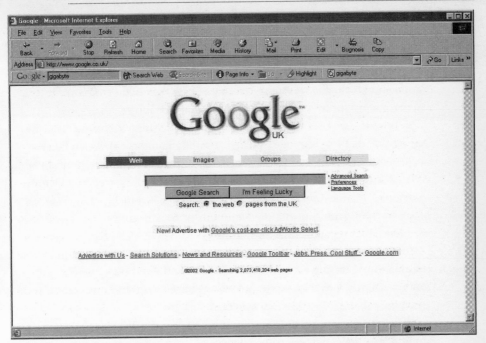

A search engine like Google can help you to find what you want quickly and efficiently.

engines also have UK-centred services; just substitute .co.uk for .com in the address. All search engines use 'keywords' to find web pages containing the information you want and this is where things can go awry. The trick is to narrow your search by choosing your words very carefully and being as specific as possible.

When you find the information you are looking for and you want to keep it or review it later you have several choices. You can save the web page as-is by clicking 'Save As' on your browser's File menu. The easiest way to save text and pictures is to highlight the block and press Ctrl + C (copy command), open a new word processor document and press Ctrl + V (paste command). Individual pictures or graphics can be easily saved by right-clicking the image and selecting Save As and choosing a location on your PC's hard drive.

PROJECT – RESEARCHING YOUR FAMILY TREE

Your PC's ability to gather, store and process information makes it a perfect tool for genealogical research, and this is a good excuse to make a start on that family tree you've been meaning to compile. It can be an absorbing and rewarding pastime and who knows where it might lead? You might discover royal ancestry, a hereditary title and coat of arms, a forgotten legacy or even an infamous mass murderer in the family. The point is you'll be creating a unique and valuable resource to share with the whole family and a fascinating insight into your own life and times for future generations.

A computer makes the task so much easier by creating a dynamic database and archive that can be easily updated as family members arrive and depart, but the real advantage lies in the ways different types of information can be collated and presented. The traditional hand-drawn family tree usually only has room for names and key dates; a PC family tree can incorporate so much more, including almost unlimited amounts of background notes, stories or anecdotes, photographs, drawings, scans of old newspapers, even sound and video clips. The PC has another equally important role to play, as a finder of information. The Internet is brim-full of genealogical sites, family home pages and email provides a fast and efficient means of communication for family members, wherever they may be.

So where do you start? You will of course need a PC but this kind of application isn't particularly demanding and any reasonably recent multimedia model will suffice. An Internet connection is vital and since you will be handling photographs and documents, a scanner is invaluable (see Chapter 13). Again, you won't need a particularly elaborate model, indeed any of the current budget models should be more than adequate.

The right software is important too. It is possible to create a basic graphical tree with standard Windows applications like a word processor. Better still would be a spreadsheet program, such as Excel. Cells can contain a mixture of information and the tabular presentation is well suited to the tree layout. However, to do the job properly and make maximum use of your PC's processing power it's a good idea to get hold of a purpose-designed family tree program. There are plenty to choose from, including some excellent freeware and shareware titles that can be downloaded from the Internet.

In addition to displaying the tree in a visually attractive format, and making it easier to access or update the archive, most family tree programs will allow you to create detailed printouts or even help compile an illustrated book for wider distribution. Many family tree programs use a common file format, called Gedcom (extension *.gft), which will allow you to exchange data with other researchers, using other types of software.

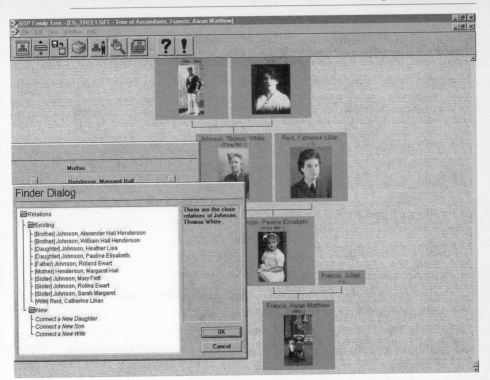

Genealogy can be a rewarding and engrossing hobby and a program like this will help you to collate your data, and allow you to share it with other members of your family.

It can be a lot of hard work so before you begin ask around to see if any of the initial research has already been done. Most families have at least one amateur historian – past or present – whose records may be able to get you off to a good start. Older family members can give you first-person access to recent family history, though remember to exercise some tact and always be sensitive to any skeletons and scandals that you may uncover. Illegitimacy and extra-marital affairs were just as common 100 years ago as they are today, our forebears were just more adept at keeping them secret.

Official documents such as old birth, marriage and death certificates are an invaluable source of raw data and family photo albums can provide a wealth of information. Don't dismiss the apparently mundane; postcards and letters often contain useful historical snippets and even obscure photographs of places or buildings can provide additional avenues for exploration.

Back to the PC. Start with an Internet search of your family name on search engines like Google, Alta Vista and Yahoo; don't forget to try some of the more obvious alternative spellings. You may well come across a family home page link to long-lost relations or overseas branches of the family. In the UK genealogists are well served by our long history of bureaucracy and record keeping by Government agencies. The Public Records Office website (see Contacts) is a good place to start with some excellent information and advice for novice family historians. Try also the Office for National Statistics and Family Record Centre and the Commonwealth War Graves Commission, all of whom host informative websites. You will also come across numerous historical societies, research agencies and magazines that specialise in genealogical research.

The world's largest genealogical database has been set up by the Church of the Latter-Day Saints in the US (see Contacts). It is extremely powerful – avoid a casual search, you will be swamped with information but it should prove invaluable once you have started work on your family tree.

Be realistic in your research and set yourself achievable goals. At first it is highly unlikely you will be able to trace your ancestry back more than a few generations, so aim to complete a tree for the past 200 years, say, and take it from there. Most researchers begin with the paternal or family name but from a genetic perspective the maternal line is equally valid and in some societies it is considered more important, though it may involve considerably more effort.

CONTACTS

Web list/resources
http://www.cyndislist.com/

UK Public Records Office
http://www.pro.gov.uk

Commonwealth War Graves Commission
www.cwgc.org]

Church of the Latter-Day Saints search
http://www.familysearch.org/Eng/Search/frameset_search.asp

PROJECT – ACCESSING NEWSGROUPS

Newsgroups are the heart and soul of the Internet. Think of them as the community halls of the global village, far removed from the slick big-city commercial and business interests on the worldwide web. They're places where like-minded individuals meet on-line to discuss and swap ideas, ask and answer questions on just about any subject you care to name (and one or two you probably wouldn't).

A Newsgroup is basically a public noticeboard where you can post email messages, articles or announcements for others to read and respond to. Unlike normal email and the web, which are immediately accessible once you've signed up with an Internet Service Provider (ISP) you have to actively subscribe to Newsgroups, though it's not like a magazine or newspaper subscription and it won't cost you a penny (apart from your normal connection charges).

If you are wondering if there's a Newsgroup devoted to your particular interests the answer is undoubtedly yes. It's impossible to give a precise figure but there are well over 50,000 of them, with hundreds more being created every day. The number of Newsgroups you will have direct access to depends on your ISP. Newsgroups are stored on computers called news servers, which are part of a wider network called Usenet; apart from the problems of finite storage space most ISPs restrict or prohibit Newsgroups devoted to activities they deem antisocial or undesirable (child pornography, bomb-making, software piracy, that kind of thing). Newsgroups may also be 'moderated', that is, monitored for abusive or offensive messages, to keep respondents on the subject and prevent blatant advertising. In fact there is a fairly strict code of conduct or 'Netiquette' that most Newsgroup users are happy to adhere to. More on that in a moment.

In order to access Newsgroups you will need a program called a newsreader. The chances are you already have one on your PC as they are integrated into most popular browsers and email programs, including Internet Explorer, Netscape and those supplied by AOL and CompuServe. Separate newsreader software programs are also available, one of the most popular being a shareware program called Free Agent, which can be downloaded from http://www.forteinc.com

The first job is to set up your newsreader. You will need a couple of items of information, namely your email address and the domain name of your ISP's news server. You should find this included in the sign-up information or you can get it from the ISP's helpline; it will usually be something like 'news.freebienet.co.uk'. In Outlook Express setup begins when you click the Read News icon on the opening page, just follow the instructions and when it has finished you will be asked if you want to download the list of

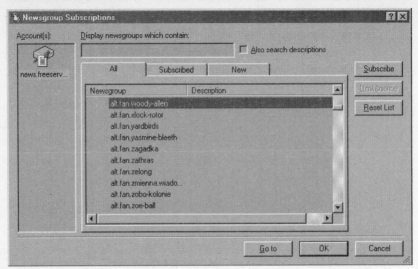

Whatever your interest there's a Newsgroup where you can share your views with other like-minded individuals.

Newsgroups on the ISP's news server. This can take several minutes depending on the speed of your connection and time of day. You have to do this only once since most newsreaders will automatically update the list when you are on-line.

The newsreader will log off and present you with a list of several thousand newsgroups. Don't bother searching through them all, it will take forever, your newsreader has a search facility that looks for groups containing a keyword. You can then select the ones that interest you by clicking on the subscribe button. Incidentally, you might be wondering what all the prefixes mean. Any Newsgroup beginning with comp. means it is computer related, misc. is miscellaneous, rec. is short for recreational subjects, sci. is used for science-related topics, soc. covers social issues, and so on. By far the largest collection of newsgroups begin with alt. for alternative. The alt. groups are a kind of fringe operation, existing outside of the official Usenet system but that doesn't imply they're any less interesting relevant or useful, though this tends to be where the dubious and doubtful Newsgroups congregate.

Once you have chosen the groups you wish to subscribe to you will have to go back on line and (if you have disconnected) the newsreader will download all of the 'headers' in your selected groups. Headers are topics or subject headings (by default OE loads 300 headers; you can change it by going to Options on the Tools menu and selecting the Read tab). Depending on the newsgroup you may see anything from a dozen to several hundred postings, those marked with a plus sign indicate the message is part of a 'thread', effectively a running conversation with other Newsgroup users contributing to the topic.

You can read any message simply by clicking on the header, however, all the time you are on-line you are clocking up the phone bill. The alternative is to download selected messages – or the whole Newsgroup, if there are not too many of them – and read them at your leisure, off-line. In Outlook Express the option to mark and download messages can be found on the Tools menu.

You will probably find that some messages or articles no longer exist or you get an error message. Don't worry, it's not a fault on your PC, messages are routinely deleted to make way for new ones and on really busy Newsgroups postings may only be shown for a couple of days. After reading a few messages you might well decide that you have something to contribute or a question to ask but it is a good idea to read all of the postings in your chosen group. It's worth monitoring a newly subscribed Newsgroup for a while to get a feel of how it works, pick up the jargon and maybe get to know the people using it. Many Newsgroups include a FAQ (frequently asked questions) file about the group and you should read it.

PROJECT – LEARNING NETIQUETTE

Having subscribed to a Newsgroup most newcomers feel an irresistible urge to join in. Don't, at least, not straight away. You will almost certainly commit some terrible *faux pas* and irritate or enrage other members of the group who will respond with 'flames' or 'mail bombs', by sending you abusive and offensive emails. If you want to get the most out of this amazing resource you must learn a few simple rules, it is called 'Netiquette' and you ignore it at your peril.

It might sound a bit precious but remember there are people on the other side of your computer screen, thousands, possibly millions of them! It is very easy to offend when your only means of communication is a keyboard. Those reading your words may well come from very different cultural and ethnic backgrounds and English might not be their first language. Without voice inflections, facial expressions and the body language of face-to-face conversation a seemingly innocent remark or gentle British irony can turn into a major insult, which in other circumstances might result in a punch on the nose!

Good netiquette isn't meant to be stuffy, your messages should be informal but be polite and above all succinct and to the point; long and wordy postings will simply be ignored. Sarcasm and humour should be used with caution, if you must try to be funny then make sure your wit is well signposted – we'll show you how to do that in a moment.

There are a few other points to bear in mind. DON'T SHOUT unless you really mean it, writing in capital letters is considered bad form. If you want to respond to a specific point or communicate directly with a member of the group on a topic outside the Newsgroup's subject area, send an email to the member concerned otherwise a Newsgroup can quickly become cluttered with irrelevant messages or 'follow-ups'. If you have a point to make it is helpful to others if you summarise what has been said before but avoid needless repetition. If you cite references or quotes make sure you mention the source, do not infringe commercial copyright and be very careful about what you say about others. Don't forget Newsgroups are in the public domain and your comments can be easily read or forwarded by email to those you've maligned. Always, always check spelling and grammar but avoid criticising others' use of English, for all you know they might suffer from dyslexia or are learning the language.

It sounds as if there's a lot to learn but it is mostly common sense and it is surprising how quickly you can pick it up by sitting on the sidelines for a few days and just reading the postings. You can get a crash course in netiquette by looking at the guidelines and FAQs in your own Newsgroup and there are some useful hints and tips on the web at: http://www.fau.edu/netiquette/net/elec.html or try the Newsgroup 'news.announce.newusers', which is aimed at newcomers.

Newsgroup postings are often littered with acronyms; used wisely they are a useful form of shorthand but too many will make your messages unreadable or difficult to follow. It's worth committing half a dozen or so of the most commonly used ones to memory. They include FYI, which means 'for your information', BTW is 'by the way', IMHO stands for 'in my humble/honest opinion', ROTFL, 'rolling on the floor laughing', RTFM means 'read the flipping manual' (or words to that effect), TIA is 'thanks in advance' and TTFN, 'ta-ta for now'; a more complete list can be found at: http://www.fau.edu/netiquette/net/acronyms.txt

Since you will be using plain text to compose your messages it is useful to

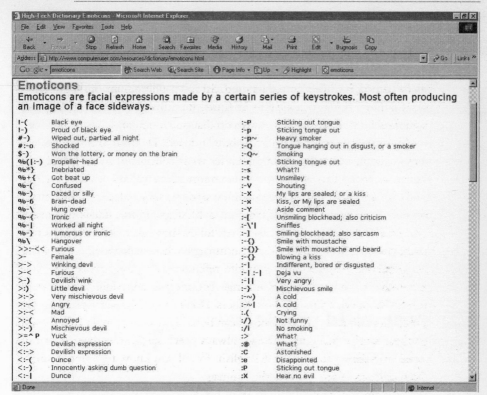

Emoticons, simple visual shorthand to help you add meaning to your messages.

know how to emphasise words or phrases. Surrounding words with *asterisks* draws attention to it, rather like an underline or a bold typeface. Names and titles, like _Boot Up_ can be signified with a single underscore before and after and it is a good idea to limit line length to no more than 60 or 70 characters as this could make your messages difficult to read on some newsreader software.

A good way of writing between the lines, to let those reading your postings know you are making a joke or what you are thinking, is to use simple graphics made up of text characters. They're called 'Emoticons' and there are dozens of them, the most familiar one is the 'smiley' made up of a colon, dash and close bracket symbol thus :-) if you don't get it, turn the page on its side. There are some really ingenious ones, like ; –) which suggests the user has just made a sarcastic remark and is winking or }:-(the user is wearing a toupee on a windy day.

Finally, a few more simple and mostly obvious 'don'ts'. Do not use Newsgroups to advertise. There's no harm in mentioning useful or apposite products and services in response to a Newsgroup posting, even if they are your own, but blatant advertising is frowned upon. It is counterproductive, you will be flamed, excluded from the group and you could end up with some very harmful things being written about you and your business. From time to time you may see or be sent chain letters promising all kinds of things or making worthy-sounding appeals. Bin them all. They are invariably scams or mathematically impossible, moreover they waste valuable network resources. If they are traced back to you your Internet account will almost certainly be closed. Once you've served your apprenticeship you will want to post your first message. Do not send a 'This is a test' message to your group, unless you want your email box filled with flames. There are Newsgroups like alt.just.testing where you can check to make sure everything is working properly.

Q&A Real world problems

Mute modem

Q   With my previous computer whenever I logged on to my server I heard the modem chirrup away as it makes contact. My new PC remains obstinately silent, but only in this respect. At all other times the machine signals me in all the usual ways. Have I inadvertently switched something off?

A   There is a control for modem sound in the Windows Control Panel. Double-click on the Modems icon, select the General tab, highlight your modem's entry, click on the Properties button, select the General tab and you'll find the speaker slider control in the middle.

Zip zap?

Q   I have downloaded several programs from the Internet in the form of .zip files which I place in a folder that I have allocated for this purpose, called (predictably) 'Downloads'. Having unzipped the programs, they then take up residence in their own specific folders as any other ordinary program would do. However, I notice that the original .zip file is still in my

'Download' folder. Would I be correct in assuming that I may safely delete these .zip files since they are now duplicates (albeit in a compressed form) of the programs that are now up and running on my computer?

A   Yes, you can remove the original downloaded .zip files but it's a bit like throwing away a program's original installation disk. You might need it one day if, for example, a program is corrupted or you want to load it on another machine and there's no guarantee the program will always be available from the Internet. If you need to recover space on your hard disk drive then copy the original .zip file to a floppy disk or another suitable backup medium.

Ten-minute rule...

Q   As a parent of three highly PC-literate children, I used to spend a great deal of time controlling and limiting their computer usage. Since installing a new home system I have overcome this problem – and seen the last of a lot of arguments – by the use of a reasonably cost-effective shareware package. This allows me to control the time an individual spends on the system, the hours of the day they can use it and several other useful bells and whistles.

There is a plethora of software to control the content that they can view from the net, but as yet I have not found anything which controls the length of time a user spends on the Internet so that I can, for instance, limit them to perhaps 10 minutes each a day. Our ISP is Freeserve, which doesn't appear to give this functionality. Have you any suggestions?

A   Only ten minutes, that's a bit mean. ... The answer to your question is yes; there are several web utilities that can be programmed to monitor the time spent on-line, sound an alarm when time has expired and even automatically disconnect the line, if required. Clockwise and TimeUp are almost certainly what you are looking for and they can be downloaded from the excellent Tucows website, along with details of more than a dozen other shareware web timers.

  http://tucows.cableinet.net/time95.html

CHAPTER 9

Websites and web cams

For most users the Internet is a passive medium but there's much more to it than web pages, email and newsgroups – why not become a part of it, create your own website or web cam and set up a videophone link with distant friends and relatives?

Setting up your own website is nowhere near as difficult as it sounds. In fact you should be able to put together a simple web page and publish it on the Internet, in less than half an hour! It may not be the smartest looking page on the net, but it's a start, it will be all yours, and in theory it will be viewable by an estimated half a billion people around the world with Internet access!

Of course you will need a few things, starting with an email account that comes with an allocation of free Internet web space (most of them do). When you signed up you should have been given details of the address of the server computer where your space is uploaded. This usually begins with the letters 'ftp' (short for file transfer protocol, a system used to move files around the Internet). If you've lost the details they should be in the support or FAQ pages on your ISP's website. You will also need your login password (usually the same one that you use to access your mailbox) and the address of your free web space.

Essentially, that's all you need because you can create web pages on any text editor or word processor, even something as basic as Windows Notepad, but that is hard work since you'll have to learn to use a text-based programming language called HTML (hypertext mark-up language). The alternative is a web page authoring program that hides HTML behind a simple point-and-click interface. You may already have such a program, there are plenty to choose from, and they are routinely given away on PC magazine disks and included in office suites; however, to keep things as simple as possible we'll be using the web page design facilities in Microsoft Word (version 97 onwards).

Creating a web page in HTML is actually not that difficult – it is based on mostly short and simple text commands – but it is very long winded and not the sort of thing you want to get involved with if you're a beginner or in a hurry. If all you want to do is make an attractive looking web page with a few pictures and words, a colourful background and maybe link it to some other pages then the ready-made web page 'templates' in Word are ideal. Once you get the hang of basic web page design and publishing you can quickly progress to more advanced techniques.

Getting your web pages onto the Internet can sometimes be a struggle. Internet Explorer and most specialist web page design programs have upload utilities but we'll be using a program called FTP Client, which will also make it easier to access pages on your website. There are many to choose from but a good place to start are freeware programs such as Smart FTP (http://www.smartftp.com/) and FTP Commander (www.internet-soft.com) because they use a familiar Windows Explorer type interface and are simple to configure, using information supplied to you by your Internet Service Provider (normally all you need to know is the address of the ISP's FTP server, your ID or log on name and your password).

Time now to create your first web page; you may want to spend a few minutes thinking about what you want to put on it but at this stage it's a good idea to keep it really simple. If you want to include a picture or graphic have one ready on your PC, preferably saved as a relatively small (preferably 50kb or less) JPEG file. Open Windows Explorer and use New on the File menu to create a new Folder, called 'mywebs' or something similar. Open MS Word, click New on the File menu and select the Web Pages tab (if it's not there you will have to run the setup program on your Word CD-ROM installation disk). In Word 97 select the Web Page Wizard icon and choose a layout and design. Don't be too ambitious, stick with the default 'Simple Layout' and 'Elegant' options for a simple, single web page template. The Web Page Wizard in Word 2000/2 takes slightly longer to configure but stick with the defaults and at the end of it you'll end up with a ready-made opening page, and 'hyperlinks' to two further pages. For the moment we'll concentrate on creating a single page.

In all versions of Word, once the template is on the screen you can click into any section of text – start with the headings – highlight and delete the original and type in your own words, then highlight and delete the bits you don't want. As you will see it works just like an ordinary Word document; you can change font size, style and add colours, effects and graphics in the

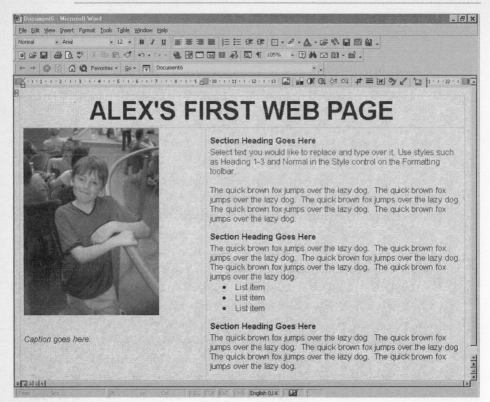

To build your own website begin with a template then type in your own words and insert the pictures.

usual way. Now try dropping in a picture. Place the cursor where you want it to go on the page, click on Picture on the Insert menu, then From File to select your image. When the image is on the page and highlighted it can be sized and positioned to suit. When you are happy with your page click Web Page Preview on the File menu. This opens an Internet Explorer window to show you exactly what your page will look like when it is on the net. Finally use Save As Web Page on the File menu, give it a name and save it in your 'mywebs' folder. Incidentally, the filename index.htm is an Internet convention that will ensure that the page opens first, when your site is accessed.

Now you are ready to upload your page. Open your FTP Client and you'll be presented with a Windows Explorer type display showing on one side the files on your PC and on the other the empty folder that represents your web space on the remote server computer, which you basically treat as another disk drive. FTP Client programs vary in the way they work but on most of them you can either drag-and-drop the folders and files that make up your website into your 'web space'. Some Client programs make it even easier with a 'wizard' type approach, where all you have to do is follow a series of on-screen prompts.

That's really all there is to it. All you have to do now is start your Internet browser, log onto your website and make sure your newly created web page is all present and correct. You should now be the proud owner of a basic but fully functional Internet website. We'll now look at some ways to liven up your web page with backgrounds, buttons and Hyperlinks, and how to get your site noticed and accessible to the millions of Internet users around the world.

The Word templates tend to be rather plain so the first thing you can do is add some background colour or texture. Go to Background on the Format menu and select one of the standard colours or better still, click on the More Colours or choose something interesting like 'Marble' or 'Tissue Paper' from the Fill Effects menu. A word of caution, darker backgrounds can make text harder to read, lighter colours and textures work best, and try not to mix red, blue and green text and graphics, it looks horrible and it may be unreadable to those suffering from colour blindness.

Don't forget you are not obliged to use the default layouts and fonts; almost everything can be changed or moved. Word also includes a small selection of graphic elements, including check boxes, drop-down menus, list boxes, forms and a scrolling text effect. In Word 97 they can all be found under Forms on the Insert menu, in Word 2000 right-click onto an empty area of the toolbar and select Web tools. Don't forget to include your email address on the page, and if you want to gauge reaction and assess the number of visitors you might also want to include a counter and a 'guest book' for comments. Note that web page elements like these are not included in Word but they can be downloaded from many sites on the Internet. Get into the habit of saving your work regularly and check the effect of any changes you make, before you upload your page, by using the Web Page Preview option on the File menu.

The most useful web page component is undoubtedly the Hyperlink, a highlighted and underlined word (or words) button or graphic that takes the reader to another location on the same page, another page on the same web site, or another page or site on the Internet. Hyperlinks come in a wide variety of shapes and sizes and the Web Page Wizard templates in Word 2000 and later make it very easy for you as it automatically creates an opening page with ready-made links to other parts of the document and two or more related blank pages. All you have to do to customise them is right-click on the link and select Edit Hyperlink from the drop-down menu that appears. The dialogue box that opens lets you change the name and the place in the document it is linked to, or you can direct it to a web page address or email address.

Word 97 is a bit more hands-on and you have to manually create your own Hyperlinks by highlighting text or a graphic then right-click on it and select Hyperlink from the menu. This opens a dialogue box that lets you specify an Internet address, a place on the document or another document.

Hyperlinks can be tricky customers and you have to be careful that they actually do what they are supposed to before you publish your web page or site. If you are going to be using more than half a dozen, say, it's a good idea to draw up a 'map' or flow chart of your web page or site on a sheet of paper, indicating where each link leads, marking the correct location or address. Once again test everything first using the Preview function.

Now that your page or site is up and running and you've uploaded it into the free allocation of web space allocated to you by your Internet Service Provider, you may want others to visit your site, in which case it might be worth registering a memorable domain name, and making use of the registration company's redirection service. You may also want to think about publicising and promoting your site, there are plenty of companies who can do it all for you, for a fee, but if you want to do it yourself, the basics are these. Register your site address or URL with as many Internet Search Engines as possible, you'll usually find a link to the URL submission form on the home page. If you have the opportunity to select keywords make sure they are succinct and focused. Seek out websites, indexes and directories that have something similar to offer, or would find the material on your site useful and offer to exchange links. Email your details to the listings editors of relevant on-line magazines, publications and newspapers.

SETTING UP A WEB CAM

Every so often a consumer electronics company claims to have re-invented the videophone. The stores dutifully stock them for a few months then they quietly disappear or are sold off, usually at knockdown prices. Occasionally the people who make and sell these things figure out the futility of being the only person with a videophone and try to sell them in pairs, but as concepts go the home videophone has been a bit of a flop.

There is a way to make sense of it; all you need is a reasonably up-to-date PC with an Internet connection. It also helps if you have a few like-minded friends or relatives with Internet PCs and it's worth pointing out that since this is an Internet facility they can be anywhere in the world.

Two-way video over the Internet is nothing new but in the past you needed to be a bit of an enthusiast with a great deal of patience and deep pockets. Two things have happened recently that now make the idea worth investigating, even if you're relatively new to PCs and the Internet. The first is the appearance of cheap 'web cams', the other is the release of programs like Microsoft NetMeeting and Messenger, which are free and simple to use and take the sting out of Internet videotelephony.

As you know, you can send reasonably high-quality still pictures over the Internet; video on the Internet works in a similar way except that instead of a single still picture you send (and receive) a succession of small relatively low-resolution still images. These are updated a few times each second, which gives a passable impression of movement. The amount of data is reduced or compressed by only sending parts of the picture that change from one frame to the next. Sound is processed in a similar way it is converted into digital data, compressed and sent in short bursts or 'packets' along with the picture information.

There is a penalty to be paid; depending on the time of day and your PC's connection type and speed there can be brief pauses in the connection, from a fraction of a second to a second or more. The resultant images are usually quite small and movement is jerky but that is something you get used to quite quickly and is more than offset by the novelty of seeing and talking to someone who may be thousands of miles away.

Unlike a normal phone call you can't simply dial up the other person, instead you both have to be on-line or logged on to a special Internet site which 'hosts' video calls, the commonest types are called Internet Locator Servers or ILS. There are lots of them and they are usually free to use. When you log on to the ILS you will see a list of all the other people using the site, including – hopefully – the person you are trying to reach. With a program like NetMeeting the usual procedure is to double-click on their name, their PC 'rings' and a message flashes up on the screen asking them if they want to accept the call. Obviously this requires prior arrangement, either you both log on at a pre-set time or you email the other person to let them know when you will be on-line.

You can also start a conversation with any of the other people logged on to the site. It works a bit like an Internet 'chat room' except that you can elect to be seen and heard, as well as exchange real-time text messages. There are scores of ILS sites including many special-interest groups – teachers, nurses, lawyers, architects and so on – not to mention a lot of 'adult' groups, but it's usually fairly clear from the name or address of the server what it's about.

Before you rush out and buy a web cam make sure your PC or laptop has a USB socket. Other types of web cam that use a plug-in card or a parallel port connection are available but they tend to be in the minority or more expensive. If you have a camcorder you could use that, in conjunction with a video capture card or a TV tuner card, most of which have video inputs.

Your PC must have a working sound system, speakers, and a microphone. If you haven't used a mike with your PC before it's a good idea to check that it's working properly. Open the Windows Sound Recorder facility (Start > Programs > Accessories > Entertainment) and make a short test recording. If you can't get it to work make sure the input hasn't been muted or the level set too low (Audio Properties on Sound Recorder's Edit menu, click on the Recording icon).

Now you can get your web cam. They're generally quite easy to install but do read the instructions. Most models come with a version of NetMeeting on the installation CD-ROM. It may be a clunky early version but install it anyway, however don't use it or try to configure it at this stage. Test the camera, familiarise yourself with the controls and settings. Most models come with utility and capture software – for video emails – and templates that can be used with captured still images to make greetings cards, so your new camera should have plenty of other uses. The last job is to obtain the latest version of NetMeeting from the Microsoft website (www.microsoft.com/windows/netmeeting/download/default.asp); it's a fairly small file (1.5Mb) and should only take a few minutes to download.

NetMeeting is a sophisticated Internet communications tool, capable of sending and receiving two-way audio, email, real-time text (chat) whiteboard (drawings and sketches) and exchanging files with other net users. However, it's the videophone bit we're most interested in and one of the first jobs is to configure NetMeeting with an ILS.

By default some versions of NetMeeting are configured to go to Microsoft ILS sites but these have been phased out, so start by using your Internet browser to go to an ILS search site like http://www.devx.com/netmeeting/bestservers.asp and http://www.meetingbywire.com/. You are looking for an ILS that is reasonably local, or at least in the same country as you or the person you are hoping to link up with. Preferably it should

Set up your own web cam using Microsoft NetMeeting.

operate in your native language, note any warnings about how busy the ILS gets and shortlist sites that are devoted to a subject that you or your contact are interested in. Jot down a couple of likely looking site addresses; you'll see that they're not like ordinary website addresses and usually look something like: ils.computebuffs.co.uk. Now you're ready to set up NetMeeting.

When you open NetMeeting for the first time it starts a set-up Wizard that asks you to enter your details (name, email address, etc.). The next page requests the address of your chosen ILS, key it in and click Next. Don't worry if this one doesn't work out, you can easily change it later on. Continue by filling in the details of your modem or connection; check the web cam name is correct and run through the audio settings. NetMeeting should now open and offer to go on-line; at this stage it's a good idea to decline and select Work Off-Line. Click on the triangular 'Start Video' icon below the screen and the 'TV' screen should activate, so you can set up your camera and lighting. Adjust your dress/expression/makeup as necessary because what you see is what will appear on the other person's screen. If necessary go back to the camera's set-up utility to tweak brightness, contrast and colour, etc. If you want to be able to see yourself when you are in a call go to the View menu and click on My Video (New Window) and a second floating screen appears which you can position to the side of the screen.

When you're happy with everything, go to Options on the Tools menu and select the Video tab and put a check against the top two items 'Automatically send video…' and 'Automatically receive video…'. Now it's time to go on-line and log on to an ILS, to make sure everything is working. Click on the Address Book (Find Someone) icon and your dial-up connection dialogue box will appear, click Connect and after a few moments the Find Someone window should show a list of all the people who are logged on to the server, including you. If nothing happens, you can't get onto the site or you get error messages, log off and change to another ILS by going to Options on the Tools menu, the ILS address is listed under Directory Settings on the General tab.

Essentially that's all there is to it, your Internet videophone is now ready to use. If you are feeling bold you can talk with any of the people logged on to the site by clicking on their name and the Call button, their PC will 'ring' and they will then decide whether or not they want to talk to you. (If you don't like the idea of them seeing you right away go back to Options on the Tools menu and deselect the 'Automatically Send video…' item.) However, remember you are effectively 'cold-calling' a stranger, so be careful, and don't forget that your email address is displayed. Better still, log off and email a friend or relative, telling them how to set up their web cam, the all-important ILS address, and the time you will be logged on.

Don't expect too much first time out, you will probably have to fine tune some settings and the jerky picture, time delay and occasional 'echos' on the line take a little getting used to but stick with it, it can be a lot of fun, seeing friends and distant relatives or maybe even grandchildren you've never seen before.

Q&A Real world problems

Website worry

Q   Is it possible to install an additional ISP (thereby having two ISPs) whilst retaining my current ISP and how do I do this? My fear is that a second ISP will delete all connections with my current ISP. My business and website is linked to my current ISP so I do not wish to sever my link with this server who, incidentally, provides a good service.

A   You can have as many ISPs as you like, the trick is to install them manually, rather than use set-up disks, which can arbitrarily change settings. You can usually obtain the necessary details by registering on-line, at the ISP's website where, after filling out the forms and creating a password, you will be given the dial-up number, your username, email address and the addresses for your new mailbox. Armed with this information you can then start the Internet Connection Wizard (Start > Programs > Accessories > Communications) and fill in the details. When the new account has been set up you can select it from the 'Connect To' drop-down menu in the Dial-Up box that appears when you go on-line, you can also use the Settings button to change the Default ISP.

Keeping watch

Q   I wish to position a camera over an entrance door with the live pictures being fed to my PC, which I can see on the screen when there is a caller. Can you suggest how to set this up and recommend any soft/hardware?

A   Virtually all web cams, even budget models, come with a monitor utility that lets you display a live image on the screen in a pop-up window. The only problem is that most web cams use a USB connection, which is very easy to configure, but is limited to a maximum cable length of five metres. However, this can be increased in multiples of five metres by the use of 'hubs' or 'active' extension cables, all of which can be obtained from PC accessory dealers.

Upgrading to XP

Q   I have an oldish web cam – bought a couple of years ago – and I now want to use it with my new PC, which has Windows XP Home installed. Unfortunately I've lost the driver disk and instructions, what are the chances of it working with XP?

A   Quite good, if you can find a maker's name it's worth visiting the website to see if there are any XP drivers for your web cam available for download. It's also worth just plugging it in and seeing what happens. XP will search its own database for a suitable driver and if it can't find one it will search the web. All this happens automatically and there's a good chance it will come up with something. Even if the driver is 'unsigned' it's worth trying, as XP will automatically create a Restore Point, so if anything goes wrong you can return to your previous, known good configuration.

CHAPTER 10 **Networking and Internet connection sharing**

Many of us now have two or more computers in our homes; connecting them together in a simple network will allow you to move files around more easily and share resources, like printers but, more importantly, you can also share your broadband Internet connection.

Broadband is coming to a telephone exchange near you. It may already be available or you might be able to hook up to your local cable TV company's high-speed network, either way, if you use the Internet for more than a few hours a week put broadband at the top of your wish list!

The cost of broadband is falling all the time and if you use the Internet for business or gaming or just heavy-duty surfing the arguments for it become very compelling indeed, particularly when you take into account the real cost of your time spent waiting for web pages and files to download via an ordinary dial-up connection.

If you're already a convert and have a broadband connection, and you fancy a challenge, then with a little effort, and a relatively modest outlay you can share that connection with several other PCs in your home or office. Unfortunately, and despite what some advertisements may suggest, there is no such thing as a simple, pre-packed, one-box solution to broadband sharing. Connecting or networking pre-Windows XP PCs is something of a black art, requiring a stout heart and a great deal of patience to master – and sort out the inevitable problems – you also need to understand a few simple concepts, and learn a lot of new acronyms.

It looks easy enough on paper; your Windows PC is connected to the Internet so a simple local area network or LAN that allows PCs to share files and a printer should by rights also be able to share an Internet connection? Wrong! The Internet, like most computer networks, relies on the fact that each PC connected to it is assigned a unique identity number – a bit like a phone number – known as an Internet Protocol (IP) Address. If a PC with an unassigned IP address – i.e., a PC on a network – tries to connect to the Internet it will not be recognised and the connection is refused.

The solution is to create a 'gateway' onto the Internet that other PCs in the LAN can access via the one with the assigned IP address, either using an extra hardware device, or a software program. In this chapter we'll be looking at the simpler, cheaper and more flexible software method. However, before you even start to think about Internet sharing your PCs must be able to connect to each other so the first job is to get your LAN up and running.

What follows applies only to Windows 98 onwards, if you're using an earlier version of Windows consider upgrading. If you are using Windows XP it's a little easier but you should use the built in 'Wizards' to set up your own network.

Step one is to decide upon the hierarchy of the PCs in your home network, and how they are going to be connected together. The computer that has the broadband Internet connection will normally be the 'Server' and the ones that connect to it and share the Internet feed are the 'Clients'. There are several connection methods but in the home or a small office environment the usual choice is 10/100 Ethernet, which can use cabled connections, or 'wireless' links, or a mixture of both.

The basics are the same for both wired and wireless systems; the only practical difference is that installing a wired system usually involves drilling lots of holes and ripping up floorboards. On the plus side, the components for a wired network are relatively inexpensive.

Wireless LANs are usually very easy to install and as an added bonus you can take your laptop into the garden and possibly log on to other public network access points when you are out and about. Wireless systems have an operating range of up to 500 metres in the open, though 50 to 100 metres is nearer the mark when the equipment is used inside a building. The downside to wireless networking is cost, which can be up to four or five times the cost of a wired network.

Be careful when shopping for wireless equipment. There are several different systems and standards and the hardware often looks similar but the different types are all incompatible. The closest thing to an international standard is generically known as 'WiFi' or IEEE 802.11b, which operates over a frequency range of 2.4 to 2.5GHz with a data rate of up to 11Mbps; remember those numbers, look for the WiFi logo and stick with a single make or brand – you can't go far wrong.

Whichever connection method you decide upon you will need to install or enable an Ethernet port on the server PC. Nowadays a lot of PCs and laptops have built-in Ethernet ports. They're easy to spot – the socket looks like a large version of the US-style phone socket similar to the type of phone line socket on the back of PCs, fax machines or cordless phones. If you have one check that it's properly configured and working by going to Device Manager (right-click My Computer and select Properties) it should be listed as working (i.e., no yellow exclamation marks) under Network Adaptors. You may find that once the adaptor is enabled you will be asked for a password every time you boot up, just accept the default entry and hit the return key.

If your PC doesn't have an Ethernet port then you need to fit an adaptor card in a vacant PCI socket on the motherboard. They're quite cheap and simple to install but if you've never worked on your PC at this level before get an expert or engineer to do it for you. The installation process is largely automatic but you may need your Windows setup disk, so make sure you have this to hand.

If you are using a wired system you must install Ethernet ports on all of your Client PCs. In a wireless system you can use adaptors that plug into the PC's USB socket, or wireless 'cards' that fit into a PCMCIA slot. These are mostly found on laptops but you can get PCMCIA adaptors for desktop PCs, which fit into a spare PCI socket. A wireless card and PCMCIA adaptor together costs only slightly more than a USB wireless adaptor, but it means that you can move the wireless card between a desktop PC and a laptop to get the maximum amount of use out of it.

The critical component in Internet connection sharing, and the last link in your network, is the Router. A router is a bit like a telephone exchange, passing data between the server and client PCs, and this applies to both wired and wireless systems. However, there are two types of router – regular and broadband (wired and wireless). A broadband router acts as the gateway between the LAN and the Internet, allowing all the PCs on the network to share the connection. It sounds like the perfect solution but there's a problem.

Most 'home' broadband packages come with a simple plug-and-play USB modem but the majority of Internet routers have an Ethernet connection for the modem. Routers with USB modem sockets tend to be in the minority and can be more expensive (especially so when it comes to wireless types) and to make matters worse, broadband modems with Ethernet connections are very thin on the ground.

If you've already got a broadband connection (using a USB modem) then you have two choices, you can pursue the more expensive 'hardware' sharing system and seek out a router with a USB socket or use software sharing. It may take a little longer to set up but it's cheaper than buying new equipment; in fact it needn't cost you anything. Windows (98 SE onwards) comes bundled with Internet connection sharing software and there are several very good freeware and shareware packages available for download from the Internet.

Whichever method you've chosen, the next step is to configure your network and be warned that by the end of it you will be heartily sick of watching Windows reboot. The first step is to check that the correct networking software or Protocols are installed on all the PCs using the network. This may have been done automatically when you installed or enabled the Ethernet card, but check anyway by clicking on the Network icon in Control Panel, select the Configuration tab and see if there are entries for 'TCP/IP' and 'NetBEUI' on the list with the name of your network adaptor. If you can't see them click the Add button, then Protocol > Microsoft > TCP/IP, then repeat for NetBEUI. You may be asked to load your Windows installation disk and the machine will ask you to reboot, click OK.

The next time Windows loads you should see a password box, hit Enter and return to Network in Control Panel (you can set up a password but do it later, when everything is sorted out). Highlight the TCP/IP entry relating to your network adaptor again and click Properties. On the IP Address tab make sure 'Obtain an IP address automatically' is checked, the field on the Gateway tab should be empty and on the DNS tab 'Disable' should be checked; the other tabs you can ignore.

Next, select the Configuration tab and click File and Print Sharing, this will allow the PCs on your network to access files on other computers and share one printer. Follow the instructions and reboot when asked. Open Windows Explorer, right-click the drive or folders you want to share with others on the network and select Sharing from the drop-down menu then check 'Shared As'. A little open-hand logo should appear under each selected drive or folder.

Return to Network in Control Panel, this time select the Identification tab, give each PC in your network a unique name or use a single name (your surname or street name), followed by 1, 2, 3, etc., then choose a Workgroup name (family, office, etc.). Note that this must be the same on all PCs! Click OK, load your Windows CD-ROM and reboot as instructed. Are we having fun yet?

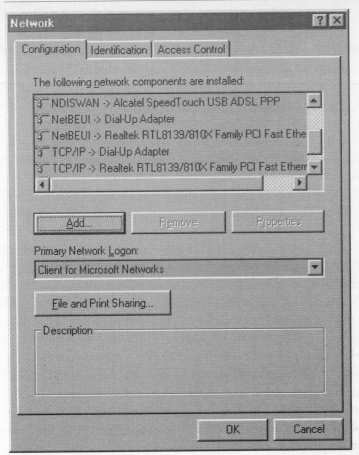

Network in Control Panel is used to configure your new Ethernet adaptor.

Hopefully that's it, now you can start to make connections. If it's a wired system plug in the cables; in a wireless system you'll have to follow the instructions for installing each of the devices but in both cases I suggest that you attempt only one connection at a time and if at all possible set up the first link with both PCs sitting next to one another. The last thing you want to do is keep running between rooms or up and down stairs. All being well, when you click on Network Neighbourhood on either the server or client you will see an icon representing the other PC you are connected to and if you click that, a list of the shared files or folders. If not go back and re-check the settings, paying particular attention to the workgroup naming (it must be the same on all PCs) and double-check the settings for TCP/IP and File and Print Sharing.

If you are struggling to get your network working then now is a good time to run through some basic troubleshooting steps for Windows 9x (Windows XP has its own troubleshooting routines and help wizards). Nine times out of ten, when you click on Network Neighbourhood and you can't see shared disk drives, file folders or resources on other PCs in the network it's due to a software problem.

Double check that you have enabled File and Printer Sharing and make sure that you have uninstalled any firewall software running on the server and client PCs. It's no good just exiting or disabling the program it must be completely removed! You should also remove any other Internet monitoring or blocking programs, including virus scanners (you can put them back later when the network is operating).

If you are still having difficulty try 'pinging' each of the PCs in the network. Ping is a simple test utility included with all versions of Windows 9x (ping is a reference to sonar detection) that checks to see if PCs in the network are connected and able to communicate with one another. It works by sending a 'packet' of data, which the other PC returns. In order to ping a computer (and this can be client to server or server to client) you need to know the other machine's IP Address.

It's a good idea to make a note of the IP addresses of the PCs in your network; you can do this by typing 'winipcfg' (without the quotes) in Run on the Start menu on each machine. Select your Ethernet adaptor from the drop-down menu. In most cases it will have been set automatically to a special networking address that won't be recognised by the Internet and usually looks something like 192.168.0.1 (the last digit or digits must be different on each PC). This is also a useful indicator that the Ethernet adaptor on each PC is functioning.

Next, open a DOS window (Start > Programs > MSDOS) and type 'ping 192.168.0.1' (or whatever the IP address is of the PC you are trying to contact). You should get a fairly immediate response from the other PC, with four lines of text showing how long it took to send and receive 32 bytes of data plus some general statistics.

If you get a 'timed out' or 'host unreachable' reply then you will have to go back and check through everything methodically. Assuming that the Ethernet adaptors are working, ensure that the TCP/IP protocol has been properly installed. Go to Network in Control Panel, select the Configuration tab and look down the list for a TCP/IP entry, followed by an arrow and then the name of your Ethernet adaptor. The arrow shows that the protocol is

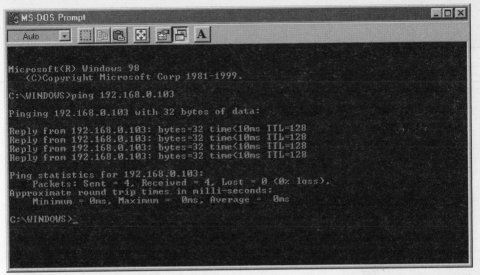

The 'Ping' utility in Windows lets you check that other PCs in the network are connected and 'listening'.

'bound' to the adaptor and that they are working properly. If not try removing and reinstalling the adaptors and the protocol. Finally, check that the physical links (cable, etc.) or wireless links are okay. If the adaptors and cable get a clean bill of health there's probably still some software running that's messing up the link so press Ctrl + Alt + Del just once to bring up the Close Program box and work your way down the list by End Tasking running programs (all except Systray and Explorer). Once you are able connect to the other PC in your network you are ready to share your Internet connection.

If you're feeling brave you might want to try your luck with a Windows utility, called Internet Connection Sharing (ICS) which is included with all versions of Windows from 98SE onwards. Apparently ICS does work though novices are advised to steer clear but in any case before you try it visit www.annoyances.org/exec/show/ics first for some useful advice.

If you have no luck with ICS, or want to try something a little simpler you will need to obtain third-party 'Proxy' software. There are plenty of commercial programs to choose from but a good place to start for novices attempting to set up a simple home network, is a shareware program called CCProxy which can be downloaded from: www.youngzsoft.com/en/index.html. Once you get past the jargon and sparse Help files it should

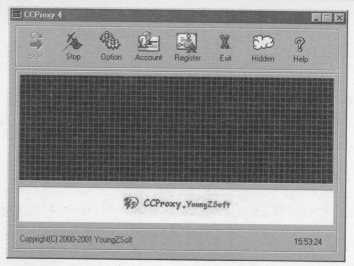

CCProxy, a simple freeware program that lets you share your Internet connection.

prove reliable and easy to use. Other programs worth investigating are WinGate (http://wingate.deerfield.com/), and SolidShare (www.solidshare. com). Time-limited trial versions of both programs are available from the respective web sites.

Programs like CCProxy and WinGate have to be installed only on the server PC (the one connected to the Internet) and more or less configure themselves. CCProxy requires some simple adjustments to the client PC's browser and email settings – this is where the Help files could be better presented – and for these you will need to know the IP Address of your server PC and some basic email settings but it shouldn't take you more than about five minutes for each machine on the network. Assuming all is well, programs like Internet Explorer and Outlook Express on the client PCs will appear to be permanently connected to the Internet – as long as the server PC is on and the proxy software is running.

It really is that simple but you may well find that the whole thing comes crashing down as soon as you re-install your firewall and Internet monitoring programs. Normally very reliable programs like ZoneAlarm (www.zonelabs.com) can prove difficult when it comes to networking. Fortunately there are alternatives. Try Agnitum Outpost, which seems to work happily with most Internet sharing programs. Outpost also has the facility to monitor Internet activity on the client PCs, which might prove useful for concerned parents. The home version is freeware and it can be downloaded from: http://www.agnitum.com/products/outpost/.

Q&A Real world problems

Parental protection

Q I am about to set up a home network, so my children can share my Internet connection – currently dial-up but I'll upgrade to broadband as soon as it becomes available. I have firewall and Internet filtering software on my main PC at the moment but will this prevent my children from viewing undesirable material on their PCs?

A Probably not, it depends on the software you are using, but in most cases the client PCs will have free access and unfettered to the Internet so you will have to install filtering software on each of the connected PCs. Also, it will not hurt to set conservative security levels on the client PC's browsers; in Internet Explorer, go to Internet Options on the Tools menu and select the Security tab.

Wireless loophole

Q I'm considering setting up a wireless network in my office, it operates around the clock so the computers would be always on and connected to the Internet. However, I'm worried about security, what can be done to stop someone with a wireless laptop sitting outside my company and accessing the Internet, or worse, the files on my computers?

A The WiFi wireless networking system has a number of very powerful security features that are more than sufficient to protect your data, but they work only if you use them! The default settings, which require you to give the network a 'name' should be enough to deter casual wireless 'sniffers', but for complete privacy and peace of mind you should enable both your PC's and wireless system's built-in password protection and encryption facilities.

CHAPTER 11 **Moving to a new PC**

At some point you will want to replace your PC, or maybe you've bought a laptop, in both cases you will be faced with the task of re-installing programs and copying across all of your important data files.

Usually it's just a tedious and time-consuming chore but things can start to get a bit awkward when it comes to transferring all of your email messages and settings, especially if you are using Outlook Express as your email client program. Part of the problem is that Outlook Express is not really a stand-alone program, it is part of Internet Explorer and bundled with Windows and although not officially a Windows component it is intimately connected with it, sharing the same filing systems, which can make it difficult to separate or extract data files.

It can be done of course but you need to give some thought to how you are going to transport the files from one PC to another. Some of them may be very large indeed. If you receive a lot of email the contents of your Store Folder can easily run to several hundred megabytes; clearly floppy disks are out of the question. The alternatives are to connect the PCs together over a network (see Chapter 10) a cable connection, such as Windows Direct Cable Connection, Laplink, or by transportable media (CD-R, Zip, etc.) which will also provide you with a useful backup. You will also need to have all of your Dial Up or Broadband connection details (phone number, passwords, mailbox settings, etc.) to hand.

Before we start it is worth knowing a bit about how and where Outlook Express stores files, and this should also help to explain why transferring from one PC to another is not as easy as it sounds. Incidentally, what follows applies to Outlook Express versions 5 and 6, which are very similar and supplied with Windows 9x and XP, and providing you are using OE 5 or 6 on both PCs you can transfer data across quite easily, even if the two machines are using different versions of Windows (i.e., your old PC uses Windows 98 and the new one is an XP machine). The files and data that make OE tick can be broken down into three basic groups: your messages, your address book and your personal settings or accounts and these are kept in three locations.

All your email messages (Inbox, Drafts, Deleted, Sent, etc.), Newsgroups and Cleanup Log plus various other housekeeping files are kept in the 'Store Folder'. In Windows 9x this can be found at C:\Windows\Application Data\Identities\{GUID}\Microsoft\Outlook Express. In Windows XP they are in C:\Documents and Settings\<yourname>\Application Data\ Identities\{GUID}\Microsoft\Outlook Express.

The {GUID} bit stands for Global Unique IDentifier and will actually be a long string of 30 or more numbers and letters that is unique to your PC. It is possible that your store folder may be located elsewhere, in which case go to Options on the Tools menu, select the Maintenance tab, click the Store Folder button and all will be revealed.

If you use Windows Explorer to look inside your Store Folder you will see a list of files with the extension *.dbx (that means database, multiple use). The master index is a file called Folders.dbx; some of the others you should recognise, as they will have the names of your various inboxes and any newsgroups that you are subscribed to. You can double-click on any of the *.dbx files and they will open in WordPad. The text of messages will be shown but can be very difficult to read as it will be jumbled in with lots of special characters (mostly squares), headers and HTML coding. Nevertheless, it's worth knowing that you can still get to your email messages in an emergency, should OE keel over and die.

Your Outlook Express address book is normally kept by default at: C:\WINDOWS\Application Data\Microsoft (C:\Documents and Settings\ <yourname>\Application Data\Microsoft in Windows XP). If you can't find it there, it may have been moved by other users or applications but you can easily track it down by opening the Address Book in OE and clicking on Help and its current location will be shown. Incidentally, if you still can't find an Address Book folder that usually means that you also have Outlook on your PC and Outlook Express has been set up to share the Contacts file.

If you take a peek inside the Address Book folder in Windows Explorer you will usually see just two files <your name>.wab and <your name>.wa~ . The 'wab' file (Windows Address Book) contains the program and the data and clicking on it will open the Address Book. The '.wa~' file is an automatic backup, usually made every time OE is running. Should your address book become corrupted or unusable you can use the backup simply by renaming the extension '.wab'.

The third and last group of Outlook Express files is what makes transferring it to a new PC so difficult. These are your email 'Account' settings, which relate to personal preferences, mail Rules and so on. Some information can be easily moved however, including the connection details to your Internet Service Provider – Dial-Up phone numbers, your email address and so on. Other items, such as your personal preferences for the way OE is set up – Views and Toolbars, etc. – Message Rules and Blocked Senders list are stored in the Windows Registry and copying them across to another PC is something only seasoned Windows users should attempt, but more on that later. That usually means when you move OE data to a new PC you will still have to enter a few details but it shouldn't take long or pose too many problems provided you make a few simple preparations. Start by creating a new folder on your original PC using Windows Explorer, call it something like OEback and this is where you will gather together all of the files to be transferred to the new PC.

Next, go to Accounts on the Outlook Express Tools menu and select the Mail tab. Highlight each entry in the Accounts window in turn, click the Export button and use the dialogue box to send the files – with the extension '.iaf' (internet account file) – to your newly created OEback folder. Next locate your Address Book and use Windows Explorer to copy and paste the Address Book '.wab' file into your OEback folder.

The OE Address Book backup/copy system isn't very reliable so as a precaution make a second copy from the File menu in OE; select Export then Address Book, highlight Text File (Comma Separated Value), click Export then send it to your OEback folder. This will create a text file with a .csv (comma separated value) extension.

Finally, use Copy and Paste in Windows Explorer to copy your Message Store folder to the OEback folder. You can copy the whole folder or just the mail folders you want to keep (<your name.dbx>, etc.) but you must copy the file Folders.dbx as this is the master index and OE won't work properly without it.

How you proceed from here depends on your chosen transfer method; if you've elected to use a cable connection like Laplink or DCC all you will have to do is access the OEback folder from the second PC. If you are using transportable media (CD-R/RW, Zip, Jaz, etc.) copy the folder to the disk and load it to the new PC. You can either read directly from the disk, or copy the folder to your new PC's hard drive.

All that remains now is to copy the files into your new PC. Incidentally, copying the Address Book and Message Store folders into the same location

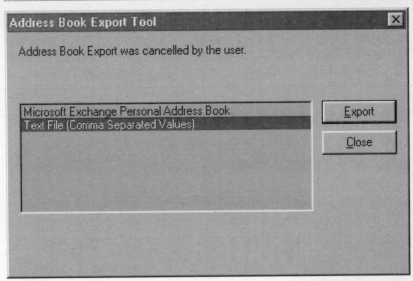

Export on the Outlook Express File menu lets you move your Address Book to another PC.

on a second PC using Windows Explorer doesn't work. Start by opening Accounts on the Tools menu, click the Import button, use Browse to find your OEback folder and click and highlight each Account in turn. Your Address Book is loaded from Import on the File menu, if you have problems with the *.wab file try using your standby *.csv file. Lastly the Messages, these are also loaded using the Import function on the File menu, from your OEback folder. This can be troublesome, especially when the message folders are really large, so rather that do them all at once (the default 'All Folders' setting) try importing a couple of mailboxes at a time. It takes a little longer but it seems to be more reliable.

Now, as promised, for Windows experts the details of the Registry keys for transferring things like Message Rules Signatures, Custom Views and Block Senders list. Please note this applies only to Windows 9x PCs and you should not attempt this procedure if you are unfamiliar with editing the Registry as really, really bad things can happen if you get it wrong and do not have a current backup. If you are in any doubt about the importance of the Registry please read Chapter 18!

Having made a backup in Regedit go to HKEY_CURRENT_USER\ Identities\{GUID}\Software\Microsoft\Outlook Express\5.0. There you will see three subkeys: \Block Senders\Rules and \Signatures. Highlight each

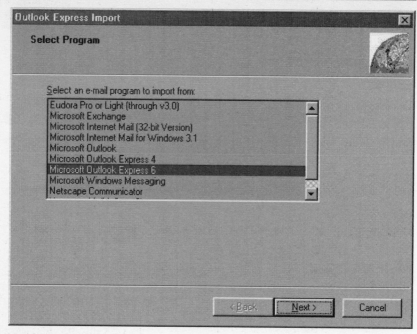

The Import utility is used to transfer the Address Book and email messages from one PC to another.

one in turn, on the Registry menu select Export Registry File and save them in your OEback folder as '*.reg' files.

On your second/new PC open Regedit and go to HKEY_CURRENT_ USER\Identities \{GUID}. In the left-hand pane right-click on the GUID key, select Rename (do not rename it!) and press Ctrl + C to copy the GUID value, brackets and all, to the Clipboard. Close Regedit and open WordPad. Open each 'reg' file in turn and use Find and Replace to change all instances of the old GUID to the new one, from the Clipboard. When that's done Save each file, making sure it retains its *.reg extension. Open Regedit again and delete the existing Block Sender, Rules and Signature keys then it's back to Windows Explorer, double-click on the modified keys in your OEback folder and they will be automatically written into the new PC's Registry. In Message Rules you may have to re-specify folder locations but this should only take a minute or so.

Q&A Real world problems

Favourite chore

Q   I have recently bought a new PC and want to be able to access my Favourite websites but I can't face the prospect of keying them all in again, there must be a simpler solution?

A   There is and all you need is a blank floppy disk and few spare minutes. On the PC where your Favourites are stored load the floppy and open Windows Explorer. Double click the Windows folder and there you will find your Favourites folder, right click on it and select Send To ... and 3.5-inch Floppy from the drop-down menu. When it has finished copying the file remove the floppy and load it into your new PC, open Windows Explorer and double click the Windows folder to open it. As a precaution drag and drop the existing Favourites folder to another location such as My Documents, so it can be easily restored if something goes wrong, now copy and paste or drag and drop the Favourites folder on the floppy disk into the Windows folder, and it's done!

The name game

Q   Having sent an email recently – not anonymously, but without my surname – I did not realise that my name was attached to the message until it was read out over the air on radio. Is it therefore possible for me to remain anonymous and if so how can I do this?

A   When you signed up for an email account or configured Outlook Express for the first time you were asked to enter your name and told that this would appear on all your email messages. This information can be edited by going to Accounts on the Tools menu, highlight your account name, click Properties and select the General tab. The Name field is what will be shown on your emails and you can edit or delete this as you see fit.

   However, it is still possible to deduce your name from your email address – very easy in your case – and your name and ISP details will also be included in hidden 'header' information that is sent with every email. This can be easily read by anyone by right-clicking on an email message in an OE Inbox and selecting Properties. The bottom line is that it is very difficult to remain completely anonymous, but it's not impossible. Websites and email servers called re-mailers can strip out any identifying data from your emails, making it impossible to trace it back to your ISP. If you want to know more there's a useful article at: http://www.stack.nl/~galactus/remailers/

Part III

IMAGES

CHAPTER 12

Pictures and pixels

What's the difference between 256-Color, High-Color and True Color and what's a megapixel when it's at home? So far we've only touched briefly on your PC's ability to process and manipulate images but this is an increasingly important facility so it's worth knowing a little about what goes on behind the scenes.

PC imaging is a vast subject that covers a lot of ground, from monitors and printers through to scanners and digital still cameras, but we'll begin with some basic principles. It all comes down to dots and pixels – they're the fundamental building blocks of all computer-generated images. For the most part pixels (short for picture elements) and dots are one and the same but you are more likely to see pixels mentioned in relation to monitor displays and digital cameras and dots when talking about printers and scanners – however, the point is a pixel or dot is the smallest individually controllable (intensity or brightness and colour) element in an image.

The pixels and dots on a monitor screen are made up of three separate red, green and blue elements, which can be mixed in varying proportions to create any one of the millions of colours and shades that our eyes can distinguish – we'll be taking a closer look at colour in a moment. The pixels in scanners and digital cameras are also made up of three elements but this time they are sensitive to red, green and blue light. The dots in printers are 'painted' on the paper using microscopic droplets of black and coloured inks or toner particles, in the case of laser printers. It's clear then that we're not talking about fixed entities, a pixel can be the size of a dinner plate, like the tri-colour display module used in one of those giant video screens you see in sports arenas and concerts whilst a pixel on the surface of a CCD image sensor chip in a digital camera is only a few microns across. It follows therefore that the amount of fine detail contained in a computer-generated image varies according to the number and size of the pixels, how close together they are, the overall size of the image or display and how far away you are from it.

To complicate matters further the number of pixels in an image is only part of the story when talking about image quality. Of equal importance is the ability of an imaging and display system to capture and faithfully reproduce or render a range of colours and shades. This is usually referred to as 'colour depth', and 'greyscale' and they all come under the general heading of resolution, a blanket term that describes how much information an imaging device can process.

MONITOR RESOLUTION

Resolution, in the context of a PC monitor, can mean two things. First there's the ability of the display to reproduce fine detail, texture and colour, and that is controlled by the number, size and spacing of the pixels on the screen, the efficiency and performance of the materials used and how well the electronic circuits in the monitor process the video signal or data coming from the computer. Second, we can also talk about the resolution of the video image displayed on a monitor screen, and that is determined by the monitor and the PC, the way the computer is configured and the performance of its video processing components.

The latter causes the most confusion, mainly because Windows lets you change resolution from the Display utility in Control Panel. Many people will have changed, or been tempted to fiddle with the 'Screen Area' setting and most recent PCs with 'standard' 15- or 17-inch monitors have at least three options (selected by moving the slider) namely 640 x 480, 800 x 600 and 1024 x 768 pixels. On systems with larger screen sizes the options may also include 1280 x 1024 and 1600 x 1200 pixels. In most cases it will be set to 800 x 600 or 1024 x 768; 640 x 480 is the 'VGA' default and the minimum resolution in which Windows can be displayed.

Windows 98 onwards lets you change the resolution temporarily so you can see what effect it has – have a go but before you do make a note of your current setting. On older Windows 95 systems there is a chance you could end up changing the setting to something your PC or video adaptor cannot handle and you'll be faced with the scary sight of a blank screen, and no obvious way of getting it back to normal. (In case that happens to you the solution is to restart the PC in Safe Mode, see Chapter 15.)

If you change the resolution to 640 x 480 you will see that everything on the screen becomes much larger and graphics and text look coarse and blocky. Change it to a higher setting and the opposite happens, everything is

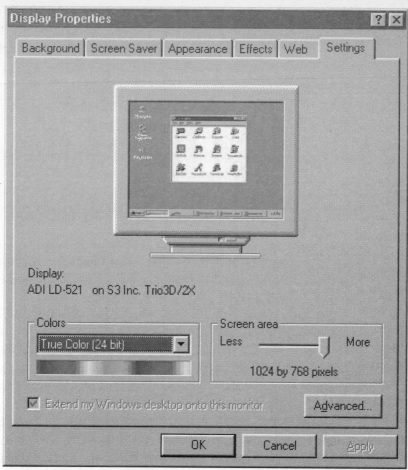

Display Properties in Control Panel lets you adjust your screen resolution.

smaller and sharper looking but text may be so small that it becomes difficult to read on a 15-inch screen, but it would be just the right size when shown on a 17- or 19-inch monitor. The conclusion you can draw from this is that the video display generated by your PC should be scaled to fit the size of the monitor screen and that higher resolutions work best on larger screen sizes. Most modern PCs, monitors and Windows 9x onwards should carry out this adjustment automatically using a system called Plug and Play (PnP) whereby the monitor tells the PC about its capabilities and which resolutions it supports.

CAMERA AND SCANNER RESOLUTION

Resolution has a slightly different meaning in the context of digital cameras, scanners and printers. Broadly speaking it is the ability of an imaging device to capture fine detail and this is determined by the number of pixels on the surface of the image sensor chip inside the camera or scanner. The sensor in a digital camera is the equivalent of a frame of photographic film so it's tempting to compare the two in terms of the number of pixels. However, film is an 'analogue' medium and doesn't easily lend itself to that kind of comparison, but we'll have a go anyway. In the case of a top-quality film camera and lens shooting a static scene in good light we can say that a frame of 35mm film contains the equivalent of 20 million or so pixels rising to more than 30 million pixels on the finest-grain professional films.

That figure falls to between 9 and 12 million pixels in the case of a mid-range camera loaded with ordinary film. Currently the best digital cameras have sensors with between 4 and 6 million pixels (megapixels) so you can see that they still have a way to go to catch up with film.

Many other factors are involved in determining the quality of a picture shot on a digital still camera, including the way the camera and PC processes the data but all things being equal and assuming a decent printer, a mid-market digital still camera with a 2- or 3-megapixel sensor can produce very acceptable looking 4 x 6-inch prints that stand comparison with photos shot on a compact film camera.

Scanner resolution is measured in a slightly different way to cameras, not by pixels but in dots per inch or 'dpi'. A dot as we explained earlier is a pixel by any other name. Inside a flatbed scanner, on the scan 'head' that moves under the glass 'platen' on which the image is placed, there is a strip of light-sensitive elements – the dots or pixels – and how many of them there are to the inch is the scanner's 'optical' resolution. This is typically 600 to 800dpi on budget models and 1200 to 2000dpi on more advanced types. A scanner's optical resolution is usually quoted as two figures (i.e. 600 x 1200dpi), the second number '1200' denotes the number of 'steps' the scanner head makes per inch as it travels down the platen.

Optical resolution is the true measure of a scanner's performance and it is not the same as the larger and more impressive-looking 'interpolated' resolution figure that many scanner manufacturers are fond of quoting. This is essentially a trick whereby the scanner software takes an educated guess and fills in the missing detail between each pixel.

How much resolution you need from a scanner depends on what you are using it for. If you only want to scan images that will appear on a video monitor – i.e., pictures for web pages, multimedia presentations, etc. — then you may be surprised to know that the resolution of most PC screens is between 75 and 100dpi; scanning at higher resolutions is basically a waste of time, effort and disk space as all of the extra detail is lost. Scanning text and documents for faxing, copying or optical character recognition (OCR) is another relatively undemanding application and a resolution of 300dpi is usually more than sufficient.

Higher resolutions start to make sense when the aim is to print out the results. Most laser printers and colour inkjets operate in the range 300 to 800dpi. Imagesetters, used in the production of books and magazines, normally require images to be scanned at resolutions of at least 1200dpi but for high-quality work it can rise to 3500dpi and above.

The resolution of a printer, which is the ability to reproduce fine detail, is like that of a scanner and measured in dots per inch (dpi). However, the numbers are not so clear-cut. There are many different printer technologies and numerous techniques for making images appear sharper, with more natural-looking colours. The type and quality of paper can also have a big impact on the finished results so it's a bit of a minefield. The simple rule of thumb is that the more dpis a printer can manage the better, and 'photorealistic' models with multi-colour (i.e., 4-, 5- or 6-colour inks) printing systems produce the best results on photographs shot on a digital still camera.

COLOUR DEPTH

Colour plays a very important role in image quality, in particular something called colour depth. In keeping with tradition the PC industry has managed to make the whole business seem a lot more complicated that it actually is but we'll try to make some sense of it.

The human eye is very sensitive to colour and we have the ability to distinguish up to ten million shades. Digital imaging systems are even more adept at processing colour and can detect and reproduce millions more colours by assigning each colour a number, and as you know computers are very good with numbers.

Most PCs and peripherals use four basic colour formats. The first is the VGA standard of 16-colors, also referred to as 4-bit color (excuse the

American spelling) which is the number of binary digits (bits) used to identify each of the colours. 4-bit color is okay for displaying simple graphics and icons but it can't handle the shades in photographic images and they look really coarse and blotchy. Next is 8-bit or 256-colors. This is just enough for a photographic image though variations in colour and shade tend to look very patchy. Picture quality takes a big leap with 16-bit color, also known as 'High Color' which can resolve 65,536 colours. Finally there's 24-bit and 32-bit 'True Color' that describes more than 16 million (16,777,216 to be precise) colours. 32-bit True Color is a special format used mainly for video games and high-end graphics applications where the extra 8-bits of information, known as the 'Alpha Channel' is used for creating special transparency and texture effects.

IMAGE SIZE

Image size is another slightly tricky subject because it means several different things in computer imaging. First there's the physical size of a picture as you see it, on a monitor screen or printed out on a sheet of paper, then there's the actual size or area of an image, measured in pixels and, thirdly, there's the size of an image file, in kilobytes or megabytes.

The size of displayed and printed images throws a lot of people. In the real world we are used to pictures and photographs having fixed physical dimensions but in computerland things are very different. Photographs in emails (as opposed to pictures sent as 'attachments') are a case in point and they can sometimes appear so large that only a small portion of the image is shown in the message window. It's due to something called 'scaling'. Basic email programs like Outlook Express show a picture 'as is' and make no attempt to resize the picture to fit the screen or compensate for the Windows resolution setting. For example, if a picture is 1000 x 750 pixels and your Windows display is set for 800 x 600 pixels then you will only see about three-quarters of the picture on the screen and you'll have to use the scroll bars at the bottom and side of the window to see the rest of it.

Picture editing programs on the other hand have the facility to enlarge or reduce the size of the displayed image – usually called 'zooming' – so an image can be scaled down to fit the screen area or blown up, to view fine detail, and enlarged or reduced to fit onto a printed page. However, it's important not to confuse this with a picture editing program's ability to alter the size of the picture by changing the number of pixels. This is quite a

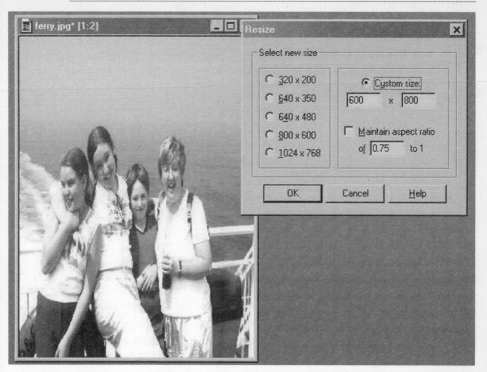

Your graphics program should have a facility to change or maintain an image's aspect ratio.

complicated business; if you reduce the width of an image by decreasing the number of pixels the picture will probably end up looking squashed. That's because in order to maintain the correct proportions the height has to be reduced by a corresponding amount.

The relationship between the width and height of a picture is called the Aspect Ratio and most picture editors have a facility to automatically maintain it; it's usually on the Size or Resize dialogue box on the Image menu. Sometimes it's clearly labelled as such, i.e., Maintain Aspect Ratio, though programs like Adobe Photoshop Elements insist on calling it 'Constrain Proportions'.

There's quite a bit more to resizing an image than simply adding or taking away pixels, and picture editing programs use a variety of exotic-sounding techniques to maintain the smoothness and preserve the sharpness of edges when enlarging or reducing an image. This comes under the general heading of Resampling and it's not something we have the room to go into here; fortunately it's not something you need to worry about if you're mainly concerned with pictures captured on a 'consumer' digital still camera or scanner but needless to say it causes a lot of arguments amongst professionals and enthusiasts.

It's worth familiarising yourself with the resizing facilities in your picture editing program as it is important to match the size of an image to its medium to ensure the best possible quality and effect. In other words there's no point trying to print or display an image that's larger than the screen or sheet of paper can handle. In fact it can actually degrade the image, so experiment with the sizing facilities and learn to keep an eye on the 'statistics' display. This is usually at the bottom of the screen and shows the actual size of the image in pixels or centimetres and the amount of magnification (or reduction) applied to the display.

FILE FORMATS

Statistics info boxes usually tell you other useful things, like the colour depth of an image and the size of the image file. This is crucially important if, for example, you want to send a picture by email or illustrate a web page as the size of the file has a direct bearing on how long it takes to download. File size is largely determined by the picture file format and there are plenty to choose from though in practice most PC users will encounter only a handful of types, namely Bitmaps, TIFFs and JPEGs.

Bitmaps (file extension *.bmp) and TIFFs (extension *.tif) are 'lossless' formats that create the biggest files and highest quality pictures because the data describes the position, brightness, colour and colour depth of every single pixel in the image. Scanners and some high-end digital cameras produce Bitmaps and TIFFs and depending on the size and complexity of the scanned image, can be anything from two to ten megabytes or more in size. Clearly, this is far too big to send easily over the Internet. On a normal dial-up connection a 5Mb bitmap file could take anything up to an hour to send or receive!

Most images sent over the Internet use the JPEG (file extension *.jpg) file format. This is a 'lossy' format, which means that the data is compressed to make the file size smaller. Compression ratios of 100 to 1 are possible, though for most applications a ratio of between 10 and 20 to 1 strikes a good balance between size and quality. There are no hard and fast rules about the size of picture files sent over the Internet or in email messages but in general it's best to keep them below 100Kb and preferably under 50Kb, especially if you are going to be sending a lot of them.

IMAGE EDITING

Once a picture has been downloaded onto your PC's hard drive there's almost no limit to what you can do to it, from relatively mundane things like cancelling 'red-eye' to inserting or removing people and objects, changing facial expressions and applying a range of exotic special effects and filters that are simply not available in conventional film photography.

You don't need a lot of skill or expensive software to prove that the camera can lie – and lie convincingly – just the picture editing software that comes with most digital still cameras and scanners. The Paint program included with Windows has some useful facilities but it's not really up to serious picture work moreover some earlier versions, included with Windows 95 and 98 cannot handle common digital still camera picture file formats like JPEG and TIFF.

We'll start with some very basic techniques to prepare your pictures for more in-depth editing. The first one is image rotation; pictures taken on a digital still camera are rectangular in shape so it's quite natural to turn the camera sideways to frame a tall object or structure. Obviously it's not a problem with pictures taken on a conventional film camera, when the print comes back from processing you simply turn it around, however you can't easily do that with a PC screen so the first thing you need to do after downloading images to your computer is turn the sideways shots the right way around and re-save them.

Virtually all photo-editing programs have a rotate facility that turns the picture right or left 90 degrees at a time, however, some programs also have a Free Rotate option that lets you rotate the image in one-degree increments. This can be handy if, for example, you were leaning to one side when you took the picture. Alternatively, you might want to deliberately tilt the image for effect, to emphasise the angle of a slope, or make it appear as though your subjects are on a hill or climbing a mountain.

The problem with free rotation is that once the image is saved the sides will no longer be parallel with the screen, and that's one of the many things our next editing technique can fix. Cropping is one of the most useful tools in any photo-editing program, it can instantly transform a dull-looking image and cut out all sorts of little embarrassments, as well as help to straighten up wonky edges.

Most of us never get close enough to our subjects, especially when taking pictures outdoors and unless your camera has a zoom lens – and you remember to use it – you end up with little people in the near distance set against a huge expanse of background. Cropping can also help when the

The rotate facility in many image editing programs lets you correct for wonky pictures.

subject isn't in the centre of the frame, there's too much sky, or you can remove someone or something you don't want in the picture.

Some programs have specific cropping tools, others have 'Selection' or 'Marquee' functions but in most cases, after the tool has been selected, the mouse cursor turns into a crosshair which you place in the top left-hand corner of the area you want to select; click and hold the mouse button and drag it to the bottom right corner of the area. When the mouse button is released the defined area is normally shown bordered by a dotted line. The size and shape of the area can then be adjusted using sizing handles, bearing in mind that as you enlarge a part of an image you reduce the amount of detail it contains.

When you are happy with it save that as a new image. Don't give it the same name as the original picture file otherwise it will be overwritten, and

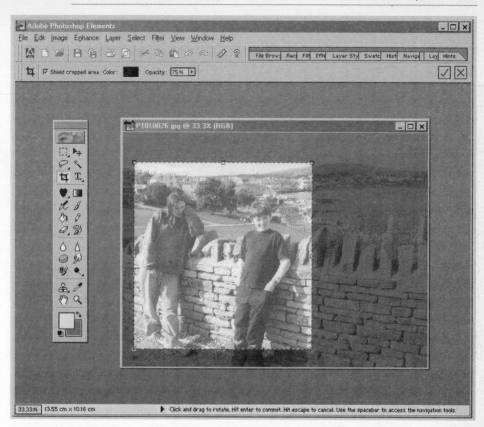

The cropping tool lets you chop out parts of an image you don't want to see.

you won't be able to use it again. Instead just add a '1' to the end of the filename (before the extension, i.e., seaside.jpg becomes seaside1.jpg), so they'll appear next to one another in your directory listings.

On some photo editing programs you can speed things up by using keyboard shortcuts; standard Windows Copy and Paste conventions often work. For example, select the area with the cropping/selection tool then press Ctrl + C to copy it to the clipboard, then Ctrl + V to paste the new image back onto the program's desktop.

ADJUSTMENTS

We take for granted the ability of our eyes and brain to adjust automatically to a wide range of lighting conditions. For example the pages in this book –

the unprinted bits at least – should appear white, whether you're reading it in natural daylight or under artificial light, and if you have normal eyesight you'll still be able to read the print with only the tiniest amount of light. Cameras, digital or otherwise struggle to achieve this kind of performance, which is why a lot of the photographs you take are bound to have some exposure or colour balance defects.

Photographic labs do their best to correct minor aberrations when you send a film off for processing but with a digital camera, once the images are downloaded onto your computer, you are in charge. With the right software you can do just about anything to an image, from adjusting colours and brightness levels, to extracting lost or hidden detail masked by shadows or poor lighting.

It all sounds very exciting, as indeed it is, but before we get started a few simple ground rules. Firstly, before you do anything make sure your computer display's picture controls are correctly aligned. Check to see if your monitor or system came with any setup or colour matching utilities and there's a set of basic test patterns at: http://arc.co.uk/setup/

Most picture editing programs have far too many options for novices and it's easy to get carried away with all the tools and end up making a mess of it. It's a good idea therefore, always to keep a virgin copy of your original picture. As soon as you make any changes to an image use Save As on the file menu to give the picture you are working on a different name (but keep to the same file format) then you will always have the original as a backup if you muck things up.

The watchword in picture editing is moderation. When you make adjustments do them singly and in small increments and preview the result each time. Most image editing programs have an undo function but in some cases they will only let you undo one or two steps, so if you've made several changes that you are not happy with you're stuck. Also bear in mind that reversing an action, i.e., reducing contrast level back to a previous setting, will not necessarily restore the image to its original state, especially if you've made other changes in the interim.

Brightness, contrast and colour are the three most basic and arguably the most important picture adjustments and they're the ones you should really get off pat before you progress to more advanced techniques. It's a largely intuitive process and there is no right or wrong way but the brightness adjustment is often the best place to start. It is usually fairly obvious when a picture is too light or too dark and you'll know when you've overdone the corrections and the image 'washes out' or becomes too gloomy; usually once the brightness level looks 'right' the rest of the adjustments usually fall into place.

When altering contrast, rather than looking at the picture as a whole, focus on changes in the amount of visible detail and texture revealed (or obscured) in the lighter and darker areas of the picture – the highlights and lowlights – and try to achieve a balance between the two. Some programs give you the option to adjust highlights, lowlights, mid-tones and shadows separately; if so experiment with the settings but remember the golden rule, only adjust one parameter at a time.

Most image editing programs let you adjust both the colour intensity or saturation and the relative levels of the three primary colours, red, green and blue (RGB). Saturation tends to be subjective, there is a correct – i.e. natural and lifelike setting – but some people prefer the colours in their photographs to look bright and vibrant, and tweaking the saturation in a picture shot on a dull day or when the light is 'flat' can make it look a little more interesting. However, it's much more likely that you will want to use the RGB levels to correct faults in the picture's colour balance.

A lot of digital cameras – even some expensive models – have trouble with colour balance (sometimes referred to as 'white balance') especially when shooting under low level or artificial light, which has a different colour 'temperature' to daylight. Tungsten light tends to give photographs a slightly warmish look, emphasising red and orange hues and the effect can be quite pleasing but tube or fluorescent light often imparts a yellowish or green cast, which can make delicate shades like skin tones look quite sickly.

Correcting colour faults can be tricky as you are juggling with three variables, which results in a lot of interaction so it is even more important to make only small changes, and – at the risk of being repetitive – only alter one thing at a time, so you can judge the effect. There are various techniques but the simplest is to choose a reference colour, and work on that. White surfaces or objects can be a very useful guide, once you get the whites right the other colours should look okay too. Alternatively when there are people or faces in the picture work on the skin tones, it's something we're acutely aware of and unnatural or unhealthy tinges stand out like a sore thumb.

DIGITAL TRICKERY

Having dealt with the fundamentals of picture editing it's now time to move on to some more advanced digital image trickery and two fairly common jobs – eliminating red-eye and removing a person or object from a picture. Between them they involve a range of relatively simple techniques that can be readily adapted to a wide variety of picture editing jobs and the tools required are common to most picture editing programs, including the sometimes fairly basic ones supplied with digital still cameras.

Red eye is caused by light from a flashgun reflecting straight back to the camera from a subject's eyes; blood vessels in the retina produce the characteristic red colour, which gives the subject a somewhat demonic appearance. Compact cameras are the worst offenders because the flashgun is usually very close to the lens.

Several picture editing programs have automated red-eye removal facilities, and some of them are quite good, but it's actually very easy to do it manually, and it will help you to become more familiar with some important features in your editing software.

Open your picture-editing program and display the image you want to work on. Get into the habit of using Save As on the program's File menu to rename and save the image straight away, so the original is preserved, just in case you make a mess of it.

Use the magnification tool to zoom in close on one of the red eyes. Now change to the freehand selection tool and carefully outline the red area of the eye. You could of course simply 'fill' or change the colour of the red area but that would look very odd – more so than red eye in fact. The trick is to remove the colour – i.e., turn the defined area black and white – using the program's colour or saturation controls. This means that texture and detail is retained and the end result will look perfectly natural. When you've removed the colour zoom back out to normal size and if you're happy with it save the image and repeat the process for all other affected eyes.

Removing people, objects or things apparently growing out of people's heads, etc., from photographs is another reasonably straightforward job, in principle at any rate, but it's easier on some photographs than others. The determining factor is the background, and what's behind the person or object you want to remove. The idea is to replace the object or person with sections of background taken from other parts of the image, preferably close to the object, so you get the best match in terms of colour, brightness and scale. The best backgrounds are either plain or blurry – the sky or the sea for example – or tightly textured or patterned with a uniform colour – grass, bricks, leaves on trees, etc. Images with irregular background, buildings, large shapes and lots of colour or perspective, etc. can be more difficult to work with.

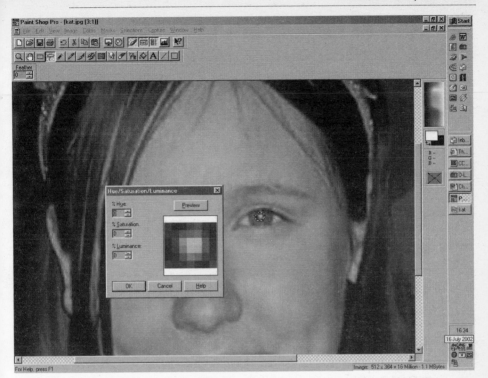

Correcting 'red-eye'; highlight the red part of the eye and reduce the colour saturation.

There are various ways of doing it but the simplest method, and the one that's applicable to most picture editing programs, is to use a combination of copy and paste – to mask out the object – and the 'clone brush' tool to tackle fine detail, tidy up edges and spot out imperfections.

As usual start by opening the photograph and use Save As to create your working copy and remember to save your work every few minutes. There's no right or wrong way to proceed but it's usually easier to enlarge or zoom in on the image and work on only a small area at a time. Use the freehand selection tool to define smallish chunks of background adjoining the object then copy and paste or 'float' the sections over the object to mask it out in several operations. The size of the chunks depends on the uniformity of the background; larger areas are more difficult to work with, and can look awkward as they may contain graduations in brightness and colour, shadows or fine details that show up as a repeat pattern or a defined edge. If available use the 'feather edge' option as this will makes the edges less distinct. Return the image to normal magnification and check your progress every so often.

When the bulk of the object or person has been obliterated you can use the clone tool to obscure edges and edit fiddly details. You will probably find it easier to work at even higher magnification levels, so you can start seeing the individual pixels. It's more accurate and the results will look a lot better. The clone tool is one of the most useful facilities in an image-editing program. It 'picks up' detail and texture from a selected part of the image and the brush tool 'paints' it back into the picture. It takes a little practice to become proficient with it and you will probably have to experiment with the brush size and shape options but once you've got the hang of it you will find that you can do some amazing tricks.

Q&A **Real world problems**

Screen test

Q   I note that a lot of books and magazines show Windows screen menus and displays as pictures. Can you tell me what software to use to capture the screen display as a file, which can be incorporated in a DTP file? I would also like to know the source of the program.

A   Windows contains everything you need to insert a 'screen grab' into a document. Simply press the Print Screen button on your keyboard and a snapshot or bitmap of whatever is on the screen is sent to the Windows Clipboard. From there it can be opened and manipulated using the Paint program, or pasted into a document using the Paste command. If you only want to capture the active window in a display then hold down the Alt key before pressing Print Screen button. If you want to do anything more complicated with the image then you will need a graphics program, such as Paint Shop Pro.

Handy scanner

Q   I've been using my scanner to scan my baby's hands and feet, which seems a marvellous method, and prevents getting paint on the child's hands. However, I cannot get a 1:1 scaled image. Even if I put the scanner into photocopy mode, the printout is a little smaller than the original. How can I print out a full size image?

A   It is not unusual for scanned and photocopied images to be a slightly different size from the original. There should be a way of compensating for this in your chosen (or supplied) paintbox/graphics software, usually under the print preview menu. Most programs have a sizing facility, to alter the dimensions of the image as it is printed. You can easily calibrate your set-up by scanning a small ruler, print it out and adjust the image size accordingly.

Prints of darkness

Q   I have recently bought a scanner; it seems to work well, if a little slowly but we have problems printing the results. The main difficulty concerns watercolour paintings that we are trying to print out. They scan well, if the results on the screen are anything to go by, but when they are printed the colours are dark and harsh. The very helpful chap in the local computer shop suggested altering the printer settings but to no avail. Any help, in words of one syllable that could be understood by a middle-aged home computer user would be appreciated. One other question, what is the light fastness of colour prints and do different models produce varying results?

A   The paint or graphics software that came with your scanner should allow you to alter basic colour and brightness settings, if not then it's worth changing to a more advanced program. Your monitor might be giving a false impression; make sure it is set up correctly. The type of paper you are using can also affect print quality. For best results use high-quality, low absorbency grades, specifically designed for inkjet printing. Most inkjet printers use water-based inks and these will begin to fade after only a few years, faster if the print is exposed to bright light or stored in a humid atmosphere. Longer lasting UV stabilised inks are available for Hewlett Packard, Canon and other makes of printer that should last 25 years or more.

CHAPTER 13 **Printers and scanners**

*Printers and scanners bring to mind Dr Johnson's
famous quip about performing dogs; the wonder is not
that they do the job so well, but they do it at all!
Printers and scanners are probably the most useful
peripherals you can have connected to your PC but
there's a bewildering choice available and it's a
potential minefield, if you don't know what you're
doing...*

PRINTERS

Basically there are four main types of printer available to the PC user: dot
matrix, thermal, laser and inkjet. Dot matrix and thermal printers are now
mostly used in specialised applications, such as printing multi-part forms, till
receipts and so on and for most users the choice is between laser and inkjet.
Laser printers tend to be single colour (i.e., black) but they produce very
high-quality output, a fast throughput and are relatively cheap to run;
therefore they are best suited to office applications. Colour laser printers are
also available but they can be expensive to buy and run and again are aimed
at commercial and business users.

The clear choice therefore for the vast majority of home and small office
users is inkjet. The technology has now reached the stage where black and
white print quality is as good as laser and colour models can produce prints
of near photographic quality; some of them are so good that only an expert
with a magnifying glass could tell the difference. They're not expensive to
buy either and there are some very capable models on the market for less
than £100, but there's a catch, well, several actually, and the most obvious
one is running costs.

Manufacturers have developed increasingly elaborate ink delivery systems
to achieve the high resolution and colour accuracy needed to do justice to a
new generation of high-performance multi-megapixel digital still cameras
(see Chapter 14). Early colour printing systems relied on mixing just three

coloured inks – cyan, magenta and yellow – and sometimes black as well; however today's photorealistic printers use four, five or even six different coloured inks.

Inevitably it's not the ink that costs the money but the disposable cartridges and the fact that the few millilitres of ink they contain often runs out at alarming speed. It's a reprise of the old story about how Kodak never made a penny selling cameras, the real money was, and probably still is, in the film and processing. The real cost of colour inkjet printing is the 'consumables' and we have reached the absurd position where the cost of replenishing the ink tanks on some models of colour printer can be as much as three-quarters of the cost of the original purchase price. There has even been speculation that one day manufacturers may just give the printers away in return for a year or two's commitment to buy only branded consumables.

Some manufacturers pile on the misery with combined multi-colour ink cartridges that have to be replaced, even if only one colour has run out and it's a little-known fact that ink cartridges on some models can be drained without printing a single page. Most inkjet printers go into a cleaning and priming routine every time they are switched on and this uses up a small amount of ink. On some the cartridge can be emptied in as few as 60 on/off cycles.

For that reason you should avoid switching inkjet printers on and off any more than is necessary. On the other hand you shouldn't let your printer remain idle for more than a couple of weeks at a time, otherwise the print head or cartridge may dry out or clog and if the cartridge has been drying out for some time it may not be recoverable. On a lightly used printer get into the habit of printing a test page every ten days or so, and make sure that the printer isn't placed near a radiator, window or source of heat.

Inkjet printer owners can often reduce running costs significantly by using third-party 'compatible' cartridges, which can sell for a fraction of the cost of the original manufacturer's product. Another way to beat the odds is to use refill kits, which although often messy and sometimes complicated, allow cartridges to be recycled several times before the print quality deteriorates. Naturally, printer manufacturers discourage both practices and issue dire warnings that warranties will be rendered null and void, performance will suffer and non-approved cartridges and inks may damage hardware. In practice most users will experience few problems and in a worst-case scenario the only thing likely to be damaged by inferior ink is the print head or cartridge, both of which are throw-away/replaceable items.

Compatible cartridges are now widely available from leading PC dealers and stationery suppliers; most of them come from entirely reputable sources, some are even made in the same factories as the originals, sold under well-known and respected brand names and are fully guaranteed. If you're still not happy about risking the manufacturer's displeasure then wait until the printer's warranty has expired before using them.

Manufacturers have come up with a variety of cunning schemes to discourage the use of compatible cartridges and refill kits, including 'smart' printer management software that decides when the cartridge needs to be replaced, and most recently, 'chipped' cartridges or ink tanks, that tell the printer when they are empty. Management programs are notoriously conservative and some models routinely report a tank or cartridge as being empty when there is clearly plenty of ink left, which is both wasteful and expensive. Within a few weeks of any new printer appearing the Internet is alive with ruses, fixes and devices that counter every new strategy the manufacturers dream up.

You can easily check to see if there are any money-saving fixes available for your printer, all you have to do is type 'refill xxxx printers' (where 'x' is the make and model number of your printer) into the find field of a search engine like Google (www.google.com). Nine times out of ten you will be rewarded with scores of hits from fellow owners and companies supplying low-cost consumables.

Chipped cartridges caused a few problems at first but devices that can reset or reprogram the chips are now widely available, that allow the use of compatible cartridges. In most cases the chip from an empty cartridge is simply removed, and after being reset inserted into the new full cartridge. It only takes a few seconds and the cost savings can be very substantial, even after taking into account the cost of the programmer.

Although most inkjet cartridges are not designed to be re-filled, and the quality of refill inks and compatible cartridges may not be as good as the original with the same light-fast/anti-fade properties, for routine jobs and printing text this probably doesn't matter. If you use a refill kit only use good-quality products but in any case do not expect to be able to refill a cartridge more than three or four times.

The fact that these complex electromechanical devices are normally so reliable is another constant source of amazement, until they go wrong that is. In fairness, much of the time it's not the printer that is at fault but the software, and quite often it's due to incorrect installation of the driver (see Chapters 15 and 16).

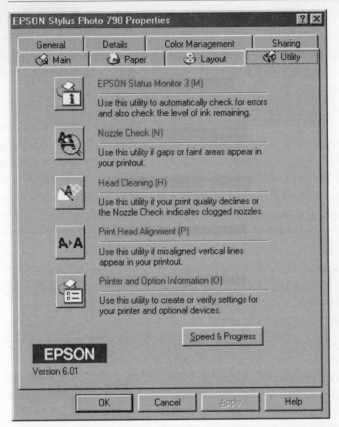

Use your printer's cleaning utility on a regular basis to ensure crisp sharp results.

If your problems are concerned with the quality of the output, rather than the operation of the printer, try changing the various performance settings that are available (depending on the make and model of printer) on the Properties tabs. However, assuming that the PC and printer between them have adopted the factory defaults, more often than not it has something to do with the printer itself, the paper, or the consumables (ink cassette, ribbon or toner cartridge).

If the microscopic holes in an inkjet printer head become blocked this can lead to partially formed characters, lines or streaking on images. If your printer has a self-cleaning routine (check the manual) you should use it regularly, particularly if the printer has been standing idle for some time, or you are about to print an important document on expensive high-grade paper. If that doesn't work, remove the cartridge and use the cleaning kit (if supplied) or gently wipe the head with a lightly moistened cotton bud; don't try poking it with a pin or any other sharp objects, you will destroy it!

Paper quality is very important, especially on inkjets. Cheap copier paper tends to be more absorbent, the ink runs – particularly watery cheap refill ink – and the characters become spidery and indistinct. Try experimenting with a variety of makes and grades of paper; special inkjet paper is usually worth the extra cost. Glossy paper, designed for use with colour inkjet printers can give excellent, near photographic results but it can be inordinately expensive, especially the small packets marketed by printer manufacturers. Try some of the cheaper brands that are coming onto the market, they cannot harm your printer – despite the dire warnings in some printer manuals – and some of them are very good indeed.

SCANNERS

Getting photographs, graphics and artwork into a PC used to be incredibly difficult but as PCs have increased in performance and the cost of memory and storage devices has fallen, so too has the cost of scanners.

Scanning is a fairly simple process, on most models the image lies face down on a glass plate or 'platen'; on the other side a bar fitted with a bright light and a row of tiny light-sensitive devices, known as CCDs (charge coupled devices), travels the length of the platen, turning light reflected from the image into a stream of digital data. This is fed to the PC, usually via the USB port though a few recent models have a FireWire connection and some older models plug into the PC's parallel printer port.

This is where it gets interesting. The data file created by the scanner represents an image and it can be used in a number of different ways by the utility software that is included with virtually all scanners these days.

Two of the most useful extras are photocopy and fax programs. Photo-copying simply involves printing out the scanned image, and don't forget that image can just as easily be a page of text or a diagram. There's more; if you have a colour printer a scanner turns your PC into a high-quality colour photocopier! True, PC photocopiers are not as fast as the real thing but if you only need to run off a few copies every now and again they're perfectly adequate, and a darn sight cheaper and more convenient than print shops or coin-operated machines.

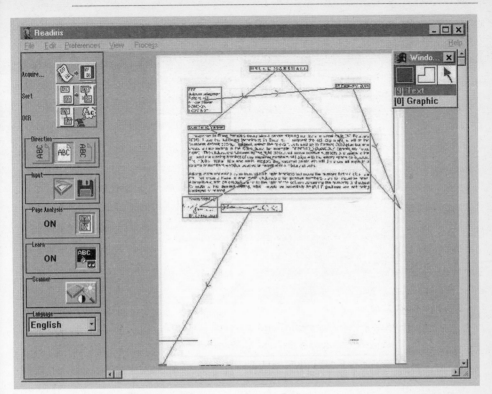

Optical Character Recognition software 'reads' a document and converts it into a word processor file.

As you probably know, with the right software you can send text documents created on a PC with a modem directly to a fax machine. However, unlike a proper fax machine, the PC fax facility can't send copies of documents on paper, handwritten notes, diagrams or drawings. With a scanner connected to your PC you can, and on some models you can fax in colour, a trick relatively few stand-alone fax machines can manage.

If you thought that was clever then how about optical character recognition? OCR is another software utility bundled with most scanners that converts a scanned image of typewritten or printed copy into a text file or word processor document. OCR software is now very efficient and can cope with a wide range of printing styles and in some cases, even neat handwriting. Most programs make a few mistakes, and they can get confused if the document is scrappy or printed on non-white, textured or patterned paper but even the most basic OCR packages can achieve at least 95%

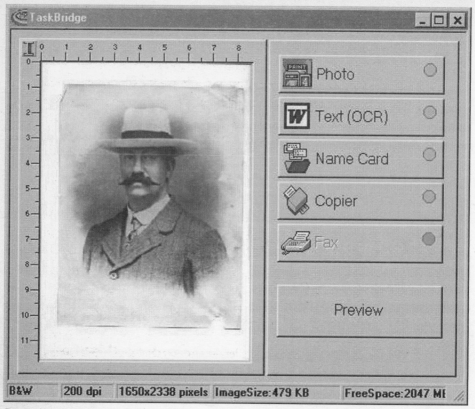

Preserving the past using your scanner, many old photographs are fading away but it's not too late to save them.

accuracy (under favourable conditions) which can mean a huge saving in time and effort if you routinely transcribe or type up a lot of documents.

Scanning photographs – which is what most people buy a scanner for initially – is the most straightforward task of all. The scanner software will usually produce a 'bitmap' or 'JPEG' image file that can be viewed directly on most graphics applications and used in word processors. Some scanners come with graphic programs of their own, usually 'lite' versions of the well-known packages.

What should you look for when buying a scanner? There are basically two types: stand-alone flatbed models, and 'multi-function machines'. The latter is a printer that scans, and sometimes has faxing facilities as well. They can be very convenient when space is at a premium, and you need a new printer, but otherwise stand-alone models tend to be a lot cheaper and usually much more flexible. Most flatbeds can accommodate documents slightly larger than A4, some models can be fitted with slide film adaptors and dedicated slide scanners are also available.

In all cases the most important considerations are resolution (see Chapter 12) which is a measure of how much fine detail the scanner can capture, and colour depth, which determines how accurately it renders colours and shades. Resolution is rated in dots per inch or 'dpi' and that is directly related to the number of light-sensitive elements on the scanning head. Needless to say the more the merrier and if you are planning to use it for demanding applications then it's worth paying more for the extra quality.

Q&A **Real world problems**

Leading question

Q What is the longest lead I can use to connect my PC to a printer?

A The maximum recommended length for parallel and USB cables is five metres, though in practice you can get away with six or seven metres, assuming you're using good-quality cables.

Paper waste

Q My Canon printer often takes in two or more sheets of paper when printing. I use ordinary photocopier paper, is that okay, or should I only use the more expensive 'inkjet' type paper?

A Copier paper is fine, but if you are working in a warm dry atmosphere the trick is to 'fan' the paper before loading, this helps separate the sheets and dissipate any static charge that may have built up, which makes the sheets stick together.

Slow print

Q What is the reason my printer runs so slowly? I have a reasonably recent Pentium PC and the printer is a new Epson model. A page can take up to a minute to print, can that be right?

A   No, that's far too long – a simple page of text shouldn't take more than ten seconds or so to print. It sounds as if you have the wrong driver installed, or it has become corrupted. Go to Printers (Start, then Settings) delete the existing driver and then go to Control Panel (Start, Settings) click on the Install New Hardware icon and follow the instructions to re-install the printer.

CHAPTER 14 **Digital cameras and camcorders**

Fading, blurred and out of focus pictures first started coming back from the chemists almost two hundred years ago. The chemists concerned were Sir Humphry Davy and Thomas Wedgwood, who outlined the basic principles of chemical photography back in 1802...

And so it was until 1981, when Sony unveiled the first prototype electronic still camera, called Mavica. It used a solid-state image sensor instead of film and recorded images on a miniature floppy disk. Pictures could be displayed directly on a TV, sent down telephone wires or printed out on paper. Electronic still photography finally came of age during the mid 1990s when the first low-cost digital still cameras (DSCs) started to appear. Ever since pundits have been forecasting the imminent demise of photographic film. Now it's finally happening. The days when you had to send your films off to be developed and printed, or even wait for an hour for on-the-spot processing, are fast coming to an end.

The benefits of DSC photography are many and varied. There's no waiting for prints to be processed, many current models have built-in LCD viewing screens so you can compose the shot and check the image straight away, and if necessary re-shoot. Running costs are minimal, there's no film to buy (though some DSCs get through batteries at an alarming rate). Storage capacity is increasing all the time, DSCs typically capture between 50 and 100 images on internal memory chips or cards and they can be downloaded onto the PC's hard disk at any time, to free up space.

Most current models look and work exactly like a compact 35mm camera, and they're just as easy to use. Almost all budget and mid-market models – like their 35mm compact and APS cousins – are geared for full or semi-automatic point-and-shoot operation. Manual exposure controls, when fitted, closely resemble those on film cameras and adjust the aperture and shutter speed over the same or similar range of settings. Exposure options on more sophisticated film and digital cameras are also broadly similar. These include programmed auto-exposure for difficult lighting situations, aperture and shutter priority, exposure bracketing and slow shutter speeds. The only unfamiliar adjustment you are likely to encounter is white balance. This is a way of compensating for variations in colour temperature, which is inherent in different types of light; on photographic film this is carried out at the processing stage. On DSCs with manual white balance control it can be with presets for different types of light (natural, tungsten, tube, etc.) or manual/manual lock, where it is necessary to give the camera's sensor a reference by pointing it at a white surface.

Flashguns are a more or less standard fitment on DSCs and the way they work is no different from most film cameras. Options typically include manual or auto operation, fill-in and red-eye reduction; a few models have level settings and exposure compensation facilities.

First-timers and even experienced photographers frequently comment that a lot of DSCs appear to have very basic or rudimentary lenses. This is particularly galling to owners of SLR-type cameras, who may have built up a collection of expensive lenses. The reason DSC lenses are so small has to do with the fact that the microchip image sensors used in these cameras are typically one-quarter or one-third of an inch across – significantly smaller than a frame of 35mm or APS film – consequently the lenses require a much shorter focal length and can be made a lot smaller, without necessarily compromising image quality.

For those who want to try their hands at digital photography but cannot bear to be parted from their lens collections or cherished 35mm cameras there may be a solution. Several camera manufacturers produce 'digital backs' for their models, which contain an image sensor and processing microchips and fits in place of the camera's normal film back. Another interesting development is 'e-film'. The idea first surfaced almost four years ago and is now poised to go into production. Basically it is a small device, shaped like a 35mm film cartridge; inside there's a battery processor and memory chips and attached to the side is a flat plate with an image sensor, that sits in place of the film. The unit fits into the film compartment of an SLR camera, turning it instantly into a digital still camera. There's more information in the website at: http://www.siliconfilm.com

Virtually all DSCs come with PC (and Mac) connection kits that include a transfer lead and a suite of operating software. In most cases that's a capture and photo album utility, for retrieving and storing images, plus one or more

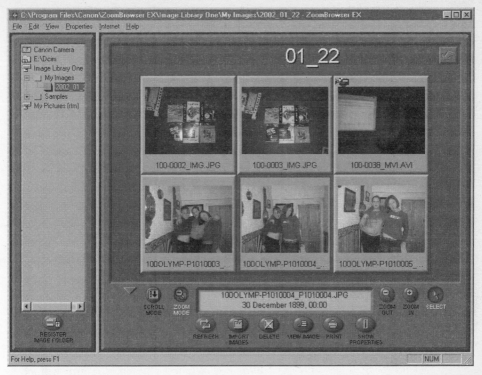

The software that comes with your digital camera will help you to organise your collection.

design and editing programs. These have templates for calendars, greetings cards and posters plus special effects and adjustments for correcting faults, like red-eye, colour imbalance, brightness and contrast. In short the software gives you the kind of creative control over your photographs normally only possible in a well-equipped film-processing lab.

Once an image is stored on your PC's hard drive you can manipulate it in an almost endless number of ways, removing people, objects and even buildings that you'd rather not have in your photographs – see Chapter 12. Digital images can be incorporated into documents, leaflets and flyers, sent around the world to friends or relatives in a matter of seconds and used to illustrate Internet web pages.

Even if you haven't yet got a photorealistic printer you can still get high-quality prints from your digital still camera. Many high-street photo and video specialists have in-store printing facilities for digital still cameras – just take along your camera or memory card and they do the rest. Alternatively,

SmartMedia and MultiMediaCard (MMC) memory cards used in many digital cameras.

images can be sent for printing over the Internet and they will be posted back to you in a day or two.

Buying a digital still camera can be quite an adventure. It is pointless trying to keep up with the technology. Whatever model you buy will be outmoded and probably selling for a fraction of what you paid for it in six months time. As a very general rule of thumb you should shortlist models with image sensors that have at least 2-million pixels (2 megapixels) which is more than adequate for the majority of PC based applications and capable of giving good results on paper (though a lot also depends on the performance of the printer).

Most DSCs store images on removable memory modules. There are four different types in widespread use, they are: MultiMediaCard or MMC, CompactFlash, Memory Stick and SmartMedia. There are no significant technical differences between the various types, but prices, and capacities vary a lot, so bear that in mind as the cards supplied with a lot of cameras often only hold 8 to 10 images at the highest quality settings. There are several ways of connecting cameras to PCs. Older and cheaper models use standard PC serial and parallel connection ports, which ensures the greatest level of compatibility but these methods are a good deal slower than the alternative USB type connection. It can take several minutes to download a dozen pictures via a serial link, but only a few seconds using a USB connection.

Images can also be downloaded directly from memory cards via an interface module, there are several types including PC-Card and floppy disk adaptor or card 'readers', the latter type includes models that can read several different types of card and they are generally quite cheap.

DIGITAL CAMCORDERS

One day – and it may be sooner rather than later – there will be a camcorder that can take high-quality still images, or possibly a digital still camera that can record a useful amount of video, but in spite of claims to the contrary it certainly hasn't happened yet. Several combination still-movie cameras have come and gone and none of them did either job particularly well.

The market is currently split between multi megapixel digital still cameras that can record a few seconds of jerky and indifferent-looking moving video, and a lot of analogue and digital camcorders with 'snapshot' still video recording modes, that at best perform as well as first generation DSCs with the sort of picture quality that is really only suitable for undemanding PC and Internet-based applications.

The basic problem – as far as recording video on a DSC is concerned – is storage capacity, or rather the lack of it. The most efficient digital video compression schemes capable of maintaining acceptable picture and sound quality gobble up between 2 and 4 megabytes of memory, per second. Currently only tape-based recording systems can provide that sort of storage space at an acceptable cost, though a new generation of DVD-RAM camcorders and micro-drives – tiny hard disk drives the size of memory cards with capacities of a gigabyte or more – are showing a lot of promise. Solid-state memory is some time away from being any use for moving video, the general consensus is that a minimum of 30 minutes recording time is needed to make the exercise worthwhile, so at the moment only disk-based media (mini PC hard disks, MiniDisk & DVD-RAM/RW, etc.) show any potential for a lightweight and pocketable still/video device at a consumer-friendly price.

Coming at it from the other direction, the main problem with camcorder-based still video cameras is the CCD image sensor, which for obvious reasons is optimised for video recording. The CCDs in 'low-band' analogue VHS/C or 8mm camcorders typically have up to 380k pixels, they don't need any more because even that comparatively modest figure produces more information than can be recorded on the tape. Needless to say, very few low-

Video editing for kids, this attractive and easy to use software package is designed exclusively for junior Spielbergs.

band machines have a still picture recording facility. Still recording is a little more common on 'High Band' S-VHS/C and Hi8 camcorders; these have CCDs with a marginally higher pixel density, in the region of 400k to 470k, which is capable of producing a VGA standard colour picture. However, this is still some considerable way behind the requirements for anything other than basic image capture for PC display.

Digital camcorders using the DVC and Digital 8 recording formats come closest to a solution and virtually all models have a still recording facility though the image sensor is still the main stumbling block. For video recording the format's basic requirement is for a sensor with 570k pixels; any more are superfluous for video recording, however, several manufacturers have upped the ante with models with sensors having more than one million pixels but even this is still some way below the two million plus pixels needed to produce a decent-looking still print.

Given the inherent limitations of sub-megapixel image sensors in camcorders manufacturers have found a number of other ways to improve the still image performance and convenience of their machines. One of the most significant advances has been the use of progressive scan techniques, when recording in 'snapshot mode'. Normally a moving video image is recorded in two interleaved 'scans', this causes problems when there is rapid movement in the scene. Progressive scan captures the image in one 'hit', more like a digital still camera in fact, resulting in a sharper and more stable image. Several makers fit flashguns or accessory shoes to their machines, which is a big help when it comes to taking pictures indoors.

Getting still images out of the camcorder and into a PC or printer is another area where manufacturers demonstrate their ingenuity. First-generation digital camcorders recorded still pictures onto tape, which made image file extraction very difficult without recourse to elaborately specified PCs and printers with exotic data input facilities. More recently there has been a steady move towards equipping machines with on-board solid-state memory and the facility to download images using a standard serial port or a cordless infra-red (IrDA) communications link. A growing number of digital camcorders now use removable memory cards, similar to those used in digital still cameras.

Q&A Real world questions

Lens lore

Q   I have a reasonably recent PC and I am interested in buying a digital camera but I am a little mystified by the lenses that they use. Most of the ones I've seen have a focal length of 5 to 10 mm, which on my SLR camera would produce a wrap-around 'fish-eye' effect. Surely this isn't the case on digital cameras, but can they be compared with 35mm SLR type lenses?

A   The lenses on most digital cameras are equivalent to SLR lenses with a focal length of between 40mm and 50mm. The apparent disparity is due to the difference in size between a frame of 35mm film, and the CCD (charged coupled device) image sensors used in digital cameras. Most models use CCDs that are only 7 to 10mm across, hence the need for lenses with a much shorter focal length.

X-rated

Q   I have just bought my first digital still camera and am concerned that it will have to go through airport security X-Ray machines, is there any chance this could damage the camera or the images stored on it?

A   It's very unlikely, most airport X-Ray scanners are 'microdose' machines, which generate very low levels of radiation, certainly not enough to fog a normal film, let alone interfere with a digital still camera, which stores images on memory microchips. If you are concerned remove the memory cards and keep them in your pocket – in their protective cases. There's not enough metal in a memory card to trigger a 'gate' type metal detector but have them ready for a hand inspection, just in case.

Part IV

RESCUE

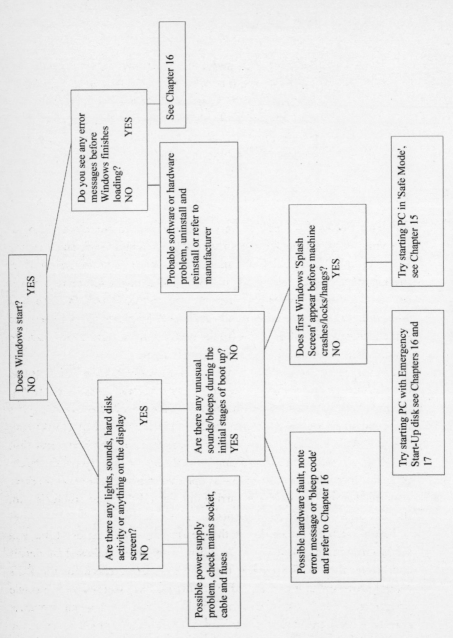

Does Windows start?
NO   YES

Do you see any error messages before Windows finishes loading?
NO   YES

See Chapter 16

Probable software or hardware problem, uninstall and reinstall or refer to manufacturer

Are there any lights, sounds, hard disk activity or anything on the display screen?
NO   YES

Possible power supply problem, check mains socket, cable and fuses

Are there any unusual sounds/bleeps during the initial stages of boot up?
YES   NO

Possible hardware fault, note error message or 'bleep code' and refer to Chapter 16

Does first Windows 'Splash Screen' appear before machine crashes/locks/hangs?
NO   YES

Try starting PC in 'Safe Mode', see Chapter 15

Try starting PC with Emergency Start-Up disk see Chapters 16 and 17

Quick start guide to common PC problems.

Crash recovery

For most of us switching a Windows PC on is only marginally more exciting than watching paint dry. The machine bleeps, lights wink, the hard disk chatters, lines of apparently meaningless text and pictures of clouds come and go then, all being well, a minute or so later the desktop appears.

Problems during boot up are very common and cause a great deal of frustration. Often the solution is reasonably straightforward, but knowing where to find it can be difficult and, in desperation, a lot of users end up making matters even worse, so it's worth knowing a bit about what is supposed to happen, when you press the 'on' button on your PC. Much of what follows applies to both Windows 9x and Windows XP but there are some relatively small differences (to the user, at any rate) during the start-up routine, which we'll deal with as we come to them.

Immediately after switch-on a small program called the BIOS (Basic Input Output System) which is stored in a 'non-volatile' memory microchip on the computer's main circuit board or 'motherboard', carries out a series of diagnostic checks called Power On Self-Test or POST. These make sure that the main electronic components, memory chips, keyboard and disk drives are all connected and working properly. By the way, having the BIOS program stored in a memory chip – as opposed to being held on a disk drive – means that the checks can be carried out, even if there are problems with the disk drives or other components.

If you watch the screen during these early stages often the first thing you see is information about the PC's video components followed by details concerning the BIOS program; then there's a name check for the PC's central processor unit or CPU. If everything is okay you will hear a single beep from the PC's loudspeaker and the first part of the boot-up sequence continues with the memory test. You may see some numbers whizzing around on the screen, stopping at something approximating the size of your

PC's random access memory (RAM) capacity. In other words if your PC has 256 megabytes of RAM the memory test number should read '262144K OK'. If you're wondering how it arrives at that particular value, that's because a kilobyte or a thousand 'bits' of information is actually 1024 bits, thus a megabyte would be 1,024,000 bits, times 256 equals 262,144,000 or 262144K.

During this part of the proceedings you may see a message on the screen to the effect that if you press the 'Del' key (sometimes F1 or a combination of keys) the PC will go into the 'setup' menu. This is a set of controls for the BIOS program and a no-go area for novices. It contains lots of critical settings that can very easily stop your PC working or make it misbehave in ways you wouldn't believe! If you're interested we'll be taking a closer look at the BIOS program in Chapter 18.

The BIOS then goes on to identify the floppy and hard disk drives and any other drives attached to the PC and instructs the PC to load a set of start-up or 'System' files into its memory. The first place it looks for them is floppy disk drive A. You may have noticed that if you've inadvertently left a

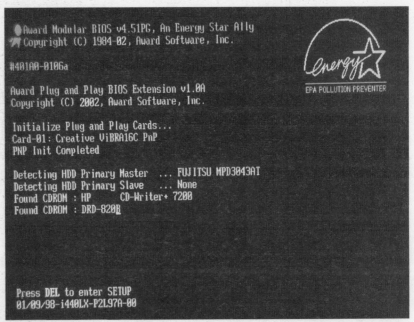

Power on Self Test – an example of a boot-up screen showing the results of the memory and disk drive checks.

floppy disk in the drive from a previous session you will be prompted to 'press any key to continue' and boot up resumes as normal.

Checking floppy drive A first is an important safety feature in Windows 9x because it means you will still be able to boot up your PC, even if the system files on the hard disk drive are missing or corrupted. Later versions of Windows 9x and Windows XP are a little more advanced in this respect and on some PCs it's possible also to boot from the setup CD-ROM.

If Windows 9x was pre-installed on your PC an emergency start-up disk or 'bootable' CD-ROM should have been provided with all the other disks and documentation, otherwise you are prompted to make one when you use your PC or Windows 9x for the first time. (A start-up disk is not strictly necessary in Windows XP as this has its own emergency recovery procedures.) If you haven't got a Windows 9x start-up disk you should make one right now. Go to Add/Remove Programs in Control Panel, select the Start-up tab and follow the instructions. We'll look at how to use it in more detail shortly.

Having confirmed that there is not a start-up disk in drive A the PC now looks for system files in a special area of the main hard disk drive called the boot sector. Incidentally, this is a hiding place for viruses, where they can remain undisturbed and do the maximum amount of damage, so make sure you have a virus checker program on your PC, and that it is kept up to date.

System files – whether on a floppy disk or drive C – contain information about the PC's configuration and in Windows 9x initiate the 'disk operating system' otherwise known as DOS. Windows XP dispenses with DOS and utilises its own start-up routine. DOS in Windows 9x tells the processor how to communicate with and process the files contained on the rest of drive C, organise its memory and look after all the input and output devices attached to the PC. When DOS has finished loading, an instruction in the start-up files tells the PC to begin loading Windows.

Now the fun really begins. Windows is a huge program comprising thousands of files the first of which is a real monster called the Registry (another topic covered in Chapter 18). This is a massive database containing everything the PC needs to know about Windows, your PC's hardware and peripherals plus the programs stored on the disk drives and your preferences for the way Windows and all the other programs are set up. Suffice it to say a lot of problems can occur at this stage if the Registry is corrupted, but it is checked automatically and if there's a problem it can load one of a number of previously saved Registry files from the last time your PC booted up successfully.

After the Registry has been installed Windows 9x next loads a series of configuration files, also stored in the boot sector (config.sys, autoexec.bat, etc.) which may also contain instructions for other programs, such as a virus scanner, to start loading. More configuration files follow, then comes the last major trouble spot, Windows drivers. These are scores, sometimes hundreds, of small data files requested by the Registry and configuration files that Windows needs to communicate with various bits of hardware, printers, the monitor, programs and so on. Finally, all being well there's a welcoming fanfare from the loudspeakers, the desktop appears and you're ready to start work.

WHEN THINGS GO WRONG

A PC that refuses to boot is one of life's more stressful experiences; when it happens to you – and it will – stay calm and take comfort from the fact that you are not alone; 99% of Windows PC users have, or will at some stage suffer the same fate. You may also be relieved to know that most start-up problems can be resolved fairly easily but please note that physical violence and abusive language definitely does not help.

As we have seen, a lot of things have to happen before the Windows desktop appears on the screen and although the boot-up sequence is a complex business it can be broken down into two fairly distinct stages: part one is before the first Windows 'splash' screen appears. If an error message appears or the machine freezes before Windows begins loading then the fault is most likely to be concerned with the BIOS program or a fault with the hardware (motherboard, memory chips, disk drives, etc.). If something goes wrong after the first Windows screen then it is almost always due to Windows or a software problem.

COMMON HARDWARE FAULTS

Thankfully hardware faults are quite rare and generally quite easy to resolve.

The obvious suspect in a totally dead PC (i.e., blank screen, no lights, stationary fan and no disk drive activity) is a loose mains cable, blown fuse or a problem with the power supply module. The fuses in the mains plug (and sometimes on the back of the PC) are easy to check and if one has blown, make sure you replace it with the same type. If it blows again there's a more serious problem, probably concerned with the power supply. That can be repaired but usually it's quicker (and cheaper) to have it replaced. If you attempt it yourself (it's not a difficult job if you're handy with a screwdriver) make sure you get the correct type, both in terms of mechanical fit, motherboard type, and power rating.

Assuming power is getting through, the first sign of trouble happens a second or two after switching on, normally most (but not all) machines emit a single beep from the internal speaker to confirm that the first part of the POST test was carried out successfully. If you hear more than one beep, or a repeating pattern of beeps that is a fault code, which requires investigation. We'll be looking at that in more detail in Chapter 16.

One very common, and serious sounding boot-up error message is 'CMOS Checksum Error' or 'Invalid Configuration', 'press F1 to continue'. After pressing the F1 key the machine will boot up normally, but you may well find that the clock in Windows is wrong, or losing time. This bizarrely worded message usually points to a dead or dying battery on the motherboard that is used to keep the PC's internal clock ticking, when the machine is switched off or disconnected from the mains. Replacing the battery is not usually a difficult job, though on some machines it can be tricky to get to and is best left to an engineer.

One of the scariest error messages is 'Cannot read from hard disk C:/' or something similar. In fact total hard disk failure is comparatively rare nowadays and the most likely cause is a loose cable from the motherboard to the disk drive. If you are familiar with the innards of your PC you may be able to fix the problem yourself. Disconnect the machine from the mains at the mains socket (see Chapters 4 and 5 for more advice about anti-static precautions) and remove the lid. Touch the metal case to dispel any static charges then check that the power and data cables going into the back of the disk drive are properly seated; do the same with the data cable connection on the motherboard.

A somewhat rarer condition, sometimes brought about by a long period of inactivity, is hard disk 'stiction' where the disk drive mechanism becomes stuck. If you cannot hear motor whine or chattering coming from the drive it is sometimes possible to get things moving again by lightly tapping the side of the hard drive case with the handle of a screwdriver. You should take any kind of problem with a hard disk drive as a warning of imminent failure, and replace it immediately.

Problems with the PC's random access memory (RAM) modules are not uncommon and they can be difficult to track down as they don't always show up during the POST check and can therefore look like a software fault. However, multiple bleeps from the PC during boot up are often a sign that there's something amiss, as are error messages that include the word 'Page Fault'. Fortunately, they are fairly simple to resolve if you are an experienced PC user and not averse to opening up your machine. If you suspect a memory fault and your PC has more than one memory module, try removing one at a time, or if you have access to a PC with a similar spec, that uses the same kind of memory module, try substituting one or more of the modules.

If your PC makes it to the first Windows splash screen and then hangs, crashes or displays an error message then the chances are the problem is software related.

EMERGENCY START UP

The all-important 'system' files stored in the 'boot sector' on the hard disk are surprisingly vulnerable and can easily become corrupted by you, a virus attack or belligerent software installed on your PC, but whatever the cause your PC and Windows cannot function properly without them. The emergency start-up disk contains a set of basic system files for your PC, so if your PC hangs during boot up and there's an error message relating to system files, switch off, pop your start-up disk into the drive and switch it back on. If you are using Windows XP you can try loading the setup or installation CD-ROM that came with your PC.

What happens next depends on what version of Windows you are using. The Windows 95 start-up disk is not especially helpful; a few moments after loading the PC displays a black screen showing a few lines of apparently meaningless gobbledegook and a flashing A: prompt. The machine is now in DOS mode, from where you may be able to get Windows going – if the files are undamaged – but at the very least you will be able to run a series of checks using diagnostic and repair tools on the start-up disk, and possibly recover files or documents.

Windows 98 users get a lot more assistance from their disks. It boots the PC and creates a temporary 'Ramdrive' in the PC's memory. This is a kind of virtual hard disk drive, used to hold all the tools and drivers on the floppy disk. The Ramdrive becomes disk D: all other drives on the PC are moved up a letter. (Don't worry, everything returns to normal once the PC boots up under its own steam.) The start-up disk gives a choice of opening a detailed help file, starting Windows in Safe mode (more about that later) and accessing help and resources on the Windows 98 installation disk. The CD-ROM drive should be accessible since the start-up disk loads the necessary drivers, but don't forget it will have been moved up a letter (i.e., if it was drive D: it now becomes drive E:).

The Windows 98 start-up disk also includes a number of diagnostic and repair utilities plus a 'Cab File' extraction tool that can copy compressed 'cabinet' files from the Windows installation CD-ROM to your hard drive. There is also a useful 'Readme' file, which is worth looking at, even if your PC is behaving normally; you never know when you're going to need it!

If the system files are successfully loaded you will see an A: prompt on the screen. Before you do anything else it's a good idea to run two simple tests on the hard disk drive and its filing system. The first is Scandisk, which looks for defects on the disk drive and the files it contains and attempts to repair simple faults. To start the program type 'scandisk' (without the quotation marks) after the A: prompt and press the Enter key. It may take a few minutes, and it's usually worth accepting any offer to carry out repairs. If you are not in a hurry you can accept the offer to conduct a 'Full Surface Scan' which will highlight any deep-seated faults on the hard disk drive, though it could take an hour or more. The other test is Checkdisk (type chkdsk at the A: prompt) and this carries out a quick health check on your hard disk's filing system. Again it will report errors and offer to fix them.

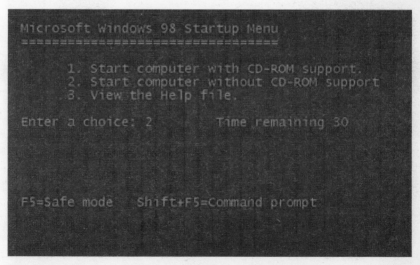

The menu choices on a Windows 98 Emergency Startup disk.

Once Scandisk and Checkdisk have passed your disk drive fit for duty you can try to start Windows. Type in 'win' (without the quotation marks of course) and press the Enter/Return key. If that doesn't work, change the drive letter by typing 'C:' then type 'cd Windows' (cd is a DOS command for 'change directory'). The screen should now show C:\Windows >, now type 'win' and press Enter and all being well it should load, if it fails to load, or crashes then it is time to move on to stage two, Windows Safe Mode.

Windows XP has a more sophisticated set of options, tools and utilities called the Recovery Console, which can be accessed by booting the PC from the XP setup or installation CD-ROM and pressing the R key. However, the Recovery Console is designed for advanced users, the simpler alternative for most boot-up problems is to start XP in Safe Mode.

SAFE MODE

In addition to reviving a dead PC, Windows 'Safe Mode' can also be used to solve a lot of the problems that generate error messages whilst Windows and other critical files are loading. Safe Mode bypasses the configuration files and start-up programs, which cause most problems and loads only the bare minimum of drivers for the monitor keyboard and mouse. These should be enough to get Windows up and running, albeit with limited functionality.

To enter Windows Safe Mode press the F8 key (on some models you may have to press the Ctrl key) after the first round of POST/BIOS checks,

The Windows Safe Mode start-up menu.

before the 'Starting Windows' message appears on the screen. A moment or two later the boot-up sequence stops and you will see a menu with a list of options (numbered in Windows 9x – there are seven in Windows 95 and four in Windows ME). Windows XP has a slightly different set of choices. We'll look briefly at the main ones and how they can be used to diagnose and solve problems.

- Normal (Win 9x) or Start Windows Normally (Win XP): use this if you entered Safe Mode by mistake; select it by pressing 1 on the keyboard, press Enter and the normal Windows boot-up sequence will resume.
- Logged (\BOOTLOG.TXT), (Win 9x) or Enable Boot Logging (Win XP). Selecting this will also make Windows resume normal loading but at the same time it creates a text file (called bootlog.txt) which is stored in the root directory of the C drive. This file records all of the actions during the loading sequence and notes whether or not each operation was successful; this detailed record, which you can save to a floppy disk, or read using a Windows Notepad or a word processor, may help you or an engineer to pinpoint an obscure fault.
- Safe Mode (Win 9x and XP) loads Windows but with a basic configuration. The words 'Safe Mode' appear on the desktop (which may be in black and white) and a warning message pops up. Click OK and loading continues. Resolution will usually be set to VGA standard (600 x 400) so the icons on the desktop and Start menu may look bigger than usual and some programs and peripherals might disappear from the desktop or stop working. Don't worry, when you have fixed the problem and Windows resumes normal operation everything will be restored though you may have to manually reset things like the hidden taskbar and small icons on Start menu features on the Setting menu. Safe Mode in Windows ME and XP starts a 'Trouble-shooter' that provides immediate access to a very useful utility called System Restore that can return the machine to a previous 'known good' configuration. If the PC fails to start in Safe Mode it could be the work of a virus, though it is possible that there is a problem with the crucially important Registry system files. Windows 98 and ME have a Registry checking utility, which can be run from the DOS prompt after booting the machine using the emergency start-up disk. At the A: prompt type 'scanreg'. Windows 98 and ME automatically make backup copies of the Registry every time Windows loads successfully. By default five copies are kept and these can be restored

from MS-DOS mode by booting your PC using the start-up disk. At the A: prompt type 'scanreg /restore' then choose a backup from which to restore your Registry.

- Last Known Good Configuration (Win XP), loads a verified backup copy of the Registry and configuration files, the best alternative for most XP start-up problems.

- Step by Step Confirmation (Win 9x) is potentially one of the most useful diagnostic options since it asks you to confirm each step of the loading sequence. Simply type 'Y' for yes at each step. If it freezes jot down the message and restart the machine in Safe Mode again. This time when you reach the suspect step type 'N'. If Windows then continues to load you will have a pretty good idea of where the problem lies. The message should point to a Windows driver or a recently installed application, which you can remove or re-install once Windows finishes loading, or from Safe Mode.

- Safe Mode With Networking (all versions) is for PCs that are connected to a network. Extra files that will allow the PC to access the network, so you can carry on working if necessary.

- Command Prompt Only (all versions except Win 98 ME and XP). This starts the PC in MS-DOS mode.

- Safe Mode Command Prompt Only (all versions except ME) also starts the PC in DOS mode but leaves out Windows start-up files, so Windows cannot be loaded. In Windows ME the option to start the PC in DOS mode is on the emergency start-up disk (press F5).

Whilst in Safe Mode you should also be able to use most of your office applications (word processor, spreadsheet, etc.) and gain access to any important files though graphics-intensive software like games probably won't work. However, the main purpose of Safe Mode is to track down faults that make Windows crash, or prevent it from loading properly.

If the problem began soon after installing a new item of hardware or software your first port of call should be the Windows Device Manager. Right-click on My Computer and select Properties > Device Manager (Hardware > Device Manager in Windows XP). Alternatively, go to Start > Settings > Control Panel > System. In both cases select the Device Manager tab and look for any yellow exclamation marks on the list that appears. These indicate that conflicts have occurred between a new hardware device or program, and it is interfering with your existing configuration. You should be able to resolve it by highlighting the item concerned, click the Properties button and a window will appear with a brief description of the problem and often a possible solution.

Safe Mode is useful for tracking down problems associated with programs that load automatically at the same time as Windows. If you suspect one of them is misbehaving you can remove them one at a time from the Start Up program group (Start > Programs > Start Up) then restart Windows as normal.

Windows 98, SE, ME and XP have some additional utilities that can help troubleshoot problems if Windows will only load in Safe Mode. Go to Run on the Start menu and type 'msconfig'. This displays all the main start-up files on a series of tabbed pages, with the option to disable individual entries,

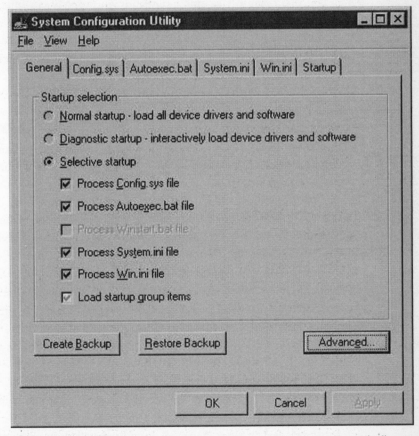

The 'msconfig' utility lets you selectively disable programs that automatically load with Windows.

there's also a Selective Start-up mode on the General tab that allows you to bypass specified files completely. This is an extremely useful facility and it can be used to solve a great many start-up (and shutdown) problems. However, it can be very time consuming but you should be able to isolate the offending file or file entry by a simple process of trial and error. In other words disable one item at a time and re-start the PC. It is vitally important that you change only one item at a time and remember to reinstate each one after every attempt.

SHUTDOWN PROBLEMS

The last thing you need first thing in the morning is a PC with attitude, telling you that because you didn't shut it down properly last time, you're going to have to wait while it checks your disk drive for errors. Needless to say you would dearly like to shut down your PC properly, but it won't let you, so you have to go through this tiresome ritual, and be cheekily chastised by your PC for something that almost certainly was not your fault.

Faced with a machine that 'hangs' during shutdown most users head straight for the on-off switch but this is really not a good idea. Most of the time, if the machine freezes in the middle of shutdown, you'll get away with switching it off but if the power is cut whilst the PC is in the middle of an operation very bad things might happen. Never switch off if the hard disk activity light is flashing or you can hear the drive chattering; if you do then critical Windows system files might be corrupted and you could be even worse off, with a completely dead machine. Suffice it to say, given the option it is far better to try a few things first, to see if you can shut down your PC in an orderly manner.

In Windows a lot of complicated-sounding things need to happen before the 'It is safe...' or 'Windows is Shutting Down' messages appear or the machine switches itself off; these include unloading and re-configuring driver files, clearing out or 'flushing' an area of the hard disk drive, called a 'cache' of temporary files, completing all disk writing operations and finally closing down programs. Whilst Windows will normally exit running applications automatically some may not respond, so before clicking Shutdown it's always a good idea to check you haven't missed something or that there's nothing happening behind the scenes by making sure the taskbar is clear of icons and pressing Alt + Tab; if nothing appears on the screen you can proceed. If the PC 'hangs' at the 'Please Wait...' screen, don't be impatient and switch off, give it a minute or two, especially if the hard disk activity light is still flickering, some programs can take a while to finish what they are doing.

Even if you do everything by the book the most well-behaved PCs can still hang from time to time. Usually the worst thing that happens after an aborted shutdown is a brief delay the next time you switch on whilst the Scandisk utility runs through a series of checks on the disk drive, after which Windows loads and shuts down normally again.

However, a small percentage of PCs suffer from persistent shutdown problems. It's not something you should have to put up with and most of the time the solution is fairly simple, usually involving uninstalling a program or changing a setting, but tracking down the cause can be time consuming. A lot of shutdown problems can be traced back to the most recent program or piece of hardware that you installed, in which case try uninstalling and re-installing it. If that doesn't work, and your PC is otherwise behaving itself, take the matter up with whoever is responsible for the errant product or visit the company's website and look for the product support or FAQ (frequently asked questions) sections for any mention of conflicts, bugs, or updates that may help.

If shutdown has always been erratic or it started playing up spontaneously you're going to have to do a bit of detective work. There are any number of possible causes so it's a process of elimination. If you have closed all running applications and your PC hangs try pressing Ctrl + Alt + Delete to bring up the Close Program menu (click the Task Manager tab in Windows XP and check Applications and Processes) to make sure no frozen programs have been left behind. Work your way down the list, highlighting each item in turn and clicking End Task, then try for a shutdown. You can do this for any entry except Explorer and System Tray, which cannot be closed.

In Windows 9x it's worth checking for a corrupted sound file so go to Start > Settings > Control Panel > Sounds. Find Exit Windows on the list and change the setting in the Sound Name field to None, then try shutting down again. Windows 9x power management system is another potential trouble spot; open Power Management in Control Panel and switch the Power Scheme to Always On and the System and Monitor standby times to Never then see what happens when you shut down.

A useful trick with Windows 9x is to disable all of the programs that load during start-up. To do that, press and hold the Shift key at switch on until after Windows has finished loading. Windows 95 machines will boot up in

Safe Mode Windows 98 and ME load more or less normally but you'll notice that there are no programs shown on the taskbar or System Tray. Now shut the PC down, if it obliges then you know that one of the programs in the start-up group is to blame.

On a Windows 95 PC open Start Up (Start > Programs > Start Up) and remove the programs one by one by right clicking on the icons and selecting Delete, then re-boot the PC each time, until normal operation is restored.

A lot of Windows 9x and XP shutdown problems can be resolved with the 'Msconfig' tool. As before, go to Run on the Start menu and type msconfig, click OK and select the General tab. Check the item 'Selective Start-up' uncheck Process System.ini file, click OK, shut down, boot up and try shutting down again. Do the same with the Win.ini file. If that doesn't help select the Start-up tab in msconfig and disable the programs that Windows loads automatically one by one, trying for a clean shutdown each time. The last thing to try is select the General tab, click the Advanced button and check the item Disable Fast Shutdown. If none of the above works remember to return all settings back to the original or default values.

The complex Windows 9x filing system has been known to cause its fair share of problems. There's an easy way to find out if this is the cause: go to Control Panel, double click the System icon select Performance, the File System button and the Troubleshooting tab. Put a check in all of the boxes, click OK, close Control Panel and shut down Windows. If it is successful go back and uncheck the items one at a time.

Advanced Power Management is another area of Windows 9x to check. In Control Panel click on the System icon, then the Device Manager tab and click the + sign next to System Devices, select Advanced Power Management and if it has been enabled, check the 'Disable in this profile' option, click OK, exit Control Panel and attempt a restart and shutdown. If that doesn't work go back to Control Panel, click on the Power Management and on the Power Schemes tab, under Power Schemes, select Always On and see if that makes a difference.

Corrupt Windows device drivers can trigger all sorts of odd behaviour; if all else has failed so far double click on the System icon in Control Panel and select the Device Manager tab (Hardware tab then Device Manager in Windows XP). Anything listed with an exclamation mark in a yellow circle next to it is worth investigating. Double click on the suspect item (or right click and choose Properties) and check the box marked 'Disable in this hardware profile' and try shutting the PC down. Don't forget to restore the original setting afterwards and only try it on one item at a time. If a driver turns out to be the source of the problem use System Properties to remove it, but before you do make sure you have the original driver disk to hand.

That covers the most common shutdown problems that users can safely tackle by themselves, but there's plenty more to try, if you know your way around Windows. There's a useful set of 'Trouble-shooters' and helpful articles on the Microsoft web site that take you through the investigative process, step-by-step. The addresses for each version of Windows are:

Windows 95
http://support.microsoft.com/support/kb/articles/Q145/9/26.asp

Windows 98
http://support.microsoft.com/support/kb/articles/Q202/6/33.ASP

Windows 98 SE
http://support.microsoft.com/support/kb/articles/Q238/0/96.ASP

Windows ME
http://support.microsoft.com/support/kb/articles/Q273/7/46.ASP

Windows XP
http://support.microsoft.com/default.aspx?scid=kb;EN-US;q307274

Shutdown problems concerning other Microsoft applications can be found at: http://support.microsoft.com/support/tshoot/default.asp

Q&A Real world problems

Check list

Q My C:\ drive is overrun by .chk files, amounting to over 200 megabytes which, when opened in Notepad, consist of gibberish with occasional snippets from Help files for a program I uninstalled years ago, and the occasional mention of the words 'Java' and 'Internet'. On a 1.6 gig hard drive, this is space I'd rather not waste. Is it safe to delete these files, or will nasty errors occur?

A Lots of *.chk files is a sure sign your PC is crashing or you haven't been shutting it down properly. They are created by Scandisk, which automatically checks the hard disk for errors after Windows or running programs unexpectedly stop running. Most programs – including Windows – create temporary files whilst they are running and they're normally deleted when the program is shut down. Following an improper shutdown Scandisk clears up the clutter left behind on the hard disk drive and converts it to a *.chk file, in case the data is important and you want to retrieve it. If the PC and your applications appear to be running normally then you can safely delete those *.chk files but the way to avoid creating more of them is to exit Windows properly, or sort out any problems that are causing your machine to crash.

Scandisk alert

Q   My problem is with Scandisk, both the Standard and Thorough tests. I find that it gets to about 50%, goes back to the beginning and starts again. This is repeated several times. If I let it continue, the following notice appears on the screen: 'Scan Disk has restarted ten times because Windows, or another program has been writing to the drive.' To my knowledge from looking at the Desktop, no other programs are operating.

A   There must be one or more programs still running in the background, the most likely ones are a screensaver or a virus scanner. Disable both and if that doesn't work press Ctrl + Alt + Delete once, to open the Close Program dialogue box, and use End Task to close everything except Explorer and Systray, then try again. If all else fails you can try the DOS Scandisk utility on your Emergency Start Up disk. Boot up from the disk and type 'Scandisk C:' at the A: prompt and press Enter.

Bad attitude

Q   I have seen the term 'bad sectors' mentioned on several occasions but it is never fully explained. Can you explain what they are, the cause, and if they show up with Scandisk, whether there is any means of clearing the fault. A friend ran Scandisk on a good computer, which he rarely uses, only to find that it indicated a large number of bad sectors. He ran Scandisk several more times and each run produced substantial increases in the number of bad sectors until about a third of his disk was shown as bad. It was suggested that re-formatting might help. In the end I suggested he continued running his computer, because the large amount of remaining good sectors was adequate for his requirements. In two years, the disk is still in good order and the level of bad sectors has remained constant.

A   A bad sector is an area of the disk that programs like Scandisk determine is not capable of reliably storing data. This can be due to a number of reasons, from defects in the magnetic material coating the disk to mechanical problems with the read/write heads and mechanism. In fact many brand-new disk drives have bad sectors but these are detected during manufacture and 'mapped out'. In other words tests show they are not going to get any worse and the rest of the drive functions perfectly well, so the 'firmware' program that controls the drive is programmed not to use those parts of the disk. However, if bad sectors develop subsequently that is a sign of potential trouble. Occasionally the problem stabilises, as in the case of your friend's drive, and sometimes reformatting makes bad sectors disappear, but this may only be temporary. It is sensible to take the appearance of bad sectors as a warning of possible catastrophic failure, backup files and replace the drive as soon as possible. These days hard disk drives are not expensive, but the data they contain can be irreplaceable!

Diligent defrag

Q   I have seen advice that hard Windows 98 drives should be defragged when fragmentation levels reach 8%. This might mean running Defrag preceded by Scandisk every month or so. A local computer technician tells me that fragmentation rapidly reaches the 10% mark then levels off between 10 and 15% and stays at these levels for months. This is quite acceptable, and defrag need not be run more than once a year as the defrag process puts a large strain on the disk drive mechanism. So who is correct? Is defrag a cunning way of drive manufacturers to get us to wear out hard drives quickly, or is the computer technician not the expert he claims to be? How harmful is Scandisk? How often should a full surface scan be carried out? Definitive advice to the confused please!

A   Whilst Defrag and to a lesser extent, Scandisk, makes the hard disk drive work a little harder than usual, it's well within normal operating parameters and there is no evidence that it has an impact on a drive's life expectancy. In fact hard disk drives are incredibly reliable and the chances are you will replace your PC long before the drive wears out. The amount of file fragmentation depends entirely on how much use the PC gets and the type of software you are using. On some heavyweight applications there can be a noticeable reduction in speed when fragmentation reaches just 5%. Running Scandisk and defragging once a month is about right for most home users. You only need to carry out a full surface scan if a routine Scandisk session reports errors, which may indicate that the drive has problems.

CHAPTER 16 **Error messages**

*The trouble with Windows error messages is that there
are so many of them and they never say anything even
vaguely reassuring, like 'don't worry, just do this or that
and it'll be alright'. Error messages are either totally
incomprehensible or littered with scary words like fatal,
invalid, illegal, corrupt, failure and missing...*

In spite of what you may think, relatively few PC problems are random or
spontaneous and taking a few simple precautions can prevent most of them.
Error messages tend to fall into one of four basic categories: missing or
damaged files, programs or Windows freezing, Windows or other programs
doing something they shouldn't and hardware faults. The majority of error
messages can usually be traced back to a deleted file or new software and
hardware installations. The fault may not show up at the time but the next
time you start up Windows, it looks for a file or application that isn't there
any longer.

Missing Shortcut message boxes (the ones with a waving torch) appear
when Windows is loading and they are fairly easy to deal with. They indicate
that a program has been improperly deleted and is still listed somewhere,
usually in the Start-Up folder or one of the Windows system files. Go to the
Start button then Programs (All Programs in XP) and locate the Start-Up
folder, right-click the folder icon, select Open then highlight and delete the
offending item. If that doesn't work try re-installing the missing program
then delete it again, this time using the program's own uninstaller, Windows
Add/Remove program utility in Control Panel or a proprietary uninstaller
program (more about those shortly).

Incorrect or missing Dynamic Link Library files (DLLs) is another
frequent source of trouble. DLL error messages often appear after installing
or removing programs and the solution is to re-install the offending
software, but this time look for dialogue boxes saying that the files being
loaded are newer or older than the ones currently in use. Check to see if any

of those mentioned are the same as that which appeared in the original error message and choose the option to load it or replace it, as appropriate. You can use a similar technique to troubleshoot error messages concerning missing or corrupt device drivers.

Windows XP has its own distinct array of error messages that pop up during installation. Warnings about 'Unsigned Drivers' usually indicate that the program you are loading may not be compatible with XP. Often the required driver is available or was released too late to be included on the installation CD-ROM. Before installing any program or peripheral on an XP machine make sure that it is compatible, if XP isn't mentioned on the packaging visit the manufacturer's website where you will usually find specific advice relating to XP. XP will usually let you continue with an installation but it will attempt to protect itself by creating a Restore Point, so that the PC can be returned to its earlier, known good configuration, should any problems arise.

General Protection Fault (GPF) error messages in Windows 9x can occur when a program has a problem with memory resources. The only thing you can do is close it down by pressing Ctrl + Alt + Delete and select End Task on the Close Program dialogue box. If you can, save any open files and re-start the computer. If Windows stopped as well you'll have to re-boot by pressing Ctrl + Alt + Delete a second time or if that doesn't work, press the Reset button.

The blue screen 'Fatal Exception' error message (aka the 'blue screen of death') is rarely seen in Windows XP but it's still a common sight in earlier

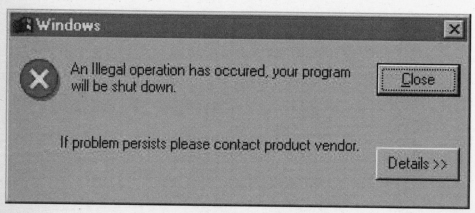

A typically anonymous error message; time for some detective work.

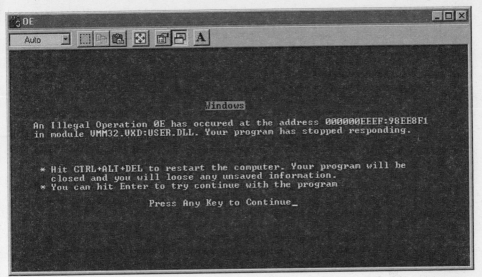

BSOD or the Blue Screen of Death, a sure sign that you've lost your work and you need to reboot.

versions of Windows and a sure sign that a program has attempted to carry out an illegal operation. It may help to know what led up to the crash. It could be a combination of keystrokes, opening a particular file, or maybe it only happens when another program is running. Try re-installing the program and if it keeps happening contact the software company to see if there's a known bug or fix available.

Following a Fatal Exception error, GPF Windows 98, ME and later versions of Windows 95 will usually run the Scandisk utility to check for errors on the hard disk. Occasionally, if the fault is deep seated, Windows will restart in the Safe Mode (see Chapter 15) loading only the bare minimum of drivers and system files; consequently the screen will usually be in a much lower resolution. Don't worry if this happens, just wait for it to finish loading then shut down; hopefully Windows should restart as normal, though you may have to reset your desktop display options (Start > Settings Taskbar & Start Menu).

Hardware faults are relatively rare and usually the culprit is fairly obvious; it's the device or component you are installing. Very occasionally faults can have a cascade effect and damage the motherboard or processor but in any event there's little you can do, other than replace the part concerned or have the PC looked at by an expert.

The root cause of many error messages is a cluttered hard disk. Every time you install a program dozens of files will be created, some of them ending up inside critical areas of your PC's operating system. Even if you delete the program lots of those files can be left behind. Most lie dormant but it takes only one minor conflict to bring the whole system down. You should install at least one PC housekeeping program. As soon as possible after you've bought a new PC or re-installed Windows, load a housekeeping utility like Clean Sweep and Uninstaller. These programs monitor every new program you put onto your PC, so that when the time comes they can be cleanly removed. They will also look for orphans, clutter, duplicate files and programs you no longer use, offer to remove them or make compressed backups, until you are ready to delete them permanently. Never install or remove more than one program at a time and afterwards always reboot the PC and watch for unexpected displays or error messages.

Without any doubt whatsoever the number one cause of PC problems is the user not reading the instructions when installing a piece of hardware or software. We're all as guilty as anyone but there is a solution. Take a Post-It note, write on it in very large letters 'RTFM' and stick it to the front of your PC. RTFM is what service engineers mutter under their breath when confronted with faults that wouldn't have happened if the user had bothered to READ THE FLIPPING MANUAL (or words to that effect).

As you add and delete software the structure of the filing system on your PC's hard disk drive becomes disorganised or 'fragmented'. Eventually it can lead to files being lost or corrupted but long before that happens, the time it takes for your PC to access information will increase as the read-write heads in the drive search for bits of files spread about your disk drive. This also increases the rate of wear and tear on mechanical components. Defragging your PC on a weekly or monthly basis, depending whether you are a light or moderate user, will keep your computer's filing system in good order.

TOP TIPS TO AVOID SEEING ERROR MESSAGES

- Never remove programs by deleting folders in Windows Explorer.
- Write down error messages, it could help you to track down errant files or assist with calls to technical support helplines.
- When you delete a program or file wait a few days before emptying the Recycle Bin.
- Always keep original program and hardware driver disks in a safe place.

- Avoid installing unnecessary programs, especially game demos and PC magazine freebies.
- Only install one new item of hardware or software at a time.
- Make frequent backups of files you are working on – every few minutes if they're really important!

Q&A Real world problems

Spare stack pages

Q   My Windows 98 computer displayed the following message just before the desktop screen appeared: 'There are no spare stack pages. It may be necessary to increase the setting of 'MinSPs' in system.ini to prevent possible stack faults. There are currently 3 SPs allocated'. What on earth are stack pages and what if anything should I do about this message? It has not appeared on subsequent occasions that I have switched on.

A   Stack pages are 4-kilobyte chunks of memory that Windows automatically sets aside for emergencies, to prevent the system from crashing if it unexpectedly runs out of memory space when loading device drivers. By default Windows allocates two spare stack pages, most of the time two is enough but occasionally – often for no apparent reason – it proves insufficient. The solution is to increase the number of spare stack pages. Open system.ini with Notepad (Start > Programs > Accessories) click on Open on the File menu (change Files of type to All Files) and look for system.ini in the Windows folder. Scroll down the list to find the section heading [386Enh], it should be fairly close to the top, at the end of that section add the following line: 'MinSPs=4' (without the inverted commas and there are no spaces), save the file and restart your PC. If it happens again try increasing the number of spare stack pages further but it must be in multiples of four.

Invalid VxD

Q   I get an error message from time to time, it says 'Invalid VxD dynamic link call from NWREDIR(04) + 000000D0 to device "0487", service 6'. I would love to have this explained in proper English.

A   Proper English is a bit of a tall order, but here goes. Invalid Dynamic Link Call error messages are usually caused by damaged, missing or incompatible drivers – data files that tell programs and peripherals how to interact with Windows. It's always worth uninstalling and re-installing the last program or device, before the problem started. The actual message is divided into three parts that can be expressed as follows: Invalid VxD dynamic link call from (Part 1) to device (Part 2), service (Part 3). Part 1 is the driver's name or identity, part 2 is the name of the device or program it is associated with, in your case 0487 refers to 'NWLINK' which is the IPX/SPX-compatible Network Protocol. Part 3 is a fault code that tells the programmer which part of the program was requested, but could not be found.

The error code suggests that the problem lies with Windows Dial Up Networking, so try removing and re-installing the Communications components on the Windows tab in Add/Remove programs in Control Panel. There are several books on the subject of error messages but they're mostly written by experts, for experts. It's always worth typing an error message into an Internet search engine's Find field, and see what that throws up.

Cannot find specified file

Q   Every time I start Windows 98 I get the following warning: 'Unable to load Dynamic Link Library msnp32.dll. System cannot find the file specified.' How can I get rid of this annoying alarm that I have to acknowledge to enable boot up to be completed?

A   This error message often follows an abortive attempt to install Internet access software, a new browser or changes to the settings in Dial Up Networking (DUN). During the installation file names are added to the Windows Registry but for one reason or another they are not copied to the hard disk. When Windows loads it looks for the files but cannot find them. Removing and then reinstalling Dial Up Networking can often cure it but before you do, make a note of all the settings. To do that double click on the DUN icon on My Computer, right click on your ISP connection icon, select Properties and note down the phone numbers and settings on each of the tabbed windows. To remove DUN go to Add/Remove Programs in Control Panel and the Windows setup tab. Double Click Communications and uncheck the box next to Dial Up Networking, select Close then OK and restart the PC. Go back to Add/Remove Programs in Control Panel, Windows setup and Communications and this time put a check in the DUN box, close and restart. Hopefully the error message will be no more. Finish off by making sure that your original Dial Up Networking settings have been correctly restored.

Spool 32

Q   Now and again a warning banner is displayed on start-up, which states that Spool 32 has performed an illegal operation and will be closed down. 'OK' removes this and nothing else seems to be wrong, all then works smoothly. What is Spool 32? Can it be removed altogether? If so, how?

A   Spool 32 is a program within Windows 9x that speeds up multiple printing jobs by temporarily storing each one on the hard disk drive, before being sent to the printer. The Spool 32 error message is very common and there are dozens of possible causes but most of them come down to other programs interfering with the print process, a corrupt printer driver or your PC is very low on resources (less than 100Mb free space, etc.). Try re-installing your printer software and have a look at your printer manufacturer's website to see if there's an updated driver for your model or anything about error messages in the support or FAQ sections. Before printing exit all other programs that use the printer, in particular any fax software you may have. If all else fails and your printer is not very heavily used you can safely disable print spooling, without any significant reduction in performance. Go to Start > Settings > Printers, right click on your printer and select Properties, select the Details tab, click the Spool Settings button and check the item 'Print Directly to the Printer'.

CHAPTER 17

Finding solutions

In an ideal world when your PC packs up, or starts behaving strangely, one phone call to the retailer or manufacturer's customer help line will resolve the problem, either with useful practical advice, or the promise of a visit from a service engineer that same day...

A great many common problems can be easily fixed over the phone but what happens when the offer of free helpline assistance or guarantee has expired? Unless you have an extended warranty, service contract or a knowledgeable friend or relative on call, you're effectively on your own, or are you?

If fact there is more free (or nearly free) help on tap for dealing with computer problems than any other commercial product, you've just got to know where to look for it and the right questions to ask. Unfortunately, much of this help is available only if you have a working PC, or access to one with an Internet connection, which is a fat lot of good if your one and only PC has turned up its toes, you don't have the Internet or the problem is you can't go online.

If you're not in an absolutely desperate hurry you can always write, fax or email a query to a newspaper or magazine problem page, though you should be aware that whilst most publications do their best they simply haven't got the space or facilities to answer every plea for help. PC agony aunts and uncles also tend to give precedence to the sort of problems that are likely to affect a lot of users in the hope that the solution will benefit the greatest number of readers. Obscure faults associated with a very particular combination of hardware and software are extremely difficult to diagnose at a distance and so stand a lesser chance of making it into print.

Keep all of the manuals and instruction books that came with your PC, peripherals and software in one place, so you can get at them easily. There are countless books on the subject and the computing section in your local library and bookshops that tolerate browsers are also worth getting to know.

It's a good idea to keep clippings of newspaper and magazine help pages as quite often you'll encounter a problem or fault that you vaguely remember reading about. Why not start your own reference library? However, without doubt the fastest and most comprehensive source of help is the Internet.

Even if your PC is out for the count you can probably still go on-line using a friend or relative's computer; publicly accessible PCs can also be found in schools and universities, libraries, motorway stations and Internet cafes or you could get an old Internet capable PC or laptop out of retirement. Either way the net is your best and fastest hope of solving a problem.

There are many ways to use the Internet to get assistance, depending on the nature of the fault. Internet help falls into two broad categories: passive help, where the information you require is on a database or forum somewhere and you have to look it up, and there's active help, where your problem is dealt with by a real person, or people and it's encouraging to know that there are lots of them out there in Internet land who give their time and expertise freely and unstintingly to help their fellow PC users.

Windows XP has a new feature called Remote Assistance that allows an engineer to connect to an ailing PC via the Internet or network and hopefully diagnose or even fix a problem. However, for obvious reasons this only works if the PC in question is still working and able to connect to the net. Since a high proportion of faults are concerned with inoperative PCs or faulty Internet connections it is often of limited value.

If the problem occurred immediately after installing a new piece of hardware or software your first port of call should be the manufacturer's website, to check whether there are any known problems or compatibility issues, drivers or patches to download and it's worth trawling through the site's FAQ sections. Many manufacturers' websites offer free on-line technical assistance and will reply by email though the speed and reliability of these services varies enormously.

A surprisingly effective method for dealing with mysterious or obscure error messages that don't appear to relate to a specific item of software or hardware is to simply type the bones of the message into the Find field of one of the main Internet search engines. This often yields useful results; it's also very reassuring to know that you're not alone.

Any problem with Windows and you should head straight for the Microsoft Windows Trouble-shooters, Knowledge Base and Error Message Resource Centre, the largest product database in existence. Unfortunately, whilst the answer to your Windows or Microsoft product related problem is

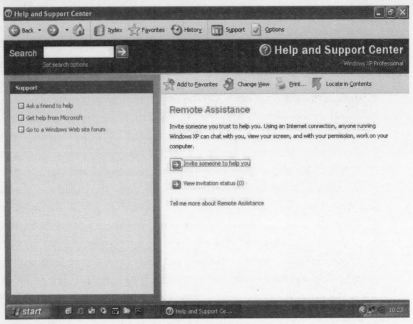

Windows XP has a facility for 'Remote Assistance' assuming of course that the PC and your Internet connection are both working.

almost certainly buried in there somewhere, finding it is another matter.

There are two points of entry, try the 'Windows Trouble-shooters' first at: http://support.microsoft.com/support/tshoot/default.asp. For reasonably straightforward configuration and common error problems, there is a helpful error message index for Windows 98 and ME and this can be found at:

http://support.microsoft.com/support/windows/topics/errormsg/emresctr.asp

Otherwise go direct to the Microsoft Knowledgebase at http://support. microsoft.com/ and click the Search Technical Database link where you will find a useful introduction to searching the Knowledgebase for help.

When it comes to seeking help from a real person then you have a number of options. Posting your query on one of the many Newsgroups, On-Line Conferences and Bulletin Boards can be a bit hit and miss. You could get lucky and be inundated with replies within minutes, or hear nothing for weeks, if ever. Generally speaking it's not something you can easily get into from cold and is perhaps better suited to experienced users who know the best places to ask for help.

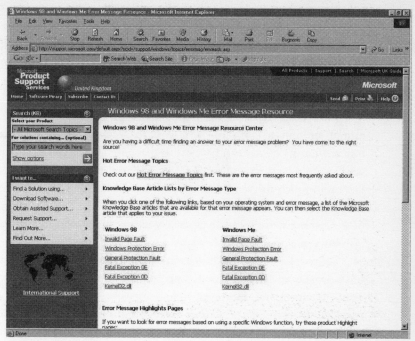

The Microsoft website can help you to track down the meaning of those obscure error messages.

Alternatively, try your luck with one of the many free on-line help websites staffed by experts, again the quality of help can be a bit variable and you may want to seek a second opinion before you do anything too drastic to your machine. Here's a small selection of sites to try to get you started:

http://www.allexperts.com/

http://www.pchelplocator.com/

http://www.freehelp.co.uk/support/swin98.htm

ELEMENTARY HELP

There's a lot you can do to help yourself and your PC contains hidden features that can make fault finding a lot easier. Sherlock Holmes's worthy companion Dr Watson might seem like an odd choice of name for a little-known Windows trouble-shooting utility but like its namesake, its special talent is gathering evidence of foul deeds. In PC parlance they're known as general protection faults or GPFs, dastardly crimes committed by malevolent computer programs carrying out illegal operations that usually result in the dreaded 'blue screen of death'. Dr Watson is known in the trade as an application error debugger and it is designed to investigate problems, stepping in at the moment a crash occurs and making a detailed record of what your PC was up to at the time it happened.

Unlike other types of PC maintenance programs or tools Dr Watson cannot prevent a crash or help you to recover lost data, instead the information it collects can be used to diagnose, and occasionally indicate a solution to a recurrent software fault, and whilst the data it generates may not mean much to you, it can be sent to manufacturers' technical support staff and the people who wrote the programs to help them fix the problem or suggest a remedy. It can be especially useful on reproducible faults, where Windows or a program crashes after a particular sequence of events.

Microsoft has included Dr Watson in Windows since Version 3 but you're unlikely to have come across it, especially if you're using Windows 95, as it wasn't in all releases. However, it does appear in most subsequent versions of Windows including XP. Part of the reason for its intermittent inclusion in Windows is that it has never been fully developed and can, in some circumstances, actually cause GPFs of its own; however, if you have a troublesome machine, and all else has failed it is definitely worth trying.

The program is very well hidden in Windows 98 and ME. It can be found by going to Start > Programs > Accessories > System Tools > System Information, and you'll see it listed on the Tools menu. It's not enabled by default, so the first task is to get it up and running on your machine. The simplest method is to type 'drwatson.exe' (minus the quotation marks of course) in Run on the Start menu. Immediately you'll see a new icon pop up in the System Tray, next to the clock display on the Task Bar. However, it makes sense to have Dr Watson running in the background, constantly monitoring your PC. To do that you'll have to create a shortcut and include it in your Start Up folder so that it launches every time you boot up your machine.

It's quite straightforward. Go to the Start button, select Programs, double-click on the Start-Up icon and an Explorer window will open. Next, go to the File menu, select New then Shortcut and the Create Shortcut dialogue box opens. In the Command Line field type 'drwatson.exe', then Next, accept the default name and click on the Finish button. Alternatively, go to Start > Settings > Taskbar & Start Menu, select the Start Menu

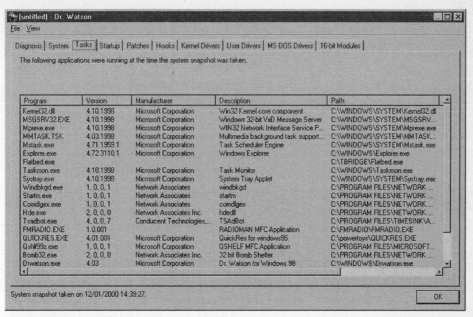

Dr Watson keeps a friendly eye on your system, logging error messages and hopefully providing a clue as to what went wrong.

Programs tab. Click the Add button then Browse and find DrWatson.exe in the Windows folder, highlight and click Open, then Next. Now select the Start Up folder from the directory tree, click Next and Finish. In the unlikely event you experience any problems after Dr Watson has been installed simply highlight the icon in the Start Up folder and remove it by pressing the delete key.

Dr Watson is also included in Windows XP but again it's buried away. To activate it go to Run on the Start menu and type 'drwtsn32 -I', then click OK and it will be installed and run automatically. To configure Dr Watson return to Run on the Start menu and type 'drwtsn32'.

From now on each time your machine suffers a GPF Dr Watson intercepts the crash and takes a 'snapshot' of your system. It identifies the program responsible and the nature of the fault and writes detailed technical information into a 'log' file (extension *.wlg) which is stored on your PC's hard disk (in the Dr Watson sub-folder in Windows). In Windows XP this log file can usually be found in C:\Documents and Settings\All Users\Application Data\Microsoft\Dr Watson as drwtsn.log. As an added bonus it gives you the opportunity to jot down a few notes of your own. This file can then be emailed to the technical support people, or printed out and sent by fax or letter.

In Windows 9x when Dr Watson is running you can get an instant appraisal of your system by double-clicking on the icon in the System Tray, it takes a snapshot and a dialogue box appears on the screen in Standard view showing the Diagnosis window along with the jotter pad for your notes. This probably won't tell you much but if you then go to the View menu and select Advanced you'll see a row of tabs that provide much more detailed insights into your system, its configuration and the software it is running. If you prefer you can have Dr Watson always open in the Advanced view by selecting Options on the View menu and checking the box 'Open new windows in Advanced view'.

You can save this data by going to the File menu, select Save and use the Browse button to locate the Dr Watson folder in Windows, give the file a name (today's date for example) and click the Save button. It's worth doing this straightaway, when your machine is operating normally as it will give you or anyone who's interested a benchmark to work from. Dr Watson is not going to stop Windows from crashing (nothing will, if it's a mind to) but the information it provides is a lot more useful than the normally meaningless error messages that appear and it just might help a software sleuth with their deductions.

Q&A Real world problems

Reporting restrictions

Q   Almost every time I boot up my new computer with Windows XP I get this error message: 'The system has recovered from a serious error. Please tell Microsoft about this problem.' I am then invited to 'send' the error message. I have done this many times and have received a reply stating that Microsoft is considering the problem. Do you think there really is something wrong with the computer or is it just an annoying feature of XP?

A   There's clearly a persistent problem that Windows XP is unable to resolve. The 'error message' you're seeing is part of Microsoft's strategy to reduce the time it takes to report bugs and glitches, which hopefully will result in drivers, patches and solutions to problems being made available much faster. However, that doesn't help you right now so I suggest you start by taking note of any error messages that might point to the cause of the crash; any recently installed software or hardware must be high on the list of suspects. You should also have a look for driver conflicts in Device Manager, which you can find by right clicking on My Computer and selecting Properties. If you click on any flagged entries Windows should offer to start one of its problem-solving 'Troubleshooters'.

Warranty worries

Q   Three years ago I bought a new PC and have religiously paid out for extended warranty cover. So far it has cost me over £500 and the PC hasn't gone wrong once! Have I been lucky, are extended warranties worth having?

A   You're paying for peace of mind, though be mindful of the fact that the quality of help and assistance you'll receive, if something goes wrong, varies enormously, so it pays to know precisely what sort of cover you're buying beforehand. However, it has to be said that the £500 you've spent so far is probably a great deal more than the PC is now worth and you could almost certainly now buy a new PC with a vastly superior specification for that sort of money. You have been lucky but PCs are getting more reliable and there is a good case for paying for service as and when it's needed, once the standard one-year warranty has run its course.

Part V

ADVANCED USERS

CHAPTER 18

The BIOS and the Registry

*Between them the BIOS and the Windows Registry are
almost entirely responsible for how a PC behaves, or
misbehaves, so they are well worth getting to know...*

The Basic Input Output System or 'BIOS' may not sound particularly
interesting but it is arguably the single most important piece of software on
your PC. The job of the BIOS is to initialise and configure a collection of
inert electronic and electromechanical components and turn them into a
working computer, ready to load and use the operating system, which for
most of us is Windows.

The BIOS program resides in a read-only memory or ROM microchip
on the PC's motherboard. It is stored in a chip because when it is powered
up your PC's processor or CPU has no idea what devices are attached to the
system, let alone how to use them, so it would be pointless storing such a
program on the hard disk drive. This also means the computer can still boot
up, even if the disk drive is faulty, or absent.

On early PCs the BIOS program was a fixed entity and the only way to
alter it was to replace the ROM chip or the entire motherboard. Nowadays
most BIOS programs are held in an erasable programmable read only
memory or EPROM chip, which means it is possible to update or change the
information to accommodate new developments in hardware and software.
However, this is a mixed blessing since virus programs have been created
that can infiltrate or corrupt the BIOS, turning a PC into a useless pile of
junk. More importantly, even minor changes to the BIOS program can have
major consequences to your PC's good nature so we'll start off with a
general warning to look but don't touch, and never fiddle with the BIOS on
your PC unless you know exactly what you are doing.

Settings and adjustments for the BIOS are held in a separate memory chip
called a CMOS (complimentary metal oxide semiconductor) which unlike
the ROM or EPROM chips used to store the BIOS program is 'volatile'. In
other words it has to be permanently powered. This is done with a backup

battery, which also maintains the PC's internal clock. Backup batteries generally last around five years; the first sign that it is failing is usually erratic timekeeping, but if after switching on you see an error message 'CMOS checksum invalid' or 'Invalid configuration, run Setup', then that is a sure sign that the battery needs replacing.

One of the BIOS program's most important jobs is to carry out a series of diagnostic checks on the main motherboard components, including the RAM memory chips and input/output devices; this is called the Power On Self Test or POST and it happens a few seconds after you've switched on. Normally the POST goes smoothly; on many PCs you'll hear a single short bleep from the internal speaker confirming that all's well, and Windows will begin loading. However, if you hear more than one bleep, a continuous tone or a repeated sequence of bleeps, that is a sure sign of trouble.

The number and pattern of bleeps or error codes indicates the nature of the fault but this varies significantly according to the make and type of BIOS. You can find out more by first noting the name and version of your PC's BIOS – it appears on the monitor screen for a few moments after switching on – and then consulting the appropriate manufacturer's website, or by visiting:

http://sysopt.earthweb.com/biosbmc.html or
http://www.pchell.com/hardware/beepcodes.shtml

These sites list the most common types of error code by manufacturer. Most faults are well beyond the scope of the average PC user but occasionally an error code points to an unseated memory module or adaptor card or a loose connecting cable, which the more intrepid amongst you can attempt to remedy.

POST error messages often appear following a major upgrade, replacing a hard drive, adding extra memory or changing the CPU. Since there are so many possibilities we can only generalise but more often than not the solution is to update the PC's BIOS. You may be lucky and find a reference to the problem in the new hardware's manual or troubleshooting guide, if not check the company's website, and the BIOS manufacturer's website for details of any known problems and solutions.

At some point you may need to access your PC's BIOS program, but you are strongly advised not to touch anything unless you know what you are doing. The precise method varies but on most BIOSs a message appears on the screen at switch on, saying something like 'Press DEL to enter SETUP',

or a combination of keys. Do so and you will see the BIOS main menu. Your
mouse probably won't be working so selections have to be made using the
keyboard arrow up/down keys; to look at a particular menu highlight the
entry and press Return. Once an item is selected changes are usually made
with the Page Up/Down keys, and confirmed with the Return key. To return
to the main menu press the Esc key and quit the BIOS by selecting the item
'Exit without saving changes' or words to that effect. You may be prompted
to confirm your decision; i.e. 'Are you sure?' in which case enter 'Y' for yes,
and press Return. The PC should now continue to load Windows as normal.

Whilst your PC is working normally it is a good idea to make a record of
your BIOS settings. You can do this easily if you have a printer connected to
your PC, though be aware that some 'Windows only' printers may not work.
Boot up your PC to the 'Setup' menu and switch on your printer. The items
we're interested in are variously labelled 'Standard CMOS setup', 'Advanced
CMOS Setup', 'BIOS Features', 'Chipset Features', 'Peripherals Setup',
'Integrated Peripherals' and 'Power Management'. The precise wording may
be different and you can ignore anything to do with passwords, auto
configuration and saving or exiting setup at this stage.

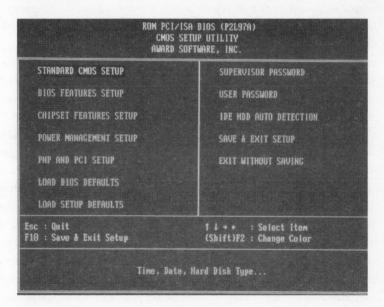

The menu screen of a typical PC BIOS program.

Select each item in turn with the arrow up/down keys and press Return, and when the menu appears press the Print Screen key. All being well your printer will leap into action and print the contents of each page. If for any reason you can't get a printout, copy the information by hand, take a photograph, video the screens with a camcorder, or use a BIOS 'viewer' utility like System Analyser. A trial version can be downloaded from: http://www.sysanalyser.com/

If you get into trouble and haven't got a record of your PC's BIOS you can usually restore some sort of order by using the default settings or auto-configuration utility on the menu (i.e., 'Load Setup Defaults' or 'Auto Configuration with Fail-Safe Settings', etc.). One last piece of advice, if you do feel inspired to make alterations only change one thing at a time. Exit the BIOS after saving each change and boot to Windows, to make sure that everything is still working properly.

CLOSE UP

The precise contents of BIOS programs vary but it's worth looking at some of the most common features. Our first port of call is the Standard CMOS Setup menu, which is usually the first item on the menu. This contains the adjustment for the PC's internal clock and calendar; you can change it if necessary using the keyboard's arrow and page up/down keys. Note that this is not the same as the Windows Time and Date settings, which get information from the CMOS clock, so if that's wrong, the Windows clock will be wrong as well. You should also see information about your PC's disk drives, though these days most BIOSs use automatic settings so there may not be much actual data on display. This page should report on your PC's RAM memory and there may be an option to change the colour of the BIOS menus (usually by pressing F2 on Award and Ami BIOSs). When you've finished press the Esc key to return to the main menu and select the next item, which is normally Advanced CMOS or BIOS Features Setup.

It probably looks a bit intimidating but don't worry, most of it is to do with motherboard configuration and only concerns manufacturers and those building their own PCs. On some BIOSs you get a short explanation of what each item does when it's highlighted, or there may be a Help facility (usually F1) but if you want to know more there are plenty of books on the subject, including the seminal work, *The BIOS Companion* by Phil Croucher (ISBN: 0968192807).

Most of the settings you should leave well alone, in any case they are likely to be the factory defaults unless your PC was specially built or configured but one item you might feel like changing is 'Boot up Num Lock', which decides whether or not the keyboard's numeric pad is enabled at switch on. Another one is Boot Up Sequence. This determines the order of the disk drives your PC accesses to look for system files when it boots up. The default is usually A:, C:, CD-ROM but if you change it to C:, A: etc., boot up may be a little quicker, and you can leave a floppy disk in the drive. Just remember to change back to A:, C:, if the PC ever fails to boot, so you can use your emergency start-up disk.

Tucked away on the list you may see a Password or Security option. By default it's usually set to 'Setup' which means you can password protect the BIOS menu, but if you change it to 'System' this will stop the boot-up process until the correct password is entered. To create a password, go back to the main menu and select the User Password option (if you also set up the Supervisor Password you'll protect the BIOS as well). This offers a high degree of protection because it prevents Windows from loading so there's no easy way to 'hack' into the machine, just make sure you remember your password!

Next is the Peripherals Setup or Integrated Peripherals setup menu: look for 'Printer Port' or 'LPT1'. Most BIOSs default to a 'standard' or 'normal' setting for data transfer through the printer port, which is safe but slow and can cause problems with some recent peripherals that share the printer port. Changing the setting to ECP or EPP (or ECP + EPP on some BIOSs) may solve current or future compatibility problems and yield a small improvement in printer performance; it's certainly worth trying. You should be warned of any conflicts when you exit the BIOS and boot to Windows.

Our final stop is the Power Management menu. This is an important one with settings that decide how your PC behaves when it's not being used. It's usually a good idea to play safe and use Windows Advanced Power Management (Start > Settings > Control Panel); the BIOS options are very detailed and really only for experts. Nevertheless there may be one or two things you might want to have a look at. Power Switch or Power Button changes how the PC's on/off switch works (Instant Off, Off After 4 Seconds, etc., manual off, etc.) and there may be an option to disable the facility that switches the PC on when the phone rings (Power on Modem Action) which some users find incredibly annoying. If you make any changes to the BIOS save and exit as normal and be on the look out for any unexpected error messages as it boots up.

Inside the BIOS, this screen contains settings for your PC's peripheral components.

THE WINDOWS REGISTRY

The Windows Registry is a huge database containing critical settings that determine how Windows and all of the software and hardware used by your PC works, which is why Microsoft has gone to the trouble of hiding it well away from novice users – you have been warned!

Changes to the Registry are carried out when you install new software or hardware, or if you alter desktop settings via the Control Panel or with utilities like Tweak UI. Under normal circumstances there is no reason why you should need to go anywhere near the actual files. However, the Registry is often directly involved in crashes or malfunctions and a little background knowledge might prove useful if your PC starts misbehaving; if nothing else an insight into the workings of your PC is empowering and can help dispel some of the mystery.

Registry data in Windows 9x is contained in two files called 'user.dat' and 'system.dat' and they are stored in the main Windows folder. In Windows XP the files are located in windows\system32\config and the Documents and settings\{username} folder.

Because of their importance they are automatically backed up. Windows 95 makes copies every time it boots up successfully, called 'system.dao' and 'user.dao'. Windows 98 and ME are even more cautious and keep up to five recent copies of the Registry and critical system files (system.ini & win.ini) in a Windows folder called Sysbckup (they're usually called rb00.cab, etc.). As a further precaution all versions of Windows also keep a copy of the Registry when it was first installed on your PC, this is called 'system.1st' and lives in the root directory of the C: drive. An expert can use this file to get your PC working when all other attempts to restore the Registry have failed. More routine problems with a 'corrupt' Registry – caused by faulty software or a failed installation – may generate an error message to the effect that Windows will revert to a saved backup, if you are given the option it is wise to click OK and let your PC carry out the procedure. If the automatic restore facility fails for some reason you can carry out a manual restoration by starting the PC in Safe Mode and using the 'scanreg' command – see Chapter 15.

Before we go any further it's a good idea to know how to make a manual backup of your PC's Registry so you can easily restore it should something go amiss. You should do it before you make any changes to the Registry; in fact get into the habit of doing it every time you open Regedit. Start by deciding where to keep your backup file, it should be somewhere you can easily find it or better still, create a special folder for the purpose. Open Windows Explorer, click once on the Drive C: icon to highlight it then go to the File menu. Select New, click on Folder and an icon called 'New Folder' appears at the bottom of the screen. The name should be highlighted, press backspace to clear the text field and rename the folder Myback, or something equally memorable, press Return then close or minimise Explorer and return to Regedit. Go to the Registry drop-down menu and select Export Registry File. In 'Save In' navigate your way to your newly created Myback folder and in the 'File Name' field call it something like Regbak, click Save and it's done. This will create a text file called regbak.reg; if you ever need to restore the Registry after an editing session simply double-click on Regbak.reg, you will be asked if you want to 'add the information to the Registry...', click yes and the file will be restored.

You can view the Registry, and make manual changes to the data (though don't be tempted just yet!) with a hidden Windows utility called Regedit. On the Start menu select Run and type 'regedit' (without the inverted commas of course) and an Explorer type window opens. To close Regedit simply click on the 'X' in the top right-hand corner or select Exit on the Registry menu.

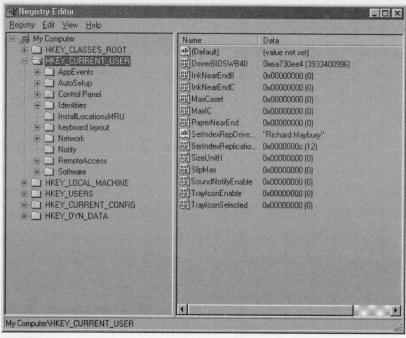

Regedit – your window into your PC's Registry showing the directory tree and file structure.

For the sake of clarity Registry data files are presented as a single directory tree with six 'branches' in the left-hand pane. At the top is HKEY_CLASSES_ROOT; this contains details about which files are associated with which programs, shortcut data and information about Object Linking and Embedding or OLE. This is the way Windows allows bits of information (text, graphics, images, etc.) to be copied between and inserted into different applications.

The second branch is HKEY_CURRENT_USER and this includes the personal preferences (appearance, colour schemes, screen saver, etc.) of whoever is logged on to the PC at the time. HKEY_LOCAL-MACHINE stores general settings and preferences for all of the PC's hardware and software. HKEY_USERS is where the details of everyone who is logged on to the machine are kept. HKEY_CURRENT_CONFIG contains more information about the way the PC is set up and lastly HKEY_DYN_DATA, which is a record of all of Windows Plug and Play features that changes as and when devices are added or removed from the system.

Each branch of the tree is known as a Hive. These contain folders called Keys and Sub Keys, which hold the 'Values', the actual data that makes the Registry tick. Values are stored in the form of alphanumeric text and binary or hexadecimal code.

One way of getting better acquainted with the Registry is to try a few simple tweaks but do bear in mind earlier warnings about always making a backup first. In fact we're not going to attempt anything too challenging or hazardous, just a few quick and simple adjustments that add some extra functionality and change the way Windows 95 and 98 works. Warning! Do not try these out with Windows ME or XP, which has a different structure.

It's all very straightforward but be aware that Regedit will not warn you if you make a mistake, or prompt you to confirm actions when you close the registry editor!

RENAME RECYCLE BIN

We'll kick off with a nice easy one, changing the name of the Recycle Bin on the desktop, which a lot of people detest.

Open Regedit and make the all-essential backup then work your way down through the following set of keys: HKEY_LOCAL_MACHINE/SOFTWARE/CLASSES/CLSID/{645FF040-5081-101B-9F08-00AA002F954E} (be warned that CLSID and that long strings of numbers and letters are a long way down the list). Click on the entry and an item called Default appears in the right-hand pane, with the name 'Recycle Bin' in the Data column. Double click on the icon next to Default and the Edit String dialogue box appears with the words Recycle Bin highlighted in the Value Data field. Press backspace to delete it and type in your new name. Click OK, move the mouse pointer to an empty area of the desktop, click the left mouse button once then press F5 to refresh the desktop and the name will change.

EDIT ADD/REMOVE PROGRAMS LIST

Here's how to get rid of a Windows annoyance, the names of programs left behind in the Add/Remove Programs list, after the program has been deleted. (Actually you can also do this with Tweak UI, but this method is much more fun.) Go to: HKEY_LOCAL_MACHINE\Software\Microsoft\

Using Regedit to change the name of your Recycle Bin.

Windows\CurrentVersion\Uninstall and the full list of titles in Add/Remove Programs appears. To remove the name key of a program you've already deleted simply right-click on it and select Delete.

SIDE-BY-SIDE PROGRAMS MENU

This one is for Windows 98 users who have upgraded from Windows 95 and miss the way the Start menu used to open with side-by-side columns, instead of the single scrolling list in Win 98. In Regedit navigate through the following list of keys: HKEY_LOCAL_MACHINE\Software\Microsoft\Windows\CurrentVersion\explorer\Advanced. Place the mouse pointer in the right-hand pane and right-click. New appears and on the drop-down menu choose String Value, rename it to 'StartMenuScrollPrograms', double click the new icon and in the Value Data field type 'false', close Regedit and give it a try.

CONTROL PANEL ON START MENU

Control Panel is probably the most frequently used Windows Utility, yet it is buried away on the Settings menu or has to be accessed from My Computer. This next Registry hack puts the contents of Control Panel in a subfolder on the Start Menu, so you can get at anything with just one mouse click. This time there's no need to actually go into the Registry to make the changes, instead right-click on the Start button and select Open. When the Explorer Window opens go to New on the File menu and select Folder and a new folder icon appears, backspace to clear the name and type in the following: 'Control Panel.{21EC2020-3AEA-1069-A2DD-08002B30309D}', do not forget the dot after Control Panel, press Return and the folder's name should now change to Control Panel. Close the Start Menu window and a new item called Control Panel appears on the Start Menu that opens to show its contents.

METAL BRIEFCASE

The brown desktop Briefcase icon is a bit dull, so why not change it for a smart metal one? Open Regedit and drill down through the keys thus: HKEY_CLASSES_ROOT\CLSID\{85BBD920-42A0-1069-AE24-08002B3 0309D}\DefaultIcon. In the right-hand pane you should see a Default icon, next to it in the Data column it should read 'c:\windows\System\ syncui.dll,0'; if so click on the icon to open the Edit String dialogue box and change the 0 at the end to a 1, click OK and close Regedit, click onto the desktop and press the F5 key to refresh the display and hey-presto, a shiny new aluminium case. (On some machines you may have to re-boot Windows for the change to take effect.)

CHANGE REGISTERED OWNER DETAILS

The name of the Registered Owner of your PC, which appears on the front page of System Properties (right click My Computer and select Properties) is often set by the vendor or manufacturer. You can easily change it to your name by editing the Registry. Click on the plus sign next to HKEY_LOCAL_MACHINE and then on the plus signs next to the following Keys: Software/Microsoft/Windows and double-click on CurrentVersion. Scroll down the list of items that appears in the right-hand pane until you come to 'RegisteredOwner'. Double-click on the icon next to it and the Edit String dialogue box opens, with the name that was entered when Windows was first installed. Press backspace to delete the entry and type in a new name, click OK and exit Regedit.

That is just a very brief taste of what the Registry can do. If you want to go any further you should read up on the subject, there are plenty of detailed books, including the inevitable 'Dummies' Guides and there's a huge amount of information on the Internet, along with very many more hacks. A very good place to start is: http://home.aol.com/AXCEL216/reg.htm

Q&A Real world problems

Wake up call

Q Every now and again I find that the ringing of the phone switches on the computer. Is there any way of preventing this happening? If I switch off at the mains, which are not easily accessible, how long will it take for the clock to cease working? I feel that this is wearing out the computer, as I have to switch it off and reboot after switching on the printer in order for the printer to work.

A 'Wake up on ring' is one of your PC's power management functions; it's controlled by the BIOS. This is normally accessed by pressing the Delete key (or a combination of keys). During boot up, there's usually a message, something like, 'to enter set-up program press…'. When the BIOS menu appears look for the Power Management menu (follow the on-screen instructions to make selections). Be very careful not to make any accidental changes, you're looking for an entry like 'Power up on modem', and disable if necessary.

Run stops

Q The AutoRun facility on my Hitachi CDR-7730 CD-ROM does not work even though the 'Auto Insert Notification' in Device Properties is checked. Have you any other ideas?

A It is possible that a Registry entry is causing the problem. Depending on your version of Windows the errant keys can be found at:

HKEY_LOCAL_MACHINE\SYSTEM\ControlSet001\Services\CDRom

or

HKEY_LOCAL_MACHINE\SYSTEM\CurrentControlSet\Services\CDRom

Change the binary value of 'Autorun' from 0 (disable) to 1 and reboot.

Memory stealer

Q   A colleague's PC displays '8Mb shared memory' (64Mb in total) shortly after the power on self-test (POST) sequence. Please advise where the setting for this is located and the likely reasons for it.

A   Some motherboards with built-in video adaptors steal a chunk of memory from the PC's RAM; it's a sneaky way for manufacturers to be able to claim that a PC has a '8Mb' of video memory. The allocation is usually best left alone but if you know what you are doing and want to try another setting you'll have to access the PC's BIOS. Look in the Advanced Setup section, where you should see an item labelled 'Shared Memory Size'. Changing the allocation probably won't make any difference on text-based office type applications but it could cause problems on graphics-intensive software and games.

CHAPTER 19

Reinstalling Windows

There's a good argument for periodically wiping or 'formatting' a PC's hard disk and starting afresh every year or so. It's one way of avoiding the inevitable build up of file clutter, glitches and the gradual slow down that occurs on any well-used PC.

For a few weeks or months after a Windows reinstall it's like having a new machine all over again. The counter argument is that if it 'ain't broke, don't fix it'. Removing and reinstalling Windows plus all your applications and data files can be a long and tedious job. Unfortunately, leaving well alone is only an option for as long as the PC behaves itself. Sooner or later most Windows users will experience a catastrophic crash or if they're really unlucky, a fatal virus infection where the only solution is to start over or, worst of all, a complete hard disk failure, necessitating a replacement disk drive.

Wiping a PC's hard disk drive to reinstall Windows or faulty applications is a fairly drastic procedure and should be considered only as a last resort. Needless to say you will lose all the programs, files, and data stored on it so make sure you have explored all other possibilities first, and backed up all non-replaceable data. Before you even think about wiping your hard disk drive you must make sure you can put everything back as it was before, so in addition to your Windows installation CD-ROM you will also need the driver programs for all of the PC's internal hardware devices (video adaptor, soundcard, modem, etc.), these will probably be supplied on a separate CD-ROM that was supplied with your PC. You will also need all of the driver disks for all your peripherals (printer, scanner, digital scanner, etc.) and any other hardware devices you may have. Make sure also that you have the disks and, where necessary, serial numbers and authorisation codes for all the software applications you want to use, plus a copy of all the email settings, PIN number and passwords you need to access any applications or services.

If Windows has become corrupted you could try reinstalling it by running the set-up program from the CD-ROM. There's a slim chance it might overwrite the damaged files. It's always worth trying the Scandisk utility to repair faults in the disk filing system and a lot of Windows problems, particularly those involving drivers, can be tracked down by starting in Safe Mode (see Chapter 15).

If you upgraded from an earlier version of Windows you will be asked to provide details of your previous setup during the installation, so before you start have the disk and its serial number to hand. Windows 95 users must also have the driver disk for their CD-ROM drive – more about that in a moment. That shouldn't be necessary if you are using Windows 98 onwards, but it's a good idea to have it handy, just in case. Finally, and most important of all, you must have an emergency start-up disk for your PC. (In case you've forgotten double click on the Add/Remove Programs icon in Control Panel, select the Start-up disk tab and follow the instructions.)

If you are installing a new hard drive then you have to go through an additional procedure called 'partitioning' before you can load Windows. This is quite different from the formatting process so don't get the two confused. It helps if you think of a hard disk drive as a filing cabinet; partitioning is akin to deciding how many drawers it will have, formatting decides how the files in the drawers are organised.

Three different types of disk formatting are in widespread use. Older PCs use the now almost obsolete FAT 16 (File Allocation Table). Most current models use the more efficient FAT 32 system, but many Windows XP machines are formatted using NTFS (New Technology Filing System) which was developed for the business-orientated Windows NT operating system.

Windows XP works perfectly well under FAT 32 but NTFS is a slightly more advanced system, there are some performance benefits and reliability and stability are improved but it is better suited to expert users therefore what follows is mostly concerned with the FAT 32 system.

Until fairly recently most hard disk drives had a single partition but in the mid-1990s the capacity of hard disk drives increased dramatically and most versions of Windows, which until then used the FAT 16 filing system, were unable to handle drives larger than 2 gigabytes. To get around the limit, larger disk drives had to be split up into 2-gigabyte (or less) partitions, which the operating system regarded as separate drives.

FAT 32 first appeared on later versions of Windows 95 and became the standard from Windows 98 onwards. It allows disk drives with a capacity greater than 2Gb to be treated as a single drive. However, some PC makers and sellers still prefer to partition drives for the sake of convenience or for extra flexibility. In most cases Windows and all the most frequently used programs will be in the C: partition whilst other partitions, assigned drive letters D:, E:, etc., can contain a complete set of Windows installation files, so it can be easily restored should something go wrong. Partitions are also used for archiving or keeping large files separate from the rest of the programs on the disk, minimising the chances of them becoming lost or corrupted through the action of a virus. Partitions can also be used for 'dual-booting' a PC, allowing the user to switch between operating systems. For example, one partition might contain Windows 98 and its programs whilst another could be used for Windows NT, 2000, XP or Linux and associated applications.

If you are starting afresh with a new hard disk drive, then before you can use it, it has to be partitioned, otherwise if you only want to erase the drive and start over you can skip the next couple of paragraphs and proceed directly to Formatting.

PARTITIONING

To partition a disk drive you need a small utility called Fdisk. Fdisk is included on your PC's Start-up or Emergency Boot disk. If the new drive is larger than 2Gb make sure the version of Fdisk supports FAT 32, i.e., the boot disk was created using Windows 98 or later.

After the new drive has been installed and all the connections checked, and double-checked the partitioning process can begin. Pop in the Start Up disk and switch the machine on. The BIOS program carries out its diagnostic routine on the motherboard, memory and disk drives and if all's well a few moments later the A: prompt appears on the screen. Type 'fdisk' (without the quotation marks of course) press return and follow the instructions. When asked you should ensure that Partition 1 is 'Active' as this will enable the PC to boot up from the new disk drive. When the job has finished reboot the PC, run fdisk again, select option 4 to display the partition information and check that there are no error messages, the capacity shown is correct and that everything is okay.

FORMATTING

Formatting a drive is quite straightforward, indeed you may already have done it before, when preparing a floppy disk for first use (though these days most floppies are sold 'pre-formatted'). Your PC must be in its default

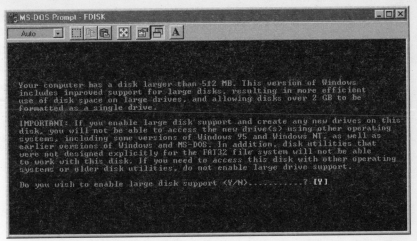

The fdisk warning message, which tells you how it will organise your disk's filing system.

condition and ready to boot from a Start Up disk in drive A:. When you are ready, load your Boot disk and switch on when the A: prompt appears. If you are installing Windows XP type 'format c:' (without the quotes) and press Enter. If you are installing Windows 98 type: 'format c: /s' and press the Enter key. The '/s' after format is a command 'switch' that instructs the PC to copy important system files onto the hard disk so that in future it can boot up on its own, without help from a floppy disk.

The length of time it takes to format a hard disk drive varies according to its capacity, so you may have to be patient. When it has finished remove the boot disk and restart the computer; this time the PC will boot up on its own and present you with a flashing C: prompt. If you get a message saying 'please insert boot disk' that means the vital system files haven't been copied from the floppy to the hard disk. In that case boot up from the floppy disk once more and when the A: prompt appears enter the command 'sys c:', and try again. If you experience recurrent problems during formatting – and that is quite unusual – it's worth starting over from the beginning and re-partitioning the drive in case vestiges of the old operating system or possibly even a virus has remained behind and is causing trouble. Occasionally there may be a physical problem with the drive, resulting in 'bad sectors' or parts of the drive that are unable to store information reliably, in which case there's nothing you can do but start again with a new drive.

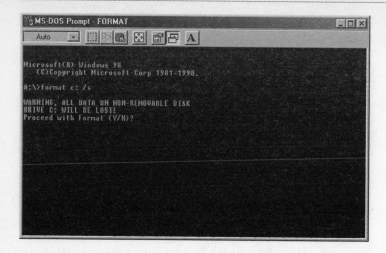

Prior to loading Windows you will need to format your hard disk drive; the command shown also copies important system files.

LOADING WINDOWS

If everything has gone to plan at this point you now have a fully working but empty PC. The last job is to load the Windows operating system. If you are installing Windows from an 'upgrade' CD-ROM you will be asked to prove eligibility by temporarily loading a previous 'full' version of Windows so have this to hand.

When loading or reloading Windows 98 or ME the system files that were copied to the hard drive during formatting should tell the PC to recognise the CD-ROM drive. The Windows 98 boot-up disk contains a number of generic CD-ROM drivers covering most common makes and types of drive; however, if your newly formatted PC doesn't recognise the CD-ROM drive, you will have to use the installation disk that came with it. Pop in the disk, change to the A: drive and type 'dir'. This will show you what's on the disk, look for something called 'install.exe', 'setup' or 'cdinstall', type it in as it appears on the screen then press return and follow the instructions, it should take only a minute or two.

If the CD-ROM driver is installed or you have successfully loaded it yourself, change to the drive letter for the CD-ROM drive, usually by typing D: (though it may be another letter if the drive is partitioned) type setup and the loading sequence will begin. You're well on the way to restoring your PC to its original condition.

Q&A Real world problems

Pound notes

Q   After reloading Windows I have found that my keyboard cannot produce the pound sign. When holding down shift and pressing 3, I get # instead of £. Each time I want to use it, I have to use character map.

A   The most likely explanation is that the keyboard language setting in Windows was left on the US American default setting during installation. It can be changed to English (British) by clicking on the Keyboard icon in Control Panel (Start > Settings), select the Language tab, click the Add button, scroll down the list to find the correct setting, highlight the entry and click OK.

Split decision

Q   I was running Windows 95 on my laptop with a 6 gigabyte hard disk drive partitioned across drives C, D and E, each of 2 gigabytes. I formatted my hard drive and installed Windows 98 in place of 95. Everything went well and it works perfectly, however, my hard disk remains resolutely split. How do I combine these three 'drives' into one C drive?

A   You cannot change disk partitions from within Windows but there are a number of utility programs on the market that can do the job, the best-known being Symantec Partition-IT Extra Strength and Power Quest's Partition Magic. However it's a bit of a palaver and unless the partitioning is causing you problems it's usually a good idea to leave well alone.

ME mutterings

Q   I have just installed Windows ME. However, Windows Explorer has vanished from the Programs list and I can't find it anywhere.

A Windows ME and Windows 98 are very similar but there have been some changes in presentation, and a few compatibility problems are coming to light. Windows Explorer has moved to the Accessories list under Programs on the Start menu, but you can place a shortcut anywhere you like by holding down the Ctrl key, right-clicking on the Windows Explorer folder icon then dragging it to your preferred location.

CHAPTER 20 **Securing Windows**

*After you've reinstalled Windows for the umpteenth
time (see Chapter 19) you might want to ask yourself
why it is so unreliable.*

On its own Windows is actually very stable, it's all the other, mostly pointless
software, that gets loaded afterwards and 'tinkering' with settings that causes
most problems. On a single-user PC you have only yourself to blame but if
your PC is shared by others you should take charge of how it is configured,
and who is allowed to mess around with it! One of the things that surprises
a lot of Window 9x users is the operating system's apparent lack of security
features (Windows XP is much more secure and easier to protect). Anyone
with a mind to do so can easily interfere with key settings that can drastically
affect the way a PC behaves, even stop it working altogether. Microsoft could
have incorporated effective security measures as standard in Windows 9x but
unless they are properly implemented they have a nasty habit of backfiring
and there is no doubt they would cause enormous problems, especially for
inexperienced users.

In fact Windows 95 and 98 come with a powerful security facility called
The System Policy Editor or 'Poledit' but it is not installed by default, or
readily accessible, unless you know what you are looking for. Microsoft in its
wisdom has decided not to include Poledit in Windows ME, relying instead
on the System Restore facility to repair damage done to PCs by the kind of
unauthorised fiddling that Poledit is designed to prevent. Some elements of
Poledit will work with ME but it is safer to assume that what follows is only
applicable to Windows 95 and 98.

System Policy Editor is meant to be used by System Administrators.
They're the folk who look after networks or a number of PCs, such as
teachers and lecturers, who use it to stop mischievous students messing
around with desktop settings and running illicit programs. Clearly, it could
also be of interest to anyone whose PC is shared by several people,
particularly if they include meddlesome children.

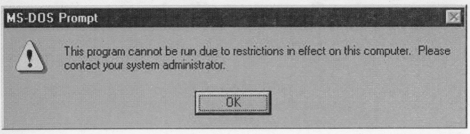

When your PC is protected anyone attempting to tinker with it will be greeted by this warning message.

Poledit is not especially difficult to use but it can easily muck up your computer so leave it alone, unless you are confident of your abilities and are prepared to accept the consequences, and don't blame us if you get it wrong!

Poledit covers a lot of ground but the part we're interested in is basically a tool for editing the Windows Registry (see Chapter 18). Poledit lives on the Windows 95 and 98 installation disks. Unlike most other Windows utilities Poledit is not loaded into the PC during setup nor is it accessible from Control Panel or the desktop. It is possible to install it on your PC's hard disk drive if you wish but that would defeat the object and compromise security. Ensuring that the installation disk has to be loaded every time in order to make changes is a useful first line of defence against casual tinkering by PC-savvy users (though obviously it can't stop determined fiddlers, who may have their own copy of Poledit on a floppy or CD-ROM).

Windows 95 and 98 have different versions of Poledit. The Windows 95 one is slightly simpler in presentation and therefore easier for beginners to get to grips with, moreover it appears to work on Windows 98 PCs without any problems; however, it's sensible to play safe and use the one that came with your version of Windows. The main difference is that Poledit in Windows 98 contains a number of extra features, mostly designed to control Internet and email facilities. To keep things as simple as possible we'll stick to the basic features common to both versions. If you want to know more about what the Windows Policy Editor can do there are plenty of websites and books covering the subject.

The changes made by Poledit on a stand-alone PC are usually global and will affect everyone who uses that computer; however it's possible to confine the changes to single 'profiles', where the PC is used by a number of people with different passwords. Before you do anything it's a good idea to work out exactly what you want to achieve since too many restrictions can be just as bad as none at all and you could end up making your PC difficult or impossible to use for routine tasks.

Poledit controls how the PC works using a series of 'administration templates'. There are several of them, mostly dealing with advanced network operations. However, the ones most home PC and small-office users will be interested in concern the Control Panel, the Desktop, access to the Windows filing system and disk drives. The Control Panel options include the facility to hide the Background, Appearance and Settings tabs on the Display icon. The latter allows users to change screen resolution, which can create a lot of

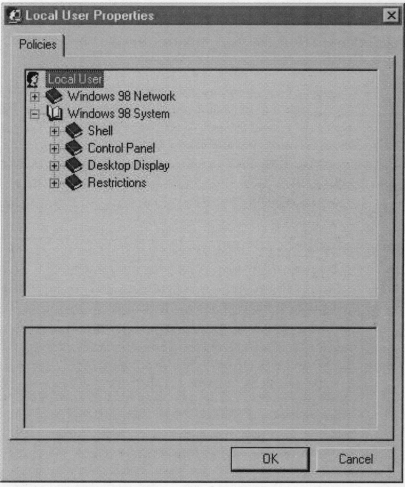

Poledit looks complicated but you quickly learn how to use it to control access to your PC's critical settings.

problems. Incidentally, Smart Alecs who know how to get into Control Panel by various alternative methods (right-clicking on the desktop and selecting Properties, My Computer, Windows Explorer, etc.) will not be able to get around the restrictions; they will be greeted with a message advising them that 'Your System Administrator has disabled the Display Control Panel' and they won't be able to make any changes. Other Control Panel items that can be restricted or disabled include Networks, Printers, Passwords and System, which includes the important Device Manager and Hardware Profiles tabs.

Poledit can lock Windows wallpaper and colour schemes and again will defeat any scurrilous attempts to make changes by backdoor means, such as using Internet Explorer to set new wallpaper. Poledit can also remove the Run Command from the Start menu, turn off Folder Options and Taskbar & Start Menu on Settings on the Start Menu. It can hide disk drives in My Computer, make everything vanish from the desktop, disable the Shut Down command and cancel the feature whereby desktop settings are automatically saved on exit. Finally, to scupper any serious attempts at sabotage, Poledit can stop editing tools making changes to the Registry, prevent DOS-based software from running in a Windows DOS session and restarting the PC in DOS mode and there's a provision to run only designated Windows programs.

USING POLEDIT

Since Poledit makes changes to your PC's Registry files it's a very good idea to carry out a backup before you do anything else, see Chapter 18 for details. If after using Poledit you get any error messages relating to the Registry you can easily restore Windows to its former condition.

The two versions of Poledit are in slightly different locations on the Windows installation CD-ROMs. On the Windows 95 disk it can be found in D:\Admin\Apptools\Poledit; for Windows 98 look in D:\Tools\Reskit\Netadmin\Poledit (where D: is the drive letter of your CD-ROM). Poledit wasn't included with Windows 95 on floppy disks, but it can be downloaded from the Microsoft web site at http://www.microsoft.com/downloads/search.asp, the file is called Policy.exe.

Step one is to install the main Poledit files on your PC. Go to Add/Remove Programs in Control Panel, select the Windows Setup tab and click Have Disk. Use the Browse button to navigate to the folder on the CD-

ROM containing Poledit and select the file Poledit.inf. Click OK, select System Policy Edit then Install. A new item called System Policy Editor will now appear in Start > Programs > Accessories > System Tools. By the way, the Windows CD-ROM must be in the drive every time you run Poledit. You can also run Poledit directly from the CD-ROM, providing you don't later restrict the use of the Run command! Go to Run on the Start menu and use the Browse button to find your way to the Policy.exe file on the disk.

When you run the Windows 95 version of Poledit for the first time you will be prompted to open a file called 'admin.adm', click Open and the main System Policy screen appears. On the Windows 98 version you normally go straight to the opening screen. Next go to the File menu and select Open Registry then click on the Local User icon.

In Windows 95 you will see a set of sub-menus called Local User Properties detailing the areas of Windows that you can control. In Windows 98 click on the item Windows 98 System and a similar set of options should appear, though it will exclude the 'Network' controls, which are dealt with separately. The four items we are interested in, and common to both versions of Poledit, are called Shell, Control Panel, Desktop Display and Restrictions; we'll look at each one in turn (in the order that they appear in the Windows 98 version of Poledit).

Click on the plus sign next to Shell and two further sub-folders appear, Custom Folders and Restrictions. Click the plus sign again and the items you can control appear, with a checkbox alongside each one. There's not much to interest the average user in Custom Folders, it's mostly concerned with changing the default locations of programs, so we'll move swiftly on to Restrictions. This contains a set of options to remove or hide Windows user interface features. The ones most users with a shared PC might want to check are: 'Remove Run Command', 'Remove Folders from Settings on Start menu', 'Hide Drives in My Computer' and 'Don't Save Settings on Exit'. Most of the others are either concerned with network features or fairly extreme things, like disabling Shut Down or hiding all the icons on the desktop.

On now to Control Panel, which opens with four or five options, depending on the version of Poledit. They are: Display, Network, Passwords, Printers and System. Clicking each item brings up a further set of options in the window below. It's worth checking everything in Display and System since these are the things that can cause the most problems through accidental and deliberate tampering. The restrictions you impose in

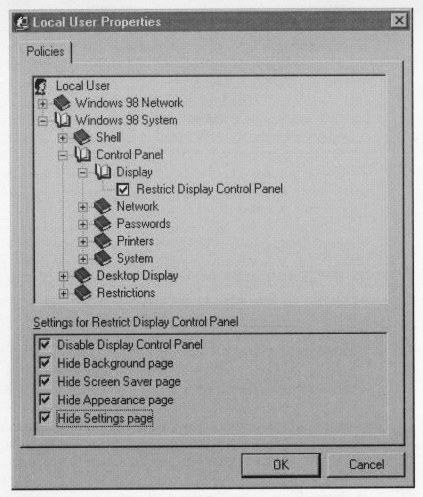

Poledit controls that allow you to hide or disable many of Windows most important configuration settings.

Network, Passwords and Printers will depend on what type of setup you have and who uses the PC.

The next item is Desktop and there are just two restrictions here that allow you to fix the wallpaper and colour scheme. Users can still make changes but they will be reset to your defaults when the machine is restarted.

Finally, Restrictions. This set of options prevents Registry editing tools being used (including Poledit – so definitely leave this one alone!) stops DOS programs running in a DOS window or restarting the PC in DOS mode and lets you specify which programs are allowed to be used on your PC. It's worth disabling the DOS options especially if the PC is under threat from knowledgeable users. Imposing restrictions on which programs may be used is actually quite difficult to use since you have to specify the full path for each program and this can be quite a chore, it's easier to remove programs you won't allow, and disable the Run command or hide the drives.

After setting your restrictions exit Poledit and you will be asked to confirm that you want to make changes to the Registry, click OK. Some of them will occur immediately, others will take place the next time the PC is booted up.

RESCUE PLAN

Using Poledit/Restrictions to prevent editing the registry stops Poledit working, so how can it be changed back again? The solution is to use Windows WordPad or a word processor to manually create a new Registry entry. Open a new document and enter the following text:

REGEDIT4

[HKEY_CURRENT_USER\Software\Microsoft\Windows\CurrentVersion\Policies\Explorer]

"RestrictRun"=dword:00000000

[HKEY_CURRENT_USER\Software\Microsoft\Windows\CurrentVersion\Policies\System]

"DisableRegistryTools"=dword:00000000

Call the file 'recover.reg' and save it in the root directory of your PC's C: drive. Reboot the PC to DOS mode and at the prompt type: 'regedit recover.reg'. Restart and the restriction should be removed.

Q&A Real world problems

Locked out

Q   I have read that that most ten-year-olds can defeat the password features of Windows. As a seventy-year-old who put an easily remembered, since forgotten, password on his taxation computations in Excel just to see what happens, is it possible to share the remedy and save several hours of work?

A   Let that be a lesson to you! Always write down your passwords and keep them in a safe place. There are many ways to disguise a set of passwords or PIN numbers, bogus phone numbers in an address book, simple scrambling – reversing the letter or number order – a diary entry using the letters to create a sentence, though of course you still have to remember how or where they're hidden…

Several companies specialise in recovering password-protected data and there are quite a few shareware programs that can also do the job. Most of them employ the 'brute force' method, which simply means they go through all the possible letter number combinations – several million per minute – until they stumble on the right one. You can find out more from the following web sites:

http://www.passwordservice.com/faq.htm
http://www.elkraft.ntnu.no/~huse/xlpassword.htm
http://www.lostpassword.com/msofpass97.htm

Child's play

Q   On a computer at school, two children pressed reset at an obviously inopportune moment and now all the windows and displays in the screens as well as the mouse pointer are very large. The Windows screens in the start-up sequence are OK but once the Windows desktop screen comes up it is huge so we only see a small amount of the screen.

I assume I need to do a change to the Settings window in the Display part of the Control Panel. I can get into this but cannot get down the window to do what I assume is the necessary change. Scrolling or page down has no effect. Am I right in my assumption and if so is there any way I can get down this screen? Is there another way of correcting the problem? Or do I have to reload Windows and so lose all the work stored on the hard disk?

A   Even if you can't actually see the selections in Control Panel you can access them by pressing the down arrow on the keyboard, try them one at a time, pressing the Return key each time, until you get to the Display option. Alternatively, restart the PC in Safe Mode by pressing the F8 key during the boot-up sequence. Windows will then load with 'standard' display setting and you'll be able to get into a normally sized Control Panel.

Lock out the Luddite

Q   My business partner is a computer Luddite and frequently messes up his PC settings. Is there a way of locking Windows settings, or fixing it so that they are restored on rebooting?

A   The simplest way to stop your partner's tinkering is to hide or restrict access to the Windows Control Panel. If you are using Windows 98 (version 1) then install Tweak UI; it's on the Win 98 CD-ROM, Tools > Reskit > Powertoy, right-click on tweakui.inf and select Install. The Tweak UI icon appears in Control Panel, select the Control Panel tab and disable all the components, or just the ones your partner interferes with. (Unfortunately this facility is only on the Windows 98 version of Tweak UI.) There are also a number of utilities that will restrict access to programs and Windows components, including Control Panel. Have a look at Sentry 98 and Security Administrator, shareware/trial versions can be downloaded from: http://www.sentry98.com/ and http://www.softheap.com/secagent.html

Junior meddlers

Q   I am having a problem with children at school moving the taskbar to the edges of the screen. We want to lock them into position at the base of the screen – the taskbar, not the children! What can you suggest apart from keep moving it back to the bottom when the little Herberts have messed around with it?

A   A shareware program called IconLock stores icon and desktop settings, so they can be easily restored if someone tinkers with them. Alternatively, the icons and the Taskbar can be locked and password protected; everything still works normally but no changes can be made. The 'zip' file is just under 900kbs and can be downloaded from:

http://www.zdnet.com/pcmag/pctech/content/18/14/ut1814.002.html

Part VI

TOP 150 TIPS

Top 150 tips

WINDOWS BUTTONS, KEYS AND ICONS

1. Help is always at hand! If you encounter a problem or get into difficulty, just press F1 and the associated Help file will be displayed. Swapping between open applications in Windows is easy; hold down the left 'Alt' key and press the 'tab' key. Pressing tab again steps through all the programs the machine is currently running. If for any reason a program freezes, or the mouse stops moving, try pressing 'Alt' and you may find that you can still select menus and options, using the four arrow cursor keys. If an application refuses to respond then press and hold down 'Ctrl', 'Alt' and 'Delete' in that order – once only – and the PC will display the Close Program window. This gives the opportunity to shut down the offending application, without having to exit Windows.

2. There are several Windows Explorer keyboard shortcuts worth remembering. Each time you press the Backspace key Explorer steps back one level up the directory tree. The F2 key allows you to rename a highlighted folder and Shift plus F10 brings up the context based pop-up menu. Clicking once or twice on the Size and Modified headings in the right-hand 'Contents' window will sort the files in descending (i.e., largest files or most recently modified first) or ascending orders.

3. Here are some more Windows Explorer keyboard shortcuts. Pressing F4 displays the full contents of the Address/location panel, F5 refreshes the windows, updating any changes you may have made and F6 switches the focus between the various window 'panes'. Ctrl + A selects everything in the right-hand window, Ctrl + Z undoes the last action and the Backspace key steps back through the parent directory tree. The asterisk key on the numeric keypad expands all of the directory branches whilst the '–' and '+' numeric keys collapse and expand the tree.

4. Windows Explorer sometimes seems to have a mind of its own and always seems to open with a different shape, position or icon and display settings. You can make it remember your preferences, for a while at least. Set it up the way you want it to look then press Ctrl + Alt + Shift when you click on the close icon (the 'x' in the top right-hand corner). It will eventually forget but it's easy enough to repeat the exercise. It's a lot easier in Windows 98. Set up Windows Explorer, go to the View Menu then Folder Options and select the View Tab and press the 'Like Current Folder' button.

5. If you have a Windows keyboard you obviously know the 'Windows' button (in between Ctrl and Alt keys) brings up the Start menu, but it can do a lot more besides. Win key (Wk) + D is a very quick way of getting to the desktop as it toggles maximise and minimise all windows. Wk + E opens Explorer, Wk + F opens Find, and Wk + R opens Run. System Properties opens with Wk + Pause, Wk + Tab steps through the programs on the Taskbar and Wk + F1 opens Windows Help.

6. There are several frequently used multiple key shortcuts in Windows, like Ctrl + Alt + Del (to bring up the close program menu) and Alt + Tab (to switch between running applications) and dozens more in applications like Word, Excel and Outlook. Windows 95/98/2000 and ME has a nifty way to avoid two- and three-finger gymnastics; it's called 'Sticky Keys' and it's one of the Accessibility Options in Control Panel. It's aptly named because instead of pressing and holding a sequence of keys, you simply press each one in turn and your PC's internal speaker bleeps at you to confirm each key press. The facility can be easily switched on and off by pressing the shift key five times in quick succession.

Sticky Keys is not always installed by default. If you can't see the Accessibility Options icon in Control Panel click on Add/Remove in Control Panel, select the Windows tab then Accessibility and follow the instructions. To enable Sticky Keys open Accessibility Options and select the Keyboard tab, use the Settings button to change the way it behaves. Whilst you're there you might also like to switch on the Caps Lock bleeper, which also uses the PC's built-in speaker.

7. It doesn't take long for the Taskbar at the bottom of the screen to fill up with icons; they get smaller as the number increases and it can be difficult to read the labels. You can easily increase the size of the taskbar by moving the mouse pointer onto the top edge of the taskbar where it will turn into a vertical double-headed arrow. Click and hold the left mouse button and you can increase the width of the taskbar by dragging it upwards; it can be expanded to fill half of the screen if necessary. Clearly this takes up more room on the desktop, so make the Taskbar disappear until it is needed. Click on the Start button, then Settings and Taskbar and check the Auto Hide option. From now on the Taskbar will be shown only when the mouse pointer is at the bottom of the screen.

8. The right mouse button in Windows has many hidden talents; here are a few to be getting on with. If you've got a lot of open windows and you want to get to the desktop, simply right click on the taskbar. This brings up a menu for minimising, tiling or cascading all windows; right click on the taskbar a second time to restore the windows. A right click on the recycle bin gives the option to empty it straight away. Disks can be quickly formatted by right-clicking on the disk drive icon in My Computer or Explorer.

9. You can do all sorts of clever things with the items on the Windows 9x Start menu, they can be copied, moved around and have their properties changed but the one thing you can't do is rename them, unless you have Internet Explorer 5.0 or later on your system. However, there is a way around that. You can change the name of an icon by left clicking on it and dragging it onto the desktop, it can then be renamed by clicking into the name field. Next, right-click on the newly named icon, drag it onto the Start button, put the mouse pointer where you want it to go on the Start menu, release the mouse button and choose 'Move Here' from the dialogue box that appears.

10. Every so often a program window opens in the wrong position or the menus and toolbars have disappeared off the top of the screen and you can't get them back. Here's a simple solution. Press Alt + Spacebar to bring up the sizing menu then hold down the letter M and use the down arrow cursor key to bring the window back on to the screen.

11. From the Start menu in Windows click on Settings, Control Panel and then on the Mouse icon. There you will find a range of settings that control the way your mouse behaves. There's also the opportunity to change the button configuration, useful if you are left-handed. The two most important parameters for PC newcomers are Motion and Click Speed; set both to slow and you'll find the mouse much easier to control. Increase the speed once you get used to how the mouse reacts. Whilst you're there click on the

Pointers tab and the Scheme menu, then select the Animated Hourglasses option. This will make waiting for things to happen just a little more interesting.

12. Bored with your desktop and all those dull little icons? Then do something about it! You can easily create your own icons in Windows using ordinary picture files or graphics created using the Paint program. You could have the pictures of the family or pets representing your programs (no jokes about using a photo of the mother-in-law to represent the word processor please), or design your own from scratch. The image can be any size – Windows will automatically adjust the size and shape – but it must be in the Bitmap (extension .bmp) format. Most paint and graphics programs have a 'Save As' facility that will convert picture files from other file types into .bmp format. Once that's done open Windows Explorer, find the picture file and click once into the name field to highlight it, then wait a second and click again to insert a cursor so it can be renamed. Change the file extension from .bmp to .ico, and hit return. Now go to the Desktop and right-click on the icon you want to change and select Properties. On the Shortcut tab you should see a 'Change Icon' button (you can't normally change the icon on Windows applications) click it and use the Browse button to find your icon picture file, press OK and it's done.

13. The double-pane view of Windows Explorer makes it easy to navigate around files and folders, if you like you can force all other Explorer type Folders (My Computer, Control Panel, Recycle Bin, etc.) to open with double panes. Open a folder, My Computer will do, click Folder Options on the View menu and select the File Types tab. Scroll down the list under Registered File Types to find 'Folder', double-click on it and in the dialogue window that appears, under Actions, highlight 'Explore', click Set As Default and then Close. To return to the original single-pane view, follow the above procedure, but this time select 'Open' in the Actions box.

14. If you've had your PC for more than a year or so the desktop is probably starting to get a bit crowded. Of course you can always remove icons and shortcuts you rarely use but if you're the sort of person who hates to part with anything, here's a simple way of packing even more icons onto your desktop by reducing the space between them. If you can find an empty area on the desktop click into it and the Display Properties window should appear. Select the Appearance tab and under Item highlight Icon Spacing (horizontal). Change the value from the default setting to 30 and click Apply. Now do the same with Icon Spacing (vertical). You may need to experiment with different values and watch out for large overlapping Icon labels. If that becomes a problem edit the text by clicking slowly into the label box three times or reduce the size of the actual icon – the option is on the same drop-down menu as Icon Spacing.

15. This tip will let you start your ten favourite applications with a single key press, and it gives the numeric keypad on the right side of your keyboard something to do. First press the Num Lock key on your keyboard then right-click your mouse on any desktop shortcut and select Properties. Click the cursor into the 'Shortcut Key' field and press the number key on the numeric keypad that you want to start the program with. Click OK and repeat for up to nine other programs. Unless you have a good memory it's a good idea to make a list. If you use the keypad then you can assign some other infrequently used key or key combination, though make sure it's not used by something else.

16. Here's a quick and simple little timesaver that will help you to make more efficient use of Windows Explorer. If you are looking for a file or folder in a large directory, rather than spend time scrolling through the list simply click into the Explorer window and type the first letter of the name of the file or folder and hey-presto, Explorer immediately whisks you down to the first file starting with that letter.

17. Make your right-click Context menus stand out! Right-click on an empty area of the desktop and select Properties or go to Display in Control panel and select the Appearance tab. In the example window display click on the menu bar below Active Window (Normal Disabled Selected) and change the colour from grey to something a bit more interesting, a light red works well; you can choose any colour by clicking the 'Other' button. Click OK and try it out by right clicking. If you click the 'Selected' label on the menu bar you can change the colour of highlighted menu items in all of your programs from dark blue – try light green for a really funky look!

18. Ctrl is a much undervalued and underused key on your keyboard and it is well worth getting to know, especially when editing, and not just in word processors, but in most text editor windows, and that includes email message windows. Holding down the Ctrl key when using Backspace or Delete erases whole words instead of single letters, and if you use the arrow keys to move the cursor around, press and hold the Ctrl key and it jumps a paragraph, or a word at a time, depending on the direction.

CRASH PROTECTION

19. A common cause of Windows crashes or lock-ups is too many programs running at the same time. You might be lucky and get a warning that something bad is about to happen – a slow running program is a sign of impending danger – but you can keep an eye on what is happening, and possibly prevent a crash, using a simple utility called the Resource Meter. It is quite well hidden. From the Start button select Programs, then Accessories and click on System Tools. Double click on Resource Meter and a small bar-graph icon will appear on the Taskbar, next to the clock. Placing the mouse pointer over the icon will give you an instant readout of the percentage of resources being used, better still click on it and a set of three bar graphs will appear. Problems can occur when any of the three meters fall below 25%. If that happens you should close one or more programs, not forgetting to save any open files first, reboot and all should be well again.

20. Thunderstorms can be fatal for PCs. Strikes on nearby overhead cables and sub-stations can send high voltage 'spikes' down mains supplies, frying computers and other electronic devices. It's sensible to switch your PC off, disconnect the mains plug and telephone modem lead during a thunderstorm, even if it's not directly overhead. If that's not possible then it is worth investing in surge-protection devices, for the mains and telephone connections. Protection devices, built into mains sockets or multi-way adaptors are relatively inexpensive – £20 to £50 – compared with the cost of a PC and loss of data. Telephone line protectors start at around £40 and are readily available from PC stockists.

21. Make sure your PC is well ventilated as the combination of a hot office and poor airflow can result in erratic behaviour. Check that the fan is working properly and if there is a build-up of dust around the grille, clear it with a clean paintbrush. Use a vacuum cleaner hose to suck out fluff and debris from the back of the machine. Remove any clutter from the front and side ventilation slots. Don't forget the monitor. Now would be a good time to file those papers that are piling up on the top and blocking the vents. Peel off any stickers and furry creatures that could obstruct cooling air.

22. This tip won't stop the dreaded 'Blue Screen of Death' (the error message that heralds a major system crash) from appearing, but you can change the colour and make it a more restful shade. Use Notepad to open the System.ini file in the Windows folder. Scroll down to the section that starts '[386enh]' and at the end type the following two lines, paying attention to the spacing, capitalisation and spelling:

MessageBackColor=
MessageTextColor=

Now you need to add a number or letter (hexadecimal code) after the equals signs for the background and text colours, the choices are: 0 for black, 1 blue, 2 green, 3 cyan, 4 red, 5 magenta, 6 yellow, 7 white, 8 grey, 9 bright blue, A bright green, B bright cyan, C bright red, D bright magenta, E bright yellow, F bright white, and here's hoping we never see the fruits of your handiwork!

FASTER WINDOWS

23. If your PC is starting to get a bit sluggish and files seem to take longer to open, you may be able to pep up its performance with a few simple changes. Open the Control Panel and click on the System icon. Select the Performance tab and click on the File System button. On the hard-disk tab you will see a box marked Typical Role of this machine. Change the selection to Network Server. While you're there, make sure the slider marked Read Ahead Optimisation is fully turned up. Click on Apply and re-start your PC.

24. Does your Windows 9x desktop PC seem to be taking longer and longer to boot up? Here's a totally safe way to claw back several valuable seconds, and it's only seven mouse clicks away! Go to the Start menu and proceed thus: Settings > Control Panel > System, select the Performance tab, then the File System button and the Floppy Disk tab and deselect the item 'Search for new floppy disk drives each time your system starts'. The facility is meant for laptop machines, which use detachable external floppy drives. Since the drive on your desktop PC is permanently attached there is no need for Windows to look for a new one; this pointless activity wastes three or four seconds of boot-up time on some machines. Don't scoff, three seconds a day, say, 250 days a year comes to twelve and a half minutes a year; in only four and a bit years this simple tweak will have saved you almost one hour – use this time wisely!

25. If you have just bought a new application or peripheral it is tempting to rip off the packaging and load or install it straight away but before you do, just ask yourself when it was made, and how long that box has been sitting around in warehouses or on dealer's shelves. The chances are, whatever it is it will be at least several months old and in the time between it being manufactured and you loading it into your PC all sorts of problems may have come to light, and you could end up spending the rest of the holidays trying to get hold of helpline support. Save yourself the inevitable headaches by visiting the manufacturer's website first, and make sure there are no compatibility issues or bugs or updates needed that you should know about.

26. If you're a real speed freak and know your way around Windows 9x here's a way to shave a few more seconds off the time it takes to boot. Open Windows Explorer, right-click on the file 'Msdos.sys', which you'll find in the root of the C:\ drive, uncheck the 'Read Only' attribute then double-click the file icon and open it with Notepad. At the end of the section labelled [Options] add the following two lines:

BootDelay=0
Logo=0

Save and re-boot. These commands disable a two-second delay during boot up and disable the Windows 'splash screen'. The delay allows time to press F8, to get to the Safe Mode start. You still can, but now you've got to be quick (Win 95), or hold down the Ctrl key at boot up (Win 98).

INTERNET AND EMAIL

27. The right button on your mouse can do some interesting tricks when you're looking at Internet web pages. Click anywhere on the page and you'll see a number of options. The most useful one is to add the address of the current page to your favourite list. If you come across a background design, that you'd like to use as wallpaper on your desktop, right click on the pattern and choose the Set as Wallpaper option. Selecting Copy Background puts the image into the clipboard memory, so you can import it into a graphics program, or it can be filed away, as a .gif or .jpg image, in the file or folder of your choice, using the Save Background As… option.

28. If your phone is connected to a digital exchange and you have BT Call Waiting or Call Minder services you may experience problems with Internet connections. Windows 9x can automatically switch the Call Waiting bleeper off before you connect. Open Modems in Control Panel and select the General Tab. Click on Dialling Properties and check the box marked 'To Disable Call Waiting Dial' (or 'How I dial from this Location'). In the adjacent box enter # 43 # (hash 43 hash). You will have to switch Call Waiting back on again manually after you log off by dialling ★ 43 # (star 43 hash). Call Minder generates a 'stutter' dial tone to let you know you have a message waiting; this does not agree with a lot of modems, so before you go on-line pick up your messages by first dialling 1571.

29. One of the main complaints about the Internet is how long it sometimes takes to access and download pages. There's an easy way to speed things up and that is to load just text. Instead of all the pictures, graphics, advertising banners and sounds you will see just icons. If you want to see or hear an item just right click on the icon and you will get the option to load it. In Internet Explorer (version 5 onwards) go to Internet Options on the Tools menu click the Advanced tab, scroll down Multimedia and uncheck the appropriate boxes. A similar facility in Netscape Navigator is listed under Preferences on the Edit menu, click Advanced and uncheck the Automatically Load Images box.

30. There are probably at least one or two Internet websites that you visit frequently – search engines or a particular home page, etc. Rather than waste time opening your browser, manually selecting the address from the favourites list and making the connection, just create a simple keyboard short cut – it's easy! Pressing the keys will take you straight to your chosen website from within any application.

   On the Start menu click Favourites, right-click the site you are interested in then select Properties and the Internet Shortcut tab. In the Shortcut Key box you will see 'None', click in a cursor and type a single letter – choose one that relates to the site you can easily remember, such as 'Y' for Yahoo, etc. – the field will now display the assigned shortcut, i.e. 'Ctrl + Alt + Y'. Click OK and try it out. Internet Explorer opens automatically and takes you straight to the website. (If IE is not your chosen browser you will have to open it and manually add the website address to the Favourites list.)

31. Web pages can often be difficult to read especially if text colours clash with fancy backgrounds and patterns. On Microsoft Internet Explorer there's a very handy feature that will allow you to make quite significant changes to the way web pages are displayed, and in particular the colours used for website addresses that you have and haven't visited and the so-called 'hover' colour. The latter is the colour change that occurs when your mouse pointer passes over and highlights a web address. Open Explorer and on the View menu choose Internet Options, select the General tab and click the Colours button at the bottom of the window. To change a default click on the appropriate colour block and choose a new one from the palette that appears or create your own custom colour. A similar feature is available on Netscape Navigator on the Options menu under General Preferences.

32. These days creating your own web pages couldn't be simpler and you can let your imagination and artistic inclinations run wild. Unfortunately some web page designers, and that includes professionals who should know better, sometimes make a right hash of it when it comes to displaying text on web pages. Coloured or patterned backgrounds and excessively light or dark text can make reading difficult, impossible in some cases, but here's a quick and easy way to make the words stand out. Just press the Ctrl + Alt keys and all the text on display will be highlighted, making it much easier to read.

33. Heavy-duty Internet users, here's a way to save yourself several seconds a week by increasing the dialling speed of your PC and modem. It may not work with some modems or phone lines but it's worth a try. Go to Control Panel click on the Modem icon, then Properties and select the Connection tab and click on Advanced. In the Extra Settings field enter S11=50 then click OK. S11 determines the duration of each tone pulse in milliseconds, the second number specifies the gap between each tone, thus reducing the number to 45 say, makes it dial even faster, increasing the number slows it down. If the connection fails or becomes unreliable simply clear the Extra Settings field to return to the default values.

34. You can check up on your PC's connection speed to the Internet with a few simple clicks. Whilst on line a small double monitor icon appears in the

System Tray, next to the clock; if you place the mouse pointer over it you will see a summary of bytes sent and received and modem connection speed. Click on the icon and the disconnect dialogue box appears with the same information displayed. However, unless the modem has been properly configured the connection speed may appear impossibly high, at 115,200 bits/sec. This is the speed at which the PC is communicating with the modem, rather than the speed of data flowing down the telephone line. To remedy that you will need to program the modem with an AT command to display transfer speed in the dialogue box. Open Control Panel and double click on the Modem icon. Make sure your modem is highlighted on the General tab, select Properties, then the Connection tab and then the Advanced Button. In the field marked Extra settings enter one of the following commands – if one doesn't work try another. W2 (for modems with Rockwell chipsets), AT&F1 (3COM and USR models) or MR=2 (later Rockwell models and PCI cards). If you still see 115,200 bits/sec try your modem manual or visit the manufacturer's website and look for the Report DCE speed (Data Communication Equipment) command line.

35. One of the most annoying tricks websites pull is to open multiple browser windows and 'pop-ups' usually without so much as a by your leave. This can happen very quickly and in some cases they open faster than you can close them, or they open in 'Kiosk' mode, where there's no close or minimise icons to click on. The trick is to use the Windows shortcut Ctrl + W to close them quickly, one, by one. You could also use the Alt+F4 shortcut, but it's more of a stretch and there's the danger that if you get a bit careless you might shut another program down as well.

36. In the previous Tip we mentioned the dreaded Internet 'Kiosk Mode', where a website opens a browser window automatically but without any toolbars, menus, minimise or close buttons. In effect you are stuck with it, unless you know the Ctrl + W or Alt + F4 shortcut to get rid of it. Kiosk mode does have its uses however. For example, when you are using Internet Explorer to display web pages on a PC at an exhibition or AV presentation and you don't want all the toolbars and other gubbins taking up screen space. Here's how to force Internet Explorer into Kiosk mode. Go to Run on the Start menu and type 'iexplore –k' (without the quotes), followed by the address of the page or website you want to display. If you just type 'iexplore -k' it will open on your selected home page.

37. A lot of people are naturally concerned that private files on their Windows PCs could be opened or 'hacked' whilst they are connected to the Internet. In practice this is extremely unlikely; however, you can reassure yourself and make sure it won't happen by ensuring that no-one has enabled the facility that allows external access to your PC's hard drive. From the Start menu select Settings then Control Panel and double click on the Network icon. Now click on the File and Print Sharing button and make sure that the item 'I want to be able to give others access to my files' is unchecked.

38. It can be incredibly frustrating waiting for Internet pages to appear, especially at peak times. You may even start wondering if you are still connected, or maybe your browser program has frozen? Here's a quick and simple test; whilst on-line with your browser open go to Start > Programs > MSDOS, to open up a DOS window. At the flashing prompt type 'ping' (without the inverted commas) followed by the Internet site address, i.e., ping www.telegraph.co.uk This will call up the website four times and measure how long it takes to reply, in milliseconds (ms), showing minimum, maximum and average times. Anything under 200 ms is normal, any longer and your connection is slow or the Internet is very busy and you should try again later.

39. Here's a quick one for people who use Outlook Express to collect their email when away from home, on other people's PCs, Internet Café PCs or laptops. By default OE downloads messages from the server to the PC, which can be awkward if it's not your machine. To stop that happening go to Tools and then Accounts, highlight the account you're using and select Properties. Click on the Advanced tab and check the item 'Leave a copy of message on server'. Now you can read your messages when you are away, and when you get home you can download them onto your main PC.

40. This simple tweak can help reduce the time it takes for your PC to make a connection to your Internet Service Provider, but try this only if it's a stand-alone machine, i.e., not hooked up to a network. Open Dial Up Networking by going to Start > Programs > Accessories > Communications > Dial Up Networking. Right click on the icon for your ISP connection and select Properties and the Server Types tab. In Advanced Options uncheck 'Log on to Networks' and below that, under Allowed Networks make sure that only TCP/IP is checked. Click OK and give it a try; if all's well Internet Explorer (or your chosen browser) should log on and establish a connection a little faster than before. In the unlikely event that anything odd happens simply go back to Dial Up Networking and restore the default settings (i.e., Log on to Networks, NetBeui and IPX/SPX all checked).

41. On Internet Explorer it is possible to open a second smaller browser window by clicking on a link so you can still see, and quickly return to, the original page without reloading it. Just hold down the shift button before left clicking on the link. Here are some more IE keyboard shortcuts. Ctrl + D adds the current web page to your Favourite list. Ctrl + H opens the History folder, Ctrl + N opens a new browser window, Ctrl + W closes the active browser window and Ctrl + R reloads the page you are viewing.

42. If you are using Outlook Express and you receive and send a lot of email then your Inbox and Outbox folders could be swallowing up a lot of valuable hard disk space. Get into the habit of regularly 'compacting' the files, this can also make them small enough to backup to a floppy disk. Click and highlight the selected Inbox or Outbox folder icon then go to the File menu, select Folder and Compact Folder.

43. This handy little trick can help make sending emails easier. It will put a new icon on your Start menu. When you click on it a blank email message window opens from where you can compose and send an email, without waiting for Outlook Express to open. Move your mouse pointer to the Start button, right-click on it and select Explore from the menu that appears. When the Explorer window opens, right-click in an empty spot in the right-hand pane and select New, then Shortcut. The Create Shortcut dialogue box should appear; under Command Line type in 'mailto:' (leaving off the quotation marks) then click on Next. Now you can give your shortcut a name, clear the highlighted default name and type in something like 'email' or 'messend', and select close. Now go to the Start menu and try out your new high-speed message system.

44. Using the same basic procedure you can create a personalised message window for anyone that you frequently send emails to, with their address automatically inserted. As before, right-click into an empty part of the desktop, select New and then Shortcut from the menu. In the window that appears, in the Command Line field, type mailto:friendsname@

freebienet.com, where the part after mailto: is the recipient's email address. Click Next, give your new Shortcut a name then click Finish.

45. Here's a way to turn your Internet Explorer/Outlook Express email Address Book into a text file that can read by a word processor, or imported into other email programs. Open Address Book and on the File menu select Export, then Address Book. In the dialogue box that appears select 'Text File (comma separated values)' and click the Export button. Type in the path (where you want the file to be stored) and give the file a name, for example: C:\my documents\adbook.txt. Select Next, check the items you wish to export and click Finish.

46. Did you know that in Outlook Express (v5 onwards) you can attach a sound file to an email that will play automatically as soon as it is opened on the recipient's computer? You can specify how many times it's played, or even make it play continuously, if you really want to annoy someone, the possibilities – for good and mischief – are endless.

First record your sound as a *.wav file using Windows Sound Recorder (Start > Programs> Accessories > Entertainment); most PCs these days have a microphone input. Create your message as usual in the New Message window, on the Format menu make sure Rich Text (HTML) is checked, click anywhere in the message window and go to Background on the Format menu, select Sound and use the Browse button to locate your sound file, set the number of plays, click OK and send your message.

47. If you receive a lot of messages on the same topic, or from the same sender (maybe you print out a lot of emails) then there is a very convenient but little-known feature in Outlook Express that allows you to combine messages into one document, for reading or printing. Open the mailbox containing the messages you want to combine and highlight them by holding down the Ctrl key and clicking on each one in turn. Now go to the Messsage menu and select Combine and Decode. You will be asked if you want to change the order of the messages, if not click OK and the new combined document will be created, use SaveAs on the file menu to save it as a new document.

48. Here is a way to send a photograph with an email, by inserting it into the actual message. This works only when your email client program – we'll assume you are using Outlook or Outlook Express – is set to send HTML

(Hypertext mark-up language) and the person you are sending it to can receive HTML messages. Click on the New Message icon, go to the Format drop-down menu and make sure 'Rich Text (HTML)' is selected. Now all you have to do is compose your message as normal and when you come to the point where you want the picture to go click on the Insert Picture icon (it looks like a postcard) then use the Browse button to locate the image file. It will appear in the message window, as the recipient will see it. Finish your message and send it as normal.

49. If you are using Internet Explorer (v5 onwards) and you haven't tried Internet radio yet, there's a radio tuner facility hidden away inside your browser. To enable it click on Tools > Internet Options and select the Advanced tab. Scroll down the list to the Multimedia heading and check the item 'Always Show Internet Explorer Radio Bar'. Click OK and exit the dialogue box. Now right click into an empty area of the toolbar and select Radio from the drop-down menu. A new toolbar appears, click on Radio Stations and Radio Station Guide, which will take you to the Windows Media radio tuner home page. From there you can select a list of stations according to style, content, language, etc. This will either take you to the station's home page, and a live 'listen' button, which lets you hear what's going on through Windows Media Player (be patient, it can take a few seconds before you hear anything, as the data has to be 'buffered' in the PC's memory to prevent breaks in sound caused by heavy traffic on the Internet). Some stations may require you to have special player software but there is usually a link on the page to the appropriate download website.

50. Some modems just won't play ball and stubbornly refuse to work with Windows or do strange things, like randomly dropping the line, or operating at ridiculously low data rates. If yours is playing up it's worth trying a standard Windows modem driver. Open Control Panel and click on Add/Remove Hardware, click Next until you get to the screen that asks you if you want Windows to look for new devices, select No, on the 'Hardware Types' list double-click the Modem icon, check 'Don't detect my modem...' and click Next. Make sure 'Standard Modem Types' is highlighted under 'Manufacturers'. In the right pane select 'Standard 56000bps V90' or the option that best matches your modem, click Next and continue to the end. To revert to your previous custom driver remove the Standard Modem entry in Device Manager (right-click My Computer and select Properties) reboot and Windows will detect your modem and reinstall the original driver (have your driver disk to hand).

51. Here's an interesting freeware (to home users) utility that claims to be able to spot and zap those incredibly annoying 'pop-up' ads that appear whilst you are browsing web pages. Adsubtract also blocks cookies and in theory will speed up download times having removed all of the clutter. If you want to give it a try pay a visit to: http://www.adsubtract.com/downloads.html

52. Are there any adware or spyware programs lurking on your PC? One easy way to find out is with a program called Ad-Aware. It's freeware and the file is around 860kB in size so it should only take a few minutes to download. Once installed it is very simple to use and normally takes just a couple of minutes to scan a 10Gb hard disk drive. If it finds any adware files it offers to safely isolate and delete them. Ad-Aware is routinely featured on PC magazine cover-mount disks but I recommend that you use the latest version (v5.5), which is now available from: http://www.lavasoftusa.com/

53. If you are going to be out of the office for a few hours or the whole day you can easily let anyone sending you emails know that they may not get a reply straight away. Outlook Express has the equivalent of an email answering machine facility built in that will automatically reply to any incoming email messages. (Note that the PC and Outlook Express both have to be running and on-line or connected to a network.)

Start by creating the message that you want anyone sending you an email to receive, something along the lines 'Sorry I'll be away until…'. To do that click on New Mail, type in the text of your message then go to the File menu and use Save As to name and save the message in a location of your choosing. Next go to Tools > Message Rules > Mail and click the New button. In the first box select 'For All Messages', in the second box choose 'Reply With Message' and in the third box click on the underlined Message and direct it to your reply email. Click OK and it's done.

54. This tip is for all Internet nosey parkers and trivia fans. If you've ever wondered what's going on behind the scenes at your favourite website a visit to www.netcraft.com will reveal all. Simply type in the address of the site you are interested in and click Search. Netcraft then carries out an in-depth survey of the workings of the site and will report back a few seconds later with information about the server and its operating system and, if available, details of when it was installed, how long it has been running, the operator, its numeric IP address and any other little titbits it can uncover.

55. You don't have to put up with the default toolbar in Outlook Express. You can add or remove icons by right-clicking into an empty area of the toolbar and selecting Customise. Scroll down the list in the left-hand pane (Available Toolbar Buttons), select one that you want to use and click Add. Two that I find very useful are Mark Read and Preview Pane. The latter toggles the Preview Pane on and off; I have it disabled by default (the option is on the View menu, under Layout) as it clutters the desktop and can activate email viruses like Nimda, but it's useful to have occasionally, when working through long lists of messages.

56. If you use Outlook Express and send your emails in plain text then you can make them much easier for others to read by changing the line length, which is set by default to 76 characters. To do that go to the Tools menu and select Options and then the Send tab. Click the Plain Text Settings button and use the down arrow to change the 'Automatically wrap text at' value to 65. If OE is set to send text as Rich Text or HTML there's no need to worry, as it will automatically wrap to fit the recipient's message window.

57. Search engines are not noted for having a sense of humour but you can brighten up your Internet exploration if you use Google (www.google.com) by changing the language. The next time you visit Google – and make it soon, it's still the best search engine around – click on the Preferences, next to the Search Field, then click the down arrow next to Interface Language. Try Hacker, it's surprisingly easy to read after a while, and Bork bork bork! might amuse anyone of a Swedish disposition but our favourite has to be Elmer Fudd. Whilst you are there you might also want to increase the number of displayed results from the default setting of 10 to 20, to speed things up a bit. Now where are awl wose wascally web pwages...?

58. Outlook Express, like most Windows programs, is a lot easier to use if you remember a few keyboard shortcuts. For example Ctrl + P prints the currently displayed message and you can view the Properties of a message (the identity of the sender, its size and even the route it took to get to you) by highlighting it and pressing Alt + Enter. There's a full list of keyboard shortcuts in OE Help (select the Index tab and type 'short').

59. Just how good is your Internet connection? There are lots of websites that can test your connection speed; however, each can give you only a snapshot of what is happening at the time. Moreover, speed will vary according to various other factors, including the geographical location of the server doing the test. For a more accurate picture you should try several sites – see below – at different times of day and average out the results. Remember, just because you have a 56kbps modem it is very unlikely you will achieve anything like that speed; in real world conditions you are more likely to get between 30 and 40kbps.

General test sites

http://bandwidthplace.com/speedtest/
http://promos.mcafee.com/speedometer/
http://www.aitsoft.com/Services/speedtest.asp
http://www.cablemusic.com/testSpeed.asp?
http://home.cfl.rr.com/eaa/Bandwidth.htm

For ISDN and ADSL connections

http://speedtest.inch.com/

60. If you are taking a laptop, organiser or mobile phone with email access on a trip create a small document file containing important numbers, names and contacts that might come in useful in case of an emergency, such as your passport number and local telephone numbers for your insurance company, etc. You can disguise or hide the numbers in an email or letter, so that no one else can understand them. Give the file an innocuous name – e.g., 'trav126.txt' – and hide it in an unrelated folder. Before you leave send the file to yourself in the form of an email, so you can access it from an Internet café for instance, using an email web server (e.g., www.mail2web.com) if your equipment is lost or stolen.

61. Here's a quick timesaving tip for advanced users. This simple Registry hack disables the Outlook Express 'Splash Screen' that appears every time you start the program. OE will then open more or less instantly. Don't forget, before you tinker around with the Registry always make a backup!

Open Regedit then go to: HKEY_CURRENT_USER \ Identities

For OE 5 go below this to { — ABC123XYZ..... long alphanumeric code } \Software \ Microsoft \ Outlook Express \ 5.0. Right click into the right-hand pane and select New > DWORD, rename the DWORD 'NoSplash' (without the inverted commas) and give it a Value of 1. Close Regedit and try it out, now all you have to do is think what you'll do with all the time you saved...

62. If you are using an older version of Internet Explorer and you are happy with it just make sure you are fully up to date with all of the latest security patches and updates at http://www.microsoft.com/windows/ie/default.asp

Since version 5 has been around for a while there are lots of extras and add-ons, which can be used to improve its functionality and appearance. A good place to start is the Microsoft website, which has a useful selection of free-to-download accessories at the following locations:

http://www.microsoft.com/windows/ie/previous/webaccess/ie5wa.asp
http://www.microsoft.com/windows/ie/previous/webaccess/default.asp

63. There are plenty of family-friendly web-filtering programs on the market but before you rush out and buy a commercial package have a look at this excellent freeware offering called We-Blocker. It's highly configurable and allows concerned parents to monitor and control their children's surfing activities, and share filtering data with other users. The file is around 2.5Mb and it can be downloaded from:

http://www.we-blocker.com/

64. Here are a couple of quick tips for Google fans. You can speed up your web searches by installing the Google Toolbar (click link on www.google.com); this puts a toolbar with a search entry field and button into your browser window so there's no need to go to the Google home page every time you want to look for something. Tip 2, Google automatically provides a dictionary definition for any word entered in the search window, simply click on the word's underlined link after 'Searched the web for', just below the Google logo.

65. Here's yet another Google tip, this time for anyone who has spent ages trying to find something on the massive Microsoft website. Google has developed a search engine specifically for searching Microsoft.com, using the usual fast and friendly Google interface. The address is http://www.google.com/microsoft.html, and don't forget to add it to your Favourites menu.

SECURITY

66. Sometimes you might want to make certain files on your computer inaccessible, especially if you share your PC with others. There are plenty of password protection and encryption programs available for download, but sometimes the simplest solutions are the best. One easy way to protect a sensitive file is to rename it, and bury it deep inside Windows, or another unrelated application. Simply open Windows Explorer, right-click on the file and give it a new name with a fictitious three-letter extension – your initials perhaps – then drag and drop it into a folder. Make sure you remember where you put it and check that you're not using a genuine file type with the extension search engine at: http://extsearch.com/

FATTER AND FASTER FILES

67. Every so often you may want to transfer files between PCs on floppy disk. It's no problem, providing the file is no larger than 1.4Mb. If it is you could compress the data, or use multiple floppies but there's another option, compress the disk. Windows 95 (and 98) has a utility called DriveSpace. It is intended to increase the capacity of hard disk drives, but it works just as well with floppies, almost doubling their capacity, to around 2.6Mb. Insert a clean disk into drive A: and from the Start Menu click on Programs, then Accessories then System Tools and open DriveSpace. Click on the disk icon or choose compress from the File menu and follow the instructions.

68. If you need to make a copy of a floppy disk quickly – maybe a colleague needs to see some files you've been working on – then Windows can help. From your desktop or the Start Button open My Computer then right-click on the floppy disk icon and select Copy Disk on the menu. Windows then reads the entire contents of the disk into the PC's memory; a bar graph shows how the copy process is progressing. When the indicator reaches half way, Copy Disk will ask you to remove the original disk and load a blank formatted floppy. Make sure there's nothing on it or it may be overwritten, click OK and the information is read back to the second disk.

69. Send To is one of the most useful facilities in Windows Explorer. By right clicking on a file, the Send To option will instantly copy the file to another folder, a floppy disk or the clipboard, but it can do many more things besides. You can add any application or drive destination to the Send To list and save yourself a lot of time moving files and opening applications.

Unfortunately, the default locations for Send To are a bit limited, but there's a way around that. Send To Toys is an invaluable little utility that lets you add to (and remove) items on the Send To list with a single click. It's freeware and compatible with all flavours of Windows 9x, 2000 and XP and the download is only 400Kb. The link to the download can be found at: http://www.gabrieleponti.com/software/

Go to the Start menu then Programs and open Windows Explorer. Scroll down the list to the Windows folder, open it, locate and double click on Send To. Now go up to File on the menu bar, select New, then Shortcut and use Browse to find the application you are interested in. Open the folder and look for the relevant *.exe file, single click to highlight and select Open. You will be asked to give the program a name – if you don't want to use the default – then click Next and Finish and the item is added to the Send To list.

PRINTER PROBLEMS

70. Having problems with your printer? You may be surprised to know Windows 95 comes with a sophisticated printer troubleshooting program. It's on the CD-ROM and you can find it with Windows Explorer. Click on the D: drive icon, then open the Other folder and inside you'll find a folder called Misc. Open that and then the Epts (enhanced printer troubleshooter). Click on epts.exe and the program starts, first analysing your printer set-up. It then asks a series of questions and suggests remedies to help you solve the problem. The troubleshooter is built into Windows 98; just open Windows Help and type Troubleshooting into the Index Windows and select Printers from the list.

71. If you have a paper jam do not force it. Always try to remove the blockage in the normal direction of travel, if it tears make sure all of the fragments are removed. If you can't clear the paper path refer to the manual. Store paper flat in the original packaging, always fan it before loading to free up the sheets and stop them sticking together. If the paper hopper is partially full always load it so the old paper is used first. Always check to make sure the paper you are using is within the printer's handling limits. Keep printers well away from radiators and out of strong sunlight – especially laser printers – as this can affect print quality.

72. If you regularly need to switch between two settings on your printer (i.e., portrait and landscape mode, etc.) when printing from different applications, you can avoid a lot of messing around by making Windows believe you have two or more printers. Open the Printers folder in My Computer and click on Add New Printer and follow through the installation procedure for your existing printer. At the point when Windows asks the printer's name, change to default, Printer 2 for example. When the setup is complete right-click on the new printer icon, select Properties and change the settings as required. Now all you have to do is select the new printer in your application's Printer Setup dialogue box, or simply drag and drop the file onto the Printer 2 icon.

73. Here's a way to squeeze a little extra speed out of most printers. By default Windows is set to spool print jobs. That basically means the data to be printed is first written to a temporary file, which allows you and the PC to get on with other jobs, whilst the printer is working. If you turn off the Print Spooler you should find print jobs take less time to complete. The option can be found by right-clicking your printer icon from the Printers Folder in My Computer or Start > Settings. Select Properties, then the Details tab and click on the Spool Settings button. Click 'Print Directly To Printer' then OK. The only disadvantage is that on long print jobs you may see the busy icon in your application more often than usual. Be warned that it doesn't work on all systems and all printers so try it on a test document first. Time a print job before and after switching off the spooler and if you encounter problems click the Restore Defaults button in the print spooler dialogue window.

74. If you have a partially filled cartridge that won't print, or the text/image is streaked or fading from top to bottom there's a good chance that the print head is partially or fully blocked by dried ink. If it won't respond to your printer's cleaning routine here's something to try, you've got nothing to lose! Find a bowl or shallow container and fill it to a depth of a few centimetres with a 50/50 mixture of very hot water and bleach or ammonia. Immerse the print head – the part where ink comes out – into the solution and leave it for a couple of minutes. If the dried ink dissolves you'll see it start to flow in the water. Dry it off carefully with a soft, lint-free cloth and try it out.

COMFORT AND SAFETY

75. Computers can seriously damage your health! Inappropriate seating is a major contributing factor to back pain. If you are going to be seated in front of your PC for more than an hour or so each day get a proper chair. Purpose-designed office chairs, with adjustable height and back support are ideal, and they're not expensive.

76. Make sure your display screen is at the most comfortable height – e.g., eye-level and that the brightness and contrast are properly adjusted. If you get a lot of reflections on the screen, from bright lights or windows, a clip-on anti-glare screen should help. Don't sit staring at the screen for hours on end without a break. Stand up from time to time, walk around, maybe do some stretching exercises.

77. Keyboards can cause a lot of problems, especially the cheap ones that come with a lot of PCs these days. Fast typists and those used to manual typewriters can find the short, sharp keystrokes of a PC keyboard uncomfortable, it can even lead to painful repetitive strain injury or RSI. If you're going to be doing a lot of typing think about buying an ergonomically shaped keyboard. Wrist support pads can help relieve the strain, though if problems persist you should consult your GP.

78. If you have poor or failing eyesight computer display screens can be difficult to read. If you find the icons and printing underneath too small to read easily try the 'large' and 'extra large' colour schemes in Display Properties. They're located on the Appearances Tab that you can find by double clicking on the Display icon in Control Panel. While you are there select the Settings tab and try the 'Larger Fonts' size. You may also find it helpful to change the Desktop Area slider to a lower value, especially if it has been set to a high resolution figure (1024 x 768 pixels, for example) and you are viewing it on a 14- or 15-inch monitor. Most word-processor packages have a 'zoom' facility, to enlarge the size of the text display.

A similar set of options is available from the Accessibility Options icon in Control Panel. Double click the icon to open the window. Select the Display tab, then Settings. The next set of options will enlarge the display, with normal black on white text, or the whole thing can be reversed, with white on black characters. Click on display, then check the Use High Contrast box and confirm the changes by clicking the Apply button. Be patient, it takes a few seconds for the display to change.

79. You can easily change the font and size of the typeface used by Windows Explorer and icon labelling. It's worth trying if you find it difficult to read, you're using an unusually large or small monitor, or you're simply bored with the default typeface. Right click your mouse on an empty space on the desktop and select Properties, when the Display window appears click on the Appearance tab. In the drop-down menu marked Item, choose Icon. You will then be able to select a new typeface from the Font menu.

80. If your vision is impaired and you are having problems reading web pages there are a number of things you can do to improve legibility. First try increasing the text size of your browser's display. In Internet Explorer this can be found on the View menu. Switching off coloured backgrounds makes a big difference (even if you have normal sight...), this option is on the IE Tools menu, select Internet Options, then the General tab and click the Accessibility button. You can reduce the clutter on web pages by disabling pictures and graphics which is controlled from the Advanced Tab in Internet Options. Scroll down the list to Multimedia and uncheck 'Show Pictures'. Finally, a lot of web pages have Text-Only versions and these are usually much easier to read.

UTILITIES AND TOOLS

81. System Monitor allows you to check visually the data throughput of an external modem in real time. It can be found by clicking the Start button, then Accessories and System Tools. Open System Monitor and click on the Edit menu then Add Item. Select Dial Up Adapter from the list in the Category Window and Bytes Received/Second and Bytes Transmitted/Second in the Item Window, then OK. (Note, System Monitor is not installed by default so you may have to load it from your Windows CD-ROM using Add/Remove Programs in Control Panel.)

82. How well do you know your Windows 98 PC? Tucked away inside your machine is a complete history of its inner workings, charting system settings and changes to the hardware and software configuration. It's useful to have a permanent record of this information, made when your PC is working normally. There are some interesting facts and figures in amongst the mass of gobbledegook and if at some stage something goes wrong, it could help you or a PC savvy friend to track down the problem more easily. To produce such a file go to Start > Programs > Accessories > System Tools > System Information. On the File menu select Export, give the file a name – something along the lines 'mypc.txt' – choose a location and click Save. You could print it out but be warned that it can run to more than 100 pages!

83. If you keep a lot of images on your Windows 95/98 PC it can be very useful to see what is stored in folders without opening a paint program and sifting through the files manually. Windows Explorer has a well-hidden utility for generating thumbnail views of picture files. It is disabled by default, probably because it slows Explorer down, but you can enable it selectively, so it works only on folders containing image files. Here's what you do. Open Windows Explorer and right click on the folder you wish to view. From the drop-down menu that appears select Properties and the General tab. Check the item 'Enable thumbnail view' and click Apply, then OK. Go to the View menu and click Refresh, and a new item 'Thumbnails' should appear above Large Icons on both the View menu and the drop-down menu next to the Views icon on the Toolbar. Select it and the display will change to a screen full of mini preview pictures.

84. Hardware Info carries out a comprehensive check on driver files and the hardware attached to the machine, flagging up potential problems with colour-coded highlights. Error information is displayed in red, and warnings in blue. To start Hardware Info go to Run on the Start menu and type 'hwinfo /ui' (omitting the inverted commas of course), and then click OK. It takes only a few seconds after which the report appears. Check through the report looking for any red or blue highlights, which may indicate trouble, or potential trouble, and require further investigation. If you know a thing or two about PCs you may want to have a look at the alternative reports on the View menu. If your PC and hardware is behaving normally it's probably a good idea to leave well alone, but take note of any warnings and save your Hwinfo file for future reference or to show to an engineer.

85. The Version Conflict Manager Utility or VCMUI should be of interest to anyone who routinely updates their software applications. This can cause problems when files from older or newer versions of a program conflict with one another. If you've had difficulty with a recent update VCMUI should track down the offending files and might even provide a solution. It can also highlight potential conflicts before they've had a chance to cause problems. To give your PC's software a quick health check go to Run on the Start menu and type 'VCMUI', without the quotes of course. All being well you'll see an empty dialogue box, indicating that your applications are conflict-free; if not just follow the instructions.

86. System File Checker can help engineers and knowledgeable users to track down and automatically correct common problems. It's worth running the SFC every now and again, especially on well-used machines, and you never know, it may help to resolve a long-running problem. However, unless you know what you are doing it is a good idea to leave the settings on their defaults. To start the program go to Run on the Start menu and type 'sfc.exe' and click Start to begin the checking routine.

87. CheckLinks can be found on the Windows 98 CD-ROM and its job is to weed out shortcuts and Start menu items that no longer do anything. It's not going to save you much disk space but 'broken links' can sometimes cause problems and point to programs that you no longer need or use. The Link Check Wizard can be found by going to the Tools folder then Reskit and Desktop. Click on the chklnks.exe icon and follow the instructions. If you like you can copy and paste chklnk.exe to your hard drive, and include it with your regular hard disk maintenance routines.

88. Sometimes you just want to switch off and go but Windows won't let you and insists that you go through the tiresome shut-down ritual. There is an easier way. This simple little tip creates a shutdown shortcut; one click is all it takes to exit Windows 9x cleanly and safely. Start by right clicking on the desktop and select New then Shortcut. In the command line type the following (minus the quotes) 'C:\WINDOWS\RUNDLL32.EXE User,ExitWindows', then click Next, give the shortcut a name, something like 'Wingo', then click Finish and it's done.

89. How many applications are running on your PC right now? It's easy to lose track and if your system's resources fall to dangerously low levels Windows will crash, often without warning. Windows 9x and ME has a built-in monitoring utility but it's not enabled by default. There are two ways to get to it, via Start > Programs> Accessories > System Tools, or simply type 'RSRCMTR' into Run on the Start menu. This will put a little bargraph into the System Tray (next to the clock). If it shows two or more green bars you should be okay; double click the icon for more detailed information. It's well worth having this on display all of the time; to do that open the Start Up folder (Start > Programs) then go to Start > Programs > Accessories > System Tools, hold down the Ctrl key and drag the Resource meter icon into the Start Up folder and it will open automatically every time your PC boots up. If by any chance you can't see Resource Meter in System tools go to Add/Remove Programs in Control Panel and select the Windows Setup tab, double click System Tools, check the item System Resource Meter, click OK and follow the on-screen prompts.

90. Adding an extra cooling fan is one way to stop your PC overheating in the hot weather, but how can you tell if your computer is suffering? It just so happens that many recent PC motherboards have built-in temperature sensors that keep a running check on vital components. Motherboard Monitor is a neat freeware utility that puts that information on the screen, so you can see for yourself what's going on. Not all motherboards are supported, but the program will check your PC for compatibility before it runs. The file is 1.5Mb and it can be downloaded from: http://mbm.livewiredev.com/

91. Whether you're going out for lunch or just popping out for a few minutes your PC is vulnerable to intrusion. Of course you could switch it off and there are plenty of programs that will password protect your PC and prevent Windows from loading or you could invoke password protection on a screensaver but all that takes time or they can be easily hacked. Quick Hide is a useful little freeware program that locks the PC when it is running with a simple keyboard shortcut. It can also be set to hide the current application, the Taskbar and desktop icons, which can be unlocked only with a password. The download zip file is under 500kb in size and it's available from: http://www.cronosoft.com/

92. Drive Rescue is a powerful file recovery utility that could save your bacon one day! If you've ever deleted a file by accident Drive Rescue is your best chance of getting some or all of it back, it even works on removable media and memory cards. The zip file is 1.2Mb, it runs on all versions of Windows and it can be downloaded from: http://home.arcor.de/christian_grau/rescue/

93. Whilst the Windows Screen Magnifier is a very useful tool for those who need an enlarged display all the time it's sometimes handy to be able to view just a small portion of the screen. A simple freeware utility called Dragnifier changes your mouse cursor into a virtual magnifying glass. It's highly customisable with variable sized 'glass' and magnification level and a measuring reticule. The download file is only around 130k and it's free (though the author says all contributions gratefully received…). For more details and a link to the self-extracting zip file go to: http://www.halley.cc/stuff/

SCREEN GEMS

94. If you want to launch a screen-saver quickly – maybe you're going out to lunch or want to prevent others from seeing what's on your screen – open Windows Explorer, go to the Windows folder and open the System file. There you will find all the Windows screen-saver files. They're easy to spot as they have monitor-shaped icons and end with the file extension *.scr. Right click on the icon, select 'Send To' then 'Desktop as Shortcut', when you want to start it in a hurry just double click on the desktop icon.

95. If you're bored with the standard Windows 98 and ME colours for title bars on windows and message boxes here's a quick way to cheer them up with a very snazzy 'gradient' colour, which changes gradually from one colour to another. This trick works best if your PC is set to True Colour or High Colour. To check right click on an empty part of the desktop, select Properties from the menu and click the Settings tab. To create your colour gradient stay with Display Properties and select the Appearance tab. Click on the Active Window title bar in the display window then click on Colour; a palette of 12 colours appears with the facility to create a colour of your choice by selecting the 'Other' button. Now click on Colour 2 and select a second colour, the effect is immediately displayed. Have fun, experiment with some bright and outrageous shades; it can really brighten up your desktop!

96. Newcomers to Windows often find the scroll bars at the side and bottom of word processors and spreadsheets screens quite difficult to use. The bars are narrow and the slider can be hard to control, until you get used to it. It's easy to change the size of the bars; even seasoned users may prefer to make them a little wider. To make the change go to Control Panel, click on the Display icon and select the Appearance tab. Click in the middle of the scroll bar shown in the 'Active Window', in the display. The word 'Scrollbar' should appear in the box below marked Item, along with a pair of up/down arrows and the default setting of 16. Try 20 or 25 but if you want to see something really funny whizz it up to the maximum of 100!

97. Create your own personal screensaver. If you have the OSR2 release of Windows 95 or Windows 98 onwards click on the Start button, go to Settings, then Control Panel and double click on the Display icon. Select the Screensaver tab and scroll down the list until you come to '3D Text'. Highlight the entry and click on the Settings button. You can enter your name or a message – up to 16 characters and spaces long – in the text field, which will bounce or wobble around the screen, or you can choose an animated digital clock display (click the time button). Click on the Texture buttons and try some of the *.bmp files in the Windows folder. This screensaver also contains an 'Easter egg', a hidden novelty feature planted by the programmers. Type the word 'Volcano' into the text field, click OK and see what happens…

98. A pound to a penny says your Windows 95/98 Taskbar is still in its default position at the bottom of the screen, taking up valuable screen space. Maybe you've enabled the Hide Taskbar facility (Start > Settings Taskbar & Start menu) so it doesn't take up any room when you are working, but it still pops into view every so often when your mouse strays close to the bottom of the screen. So why not move it? The most logical place has to be the right or left side of your screen. The right-hand side in particular is often a 'dead' area in programs like word processors and since a VDU screen is over 30% wider than it is tall you can afford to lose a little room at the side. To move the Taskbar simply put the mouse pointer into an empty area of the Taskbar, right click and hold and drag it to its new location. You can enable Auto Hide, or better still, leave it on show and more accessible, then re-size your application to fit, so that it doesn't obscure scroll bars. Most Windows programs will 'remember' a new layout whenever they are opened.

99. It's all very well your PC being able to process over 16 million colours but can you see them all on your monitor screen? This simple little freeware monitor test program will help you find out and adjust your settings to produce the best possible picture. The self-extracting 'zip' file is only 278Kb and should take only a couple of minutes to download from: http://www. monitortest.net/monitortest.html

100. When you see a picture displayed on your monitor how big is it and what size will it be when it's printed out? Screen Ruler is a brilliant little freeware program that superimposes a ruler on your screen. You can move the ruler around the screen and make it longer or shorter with the mouse; a right-click menu sets the scale and units (pixels, inches, centimetres or picas) and flips between horizontal or vertical layout. The download zip file is only 143kb and it can be downloaded from: http://www.spadixbd.com/freetools/jruler.zip

101. Whilst it's easy enough to remove red-eye in a digital image, it makes sense to avoid it happening in the first place. You can't do much about the position of the flashgun on most compact cameras but a lot of models nowadays have a red-eye reduction mode. This is usually a bright light or weak 'pre-flash' before the main flash that reduces the size of the subject's pupils. If your camera hasn't got this facility you could try asking the subject to look at a bright light, just before you take the picture. Alternatively try covering the flashgun with a paper tissue or handkerchief, which has the effect of diffusing the flash.

102. If you have a scanner here's a quick, simple and very cheap trick that might help to improve picture quality, especially if it's a budget model with only rudimentary scan controls. Try this – place a sheet of black paper or card behind the picture or image that you are scanning. The card will cut down reflections and glare from the normally white backing pad, which can result in better contrast, crisper colours and more accurate mid-tones.

103. If your screen resolution is set to 1024 x 768, or higher, you may find your desktop icons are a bit on the small side and any you've made from pictures may look indistinct. You can change the size of icons (make them smaller as well as bigger) by right-clicking into an empty area of the desktop, select Properties then the Appearance tab. In the 'Item' drop-down menu select Icon and in the Size box increase or decrease the value as necessary.

SOUNDS INTERESTING

104. If you're bored with the cheesy tunes, 'pings' and 'ta-da' Windows sounds create your own from snippets of audio CDs, played in the CD-ROM drive. Load the CD and open the Sound Recorder by clicking on Start then Programs, Accessories and Multimedia (or Entertainment in Windows 98). Play the CD (the Audio CD player is also in Accessories > Multimedia/Entertainment), and click on the Sound Recorder red record button. You may need to adjust the level or enable the input from the CD player from Volume Control on the View menu on CD Player. Sound Recorder can also add special effects (echo, play backwards, change speed), and edit the sound (Delete Before/After on the edit menu). When you are happy with it, give it a name and save it in the Media folder in Windows. It can then be easily accessed from the Sounds utility in Control Panel and assigned to an event of your choice. Remember, no public performances if you're recording Copyright material!

105. Why not create your own sounds? All you need is a microphone; plug it into the 'mic' jack socket on the PC's sound card or audio input. It should be on the back of your PC, close to the speaker plug. Find the sound recorder utility, it's in the Multimedia folder in the Accessories directory. It's easy to use, just like an ordinary tape recorder; full instructions are in the associated help file. When you've recorded your sound give it a name. From the File menu choose 'Save As' and put it in the Media directory in the Windows folder, then go back to the Sounds icon in Control Panel and assign it to the event of your choice.

106. You will often find that you want to change the volume of your PC's sound system, however, the volume control is not very accessible on a standard Windows installation. Normally most users get to it via the View menu option in CD Player (Start – Programs – Accessories – Multimedia – CD Player – View – Volume Control) but there's a quicker way, and you can have it permanently on the taskbar if you so wish. From the Start menu click on Settings, then Control Panel and the Multimedia icon. Click on it and select the Audio tab. About halfway down there's a small box marked Show Volume Control on the Taskbar. Check the box and it's done. On the far left side of the taskbar you will see a small loudspeaker symbol; when you click on it a volume slider and mute switch will appear on the screen.

107. If you're in the habit of playing audio CDs on your PC it's a good idea to put the CD Player on the Start menu. From the Start menu click on Settings then Taskbar and select the Start Menu Programs tab. Click on the Add then Browse buttons and look for the Windows folder. Double click on it to open it up then move the horizontal slider along until the CD Player icon appears. Highlight it, click open, then next and select the Start Menu folder at the top of the file tree. To complete click next and then Finish.

108. Your multimedia PC has a sound system that is capable of hi-fi performance but you're never going to realise anything like the full sonic potential of audio CDs and games with those speakers. The speakers supplied with most PCs have the acoustic properties of baked bean tins. If you've got a redundant hi-fi system or some half-decent speakers lying around, try connecting them to your PC and hear the difference! The soundcards used on most PCs have an amplified output and can drive speakers directly. Suitable leads are available from electrical accessory dealers. Make sure the speakers are at least a foot away from the monitor screen, otherwise the speaker magnets may cause colour staining on the display.

109. Windows 98 and ME have a little-known speaker configuration utility that allows you to tailor the sound of your PC according to the size and type of speakers. Go to Start > Settings > Control Panel and select Multimedia, make sure the Audio tab is selected and click the Advanced Properties button. On the Speakers page Desktop Stereo Speakers will probably be selected, but it's surprising how many laptops have that setting too. Try some of the other options – you may have to reboot for any changes to take effect – and the differences can be quite small but it's well worth trying. Whilst you are at it you may want to look at the Performance tab and if your PC is a relatively speedy model with a plenty of RAM, move the two sliders to the maximum setting.

110. To play .wav sounds and music through the built-in loudspeaker of your PC or laptop you will need a little piece of freebie software from Microsoft called Speak.exe. There's a chance it is already on your PC. Use the Find utility on the Start menu to check, otherwise you can download it from one of scores of Internet websites, or direct from Microsoft's own file library:

http://support.microsoft.com/download/support/mslfiles/Speak.exe

Next, go to Add New Hardware in Control panel, double click Add, then Next, followed by No, then Next and in the Hardware Types box select Sound Video & Game Controller. Click Next again and Have Disk. Use Browse to find your copy of Speak.exe and click OK. Select Sound Driver for PC Speaker and click OK, then Finish and when prompted re-start the PC. You will find the controls for the PC speaker in Multimedia on the Control Panel; on the Devices tab click the Audio Devices branch and Audio for Sound Driver for PC speaker and then Settings. On Windows 98 you'll find it on the Advanced tab.

111. Here's a nifty freeware program that turns sounds on your PC into visual displays. Although the Sound Frequency Analyser download is only 31k this powerful little utility shows both the amplitude of sounds passing through your PC as a constantly changing waveform and as a colourful Fourier Transform, which represents the spectrum of the frequencies contained in the sound. Even if you're not interested in the science and mathematics of sound analysis it's fascinating to watch the patterns on your PC screen. Sound Frequency Analyser is a zip file and it can be downloaded from: http://www.relisoft.com/freq.zip

112. The quality of your CD recordings is dependent to some extent on the capabilities of your PC's sound card. Sound Card Analyser is a small program that tests the performance of your PC's sound system, measuring frequency response, dynamic range, noise levels, crosstalk and distortion. It's simple to use – all you have to do is connect the sound card's input to the output and click the Run Test button – and it generates a comprehensive report, complete with comments and impressive-looking graphs. Sound Card Analyser is freeware, the program's 'zip' file is quite small (454kb) and it can be downloaded from:

  http://chronos.cs.msu.su/~andre/alex/scan20.zip

113. Does your PC talk to you? If it does, and you haven't got Windows XP or installed a speech synthesiser program you might need help, but if it remains stubbornly mute, and you'd like it to read back your word processor documents, emails or web pages then have a look at a shareware program called TextAloud. It's a sophisticated text to speech program and the delightful 'Mary' will read anything you paste into the Windows Clipboard or type into the text window. If you'd prefer to listen to another voice, or even another language there's a good selection of free add-ons from the TextAloud website. The program file is 4.2Mb and the trial lasts for 20 days but it's all yours for a registration fee of around £15. More details and the link to the download can be found at:

http://www.nextup.com/

114. Here's a useful freeware program for anyone who listens to music on their PC and has scrabbled around with the mouse, trying to mute the sound or lower the volume when the phone rings. Global Audio Control (900kb) assigns simple keyboard shortcuts to all of your PC's audio controls. It's a real time-saver and you'll wonder how you ever managed without it. Suitable for Windows 9x/NT/2000 it can be found at:

http://www.globalaudiocontrol.cjb.net/

115. This freeware program is an add-on for WinAmp, but it's also available as a stand-alone program that works with Windows. G-Force is similar in concept to the 'Visualisations' in Windows Media Play 7, except that the pictures and patterns it generates – that gyrate and pulsate in time with the music — are about a hundred times more dazzling and colourful. Be warned, it's hypnotic, and works best on reasonably quick PCs, preferably 500MHz or faster.

G-FORCE, 2.1Mb, Windows 95/98/SE/ME/NT/2K, freeware
http://www.55ware.com/gforce/

WORD PROCESSING AND SPREADSHEETS

116. The bright white text area of most word processors can become quite tiring on the eyes after a few hours. You can of course jiggle the brightness and contrast settings on your monitor but a far better solution is to give your blank pages a light grey tint. Open your word processor and load a page of text, so you can judge the effect. Next, from the Start button select Settings, Control Panel and the Display icon. Select the Appearance tab and click into the area marked Window Text. Next click on the Color box and choose the Other option. This will bring up a colour palette, select grey or white from the block of colour options and use the slider to the right of the multi-colour panel to adjust the level. Click OK and if necessary readjust until you are satisfied with it. The tint applies only to the display and will not affect the way documents look when they are printed.

117. If you are constantly fussing over fonts for your documents then there's a very handy feature in Windows that allows you quickly to compare typefaces according to style and design. From the Start menu go to Settings, then Control Panel and double click the Fonts icon. Go to the View drop-down menu and click on 'List Fonts by Similarity'. Now all you have to do is click on the drop down 'List Fonts…' choose a font and you will be presented with a list of comparable typefaces, ranked according to similarity.

118. Generally speaking Microsoft Word is fairly reliable but when it does go wrong it does so in spectacular fashion and in addition to closing itself down without warning, it can also take Windows with it. Word users plagued by persistent problems usually give up and reinstall the program, only to find that nothing has changed. In those circumstances there's almost always a glitch in a file called 'Normal.dot' that contains all of the user's settings and includes macros and other mischief-makers. If you are about to reinstall Word for the tenth time, try this. Make a copy of your Normal.dot file (just in case it's not corrupt) and save it in another folder, it can usually be found in Windows\Application Data\Microsoft\Templates. Delete the original Normal.dot and reboot. Word will automatically create a new Normal.dot and return to its default settings.

119. Word users usually manage to find Word Count in the Tools menu; it may be more versatile than you think. As it stands it will count all of the words in an open document, but if you want to know how many words there are in a paragraph, or block of copy, just use the highlight function, then click on word count. You can create a simple keyboard shortcut to Word Count by going to the Tools menu and click on Customise. Select the Command tab; highlight Tools in the list of Categories and scroll down the list of Commands until you come to Word Count. Highlight it, then click on the Keyboard button, put the pointer into the Press New Shortcut field and press the mouse button. Decide which keys you are going to use (Ctrl and backslash '\' are usually free) finish off by clicking Assign and Close.

120. If you habitually work with a lot of open documents in Word you will know how time consuming it can be to save and close each document separately, when you exit the program. There's a hidden set of commands that will speed things up considerably. All you have to do is hold down the shift key and then move the mouse pointer to the File drop-down menu. You will see that Close has changed to Close All, and Save is now Save All. To exit Word in double quick time click Save All, followed by Close All and watch those documents disappear! Incidentally, Word will prompt you to name any untitled documents, so there's no fear of losing track of anything.

121. In Word there's a useful unpublished facility called Random Word. Every so often you might want to create a block of text quickly to test out your faxing or email facilities or produce dummy text to check a page layout. You can of course copy and paste text from another document but Random Word is far quicker. Simply type in the following: =rand() and press Return. Word will then generate three paragraphs, each containing the sentence 'The quick brown fox jumps over the lazy dog', five times. You can alter the number of paragraphs and sentences by inserting numbers into the brackets. For example, =rand(6,8) generates a text block of six paragraphs, each containing eight sentences.

122. If you frequently need to insert a word, line or block of text into MS Word documents you can easily automate the process with a simple keyboard shortcut. Highlight the text and press Alt + F3, to create an AutoText entry, then give it a name or accept the default that appears in the dialogue box that appears and click OK. Now go to the Tools menu; select Customize and the Commands Tab. Click the Keyboard button then AutoText in the Categories window. Highlight your new entry in the Commands Window, click a cursor in the Press New Shortcut Key field, choose a key combination then click Assign. To remove an AutoText entry go to the Insert menu, click AutoText, then AutoText, select the AutoText tab, highlight the entry and click Delete.

123. There's a hidden feature in Word 97 onwards that automatically scrolls the page or document you're watching. It's really handy for reading long documents, or you can use it to turn your PC screen into a teleprompter or autocue, for displaying speeches and scripts. It was originally designed to be used with 'wheel' type mice but it works on any standard two or three button mouse. Click on Customise on the Tools menu, select the Commands tab, scroll down the list and highlight 'All Commands' in the Categories window. In the right-hand Commands window find, single click and hold on Auto

Scroll, drag and drop it onto a toolbar and a button will appear. Close Customise and click on the Auto Scroll button, you can vary the speed and direction using the arrows that appear in the left-hand scroll bar.

124. As you may have discovered, there is no master list of keyboard shortcuts in Word Help and tracking down a specific command – there are more than 200 of them – or finding out if a particular one even exists, can be a frustrating and time-consuming business. Wonder no more, here's an easy way to print out a complete list of Word shortcuts and commands, to keep by your PC for quick reference.

Go to the Tools menu and click on Macro then Macros. In the 'Macros In' drop-down menu select Word Commands. Now move your mouse pointer to the Macro Name pane and highlight ListCommands, click Run and in the dialogue box that appears select Current Menu and Keyboard Settings and click OK. A new document will open, with a table showing all the available commands and shortcuts. Just use Save As to give it a name and print it out. Be warned, in its raw form it runs to around nine pages (12pt text) but with a little judicious editing of the commands you'll never need or use it can be trimmed to a more manageable five to six pages.

125. As you know, you can insert pictures and graphics into Microsoft Word documents but did you also know you can add sounds? Try it, it's fun! It works on most recent versions of Word (97 and 2000). Before you start select, create or record the sound you want to use with Windows Sound Recorder (Start > Programs > Accessories > Entertainment) or your preferred audio editing program and save it as a *.wav file. Open Word and position the cursor in the document where you want the sound to be then go to the Insert menu and select Object. Make sure the Create New tab is displayed then scroll down the list to Wave Sound and click on it. Press OK and a speaker icon appears on the page and Windows Media Player opens. Go to Insert File on the Edit menu, select your audio file and it's done. When anyone double clicks on the speaker icon the sound file will be played.

126. Here's an easy way to find out what the Function keys along the top of the keyboard do in Word 2000. Right click into an empty area next to the Toolbar at the top of the screen, and select Customize from the drop-down menu. Put a check mark next to 'Function Key display' and a new toolbar will appear at the bottom of the screen, with clickable buttons showing what each key does, plus their alternative functions, when you press the Alt, Shift or Ctrl keys.

127. Microsoft Word has lots of useful undocumented features; here's one that will save you a lot of time and trouble. The next time you want to replace a chunk of text forget the backspace or delete keys, just highlight the block and continue typing. One click, that's all, Word automatically places the cursor at the start of the highlighted section and replaces the text as you type.

128. Did you know that Word has a built-in calculator function? Call up the Customize dialogue box (see Tip 1) and select All Commands in the Categories menu then find and highlight ToolsCalculate in the Command list. Drag and drop it onto a toolbar and it's ready to use. Enter in a sum, using the normal mathematical operators (plus +, minus – , divide / and multiply *, etc.) highlight the equation and click your ToolsCalculate button and the answer will appear in the left-hand corner of the status bar at the bottom of the screen.

129. If you use Microsoft Word it's worth remembering this very useful keyboard shortcut for quickly increasing or decreasing the font size of a selected letter, word, paragraph or even a whole document. Simply highlight the text then press and hold the Ctrl and Shift keys, to increase the font size (in 1 point increments) repeatedly press '>' (right-facing open arrow) and to reduce size press '<'. The size of the highlighted text will be shown in the toolbar display.

130. Word has a useful hidden utility called the 'Work' menu that lives on the Word toolbar giving single-click access to selected documents. To install the Work menu right click in an empty area of the toolbar, select Customize, then the Commands tab, scroll down the Categories list, select Built In Menus, go to the Command list, scroll down to Work then drag and drop it onto a toolbar. To include a document on the menu open it and click 'Add to Work Menu'. To remove an entry press Ctrl + Alt + - (hyphen), the cursor changes to a bar, go to the Work menu and click on the item you want to delete.

131. Excel users, here's a neat little trick that old hands are probably familiar with but newcomers might find useful. If you have a column of numbers that you want to add up quickly, simply highlight them and the sum of the numbers appears in the Status bar at the bottom of the screen. There's more. If you now right click on the Status bar result you'll see a set of extra options, including Average, Count, Count Numbers, Min and Max.

JUST FOR FUN

132. The Solitaire game in Windows must be one of the greatest time-wasters of all time – it drives office managers crazy – but even though it is so simple it can be highly addictive. If you're one of the millions hooked on it then you have probably figured out by now that the Draw 3 option – selected by default – slows the game down, increases the odds against you winning and makes it harder to play. Of course you could just switch to easy-peasy Draw 1 setting and play it that way but where's the fun in that? The next time you're in a fix try this simple little cheat. Press and hold down the Ctrl, Alt and Shift keys, then click on the top card and you'll find that you can now select cards one at a time.

We know that the FreeCell and Minesweeper games included in almost all versions of Windows have a devoted following and some may consider what follows as heresy so if you're a purist avert your eyes now because we are about to reveal some simple cheats and enhancements.

In FreeCell you can win instantly by holding down Ctrl + Shift + F10, choose Abort from the menu that appears and drag any card to the top.

To switch off the Minesweeper timer, position the mouse pointer on any grey part of the game window, press and hold the right and left mouse keys and press the Escape key.

Finally, you can add some simple sound effects to Minesweeper by opening Windows Notepad (Start > Programs > Accessories) select All Files then open the 'Winmine.ini' file in the Windows folder (you might want to make a backup copy, just in case). Add the line 'Sound=3' to the end, Save and exit Notepad. If you add a subsequent line 'Tick=1', you'll hear a bleep as the timer counts up.

133. 'Easter Eggs' are diverting little features hidden away inside software applications, and another reason why programs take up so much hard disk space these days. This one is in both Windows 95 and 98. Open Display Properties in Control Panel, select the Screensaver tab, choose 3D Pipes, click the Settings button and check 'Multiple', 'Traditional' and 'Solid'. In Joint Type select Mixed, click OK then Preview and look out for Teapots. No prizes, but can anyone tell us what's so special about this particular teapot?

134. This next one can be found in Windows 98 and is quite challenging, calling for a very steady hand, and possibly an atlas. Double click on the time display on the Taskbar or click on Regional settings in Control Panel and select the Time Zone tab to display the world map. Hold down the Ctrl key and move the mouse pointer to Cairo, at the northern end of the Red Sea, click and hold the left mouse button then move the mouse pointer to Memphis Tennessee (above Florida) release the mouse button, then without moving the pointer click and hold and move the pointer to Redmond in Washington State (just North of San Francisco) release the mouse button, watch, listen and be amazed (well, mildly surprised…). Don't give up if it doesn't work first time, you have to be very precise.

135. This Easter Egg is quite diverting and it lives in Excel 2000. It's a challenging driving game with excellent graphics; note that you will also need DirectX 6 or 7 on your PC, if not you'll find it on most PC magazine cover-mount CD-ROMs.

Pay attention, it's quite involved, but well worth the effort. Open Excel 2000, on the File menu select 'Save As Web Page' then check the items 'Save Selection Sheet' and 'Add Interactivity', click Save and a file called 'page.htm' should end up in My Documents (or wherever else you choose to put it). Exit Excel and open Internet Explorer and open the saved 'page.htm' file. Scroll all the way down to row 2000 and along to column WC, check the cell, highlight the whole line and use tab to select cell 2000 WC again. Next, hold down Ctrl + Shift + Alt and click on the Excel logo in the top left-hand corner. The screen goes black and after a few seconds the game starts. Use the arrow keys to steer, the spacebar to fire your guns, H for headlights, O to spray oil and Esc to exit. Good luck!

136. This is actually more of a curiosity and it concerns most versions of Windows 98. Try this: right click on the taskbar, select Properties and the familiar Taskbar Properties dialogue box opens. Close it and this time hold down the Ctrl key and keep it pressed while you right click on the taskbar and select Properties. The same dialogue box opens but this time there's an extra tabbed item called Deskbar. If you click on it a new dialogue window opens but all of the options are greyed out. It's almost certainly an unfinished or deleted feature but what it was for or supposed to do is one of life's little mysteries…

WINDOWS XP

137. Shortly after you have started using your new XP computer you will receive messages telling you that your password will expire, usually in 14 days. If you are happy with your passwords and do not want to change them go to Run on the Start menu and type 'control userpasswords2' (without the quotes of course) and on the dialogue box that appears select the Advanced tab then the Advanced button. Double click the Users folder and right click the user name whose setting you want to change and select Properties then check the box 'Password never expires'.

138. You half expect the Tellytubbies to come waddling over the rolling green desktop and where would Windows XP be without little balloons appearing every five minutes, telling you about something or other it has just done? Some find the cutesy design theme quite endearing; others would like to have a few words with the designers but the good news is that almost everything can be changed, and the dreaded 'Balloon Tips' can be banished forever using the XP version of our old friend Tweak UI. As you regular readers will know, Tweak UI is part of a suite of tools called Power Toys, which are unsupported by Microsoft but don't let that worry you, they're usually very safe to use. Power-Toys are free and can be downloaded from: http://www.microsoft.com/windowsxp/pro/downloads/powertoys.asp and the Tweak UI utility is only around 500kB. After it's installed you'll find it on the Programs menu, double click the Taskbar option and in the Settings Window deselect 'Enable Balloon Tips' then OK.

While you are at it have a look through some of the many other useful things Tweak UI can do, including an auto log-on facility, which is useful if you are the only user.

139. Windows XP is very stable but it's certainly not immune to crashes and when it does you are presented with an offer to report the error to Microsoft. It's well meant and should, in theory, help Microsoft to identify bugs and glitches a lot faster, but it can become very annoying when you are trying to install a piece of hardware or software and the message keeps popping up. To switch it off go to Control Panel and click System, select the Advanced tab then the Error Reporting button at the bottom and check the item 'Disable Error Reporting' and click OK.

140. Generally speaking, automatic updates are quite a good idea and it means your PC will always have the most up-to-date security patches and bug fixes but a lot of people don't like the way that Windows automatically decides for itself when to search and download updates and for those with slower dial-up connections it can be inconvenient. To switch off automatic updates completely, or tell Windows to ask permission before accessing the Internet go to System in Control Panel, select the Automatic Update tab, change the Notification Settings as appropriate then click OK.

141. Microsoft are keen for us all to start using MSN Messenger (.NET Messenger) for chatting and video telephony but a lot of people still prefer the much friendlier NetMeeting program. The good news is that it is included with XP but it has been buried away; to get it up and running all you have to do is go to Run on the Start menu and type 'conf'.

142. For some reason best known to Microsoft, Windows Explorer in XP opens on My Documents, which can be incredibly frustrating if you're trying to access the contents of your C: drive. Fortunately there is a solution, the first step is to create a desktop shortcut to Windows Explorer, so go to Start > Programs > Accessories and right click on the Explorer icon and select Send To > Desktop (Create Shortcut). Return to the desktop and right click on the new Windows Explorer icon and select Properties. In the Target line, after explorer.exe, add the following '/e,c:\', so it should now read … explorer.exe /e,c:\ (note the space between .exe and /e, there's a comma after the /e and it's a backslash, not forward slash after c:). You might also want to put a copy of this shortcut onto the Quick Launch toolbar, under the Start button. To do this hold down the Ctrl key (to make a copy) then drag and drop the new Windows Explorer icon.

143. You probably know that you are using Windows XP and may not want to be reminded every time you boot up, in which case why not disable the XP opening screen? This is easy; just go to Run on the Start menu and type 'msconfig' then select the Boot.Ini tab. Check the item '/NOGUIBOOT', click OK and when prompted restart your PC. This time it will go straight from the opening white progress bar or a blank screen to the XP desktop. You may get a warning message from the System Configuration Utility telling you the PC is in Selective Startup Mode. This is not a problem though and you can safely tick the 'Do not show this message…' check box.

144. XP has a wealth of alternative mouse pointer and cursor schemes. Go to Mouse in Control Panel and click the Pointers tab then the Scheme's drop-down Menu. (If you are in Category View click Appearance and Themes then Mouse Pointers.) If you are using XP Pro have a look at Dinosaur or if you are of a musical disposition try Conductor; in XP Home you should also find Ocean and Sports schemes.

145. Windows Explorer has several new features for displaying and sorting files and folders. One of the most useful is Show In Groups, which is enabled on the View menu. You can now select the type of grouping that you require. If you click on the Name header the groups will be alphabetical, click on 'Type' and they will be sorted so that documents, images and spreadsheets, etc., are grouped together. As a further enhancement you can enable Show In Groups in Details, Icons, Tiles and Thumbnails Views.

146. The security features in XP are obviously a welcome change from Windows 9x, which is about as secure as a wet teabag; however, forgetting your log-on password could be a major inconvenience. You could write it down somewhere, rather defeating the object, but XP does have a recovery utility that you should make use of if you are prone to forgetfulness. With a blank formatted floppy to hand go to Control Panel, click on User Accounts then your account name. In the Related Tasks pane on the left select the item 'Prevent Forgotten Password', pop in the floppy and follow the on-screen instructions. If you forget your password XP will give you the option of using your recovery disk to help you to reset your password so keep it in a safe and secure place and don't for heaven's sake label it 'Password Recovery'!

147. Sooner or later XP, like all incarnations of Windows, slows down as it becomes overloaded with redundant files and Registry entries so if your machine is starting to get a bit sluggish try this quick and simple trick that should help to speed it up a bit (or maybe even a lot). Go to User Accounts in Control Panel and create a new account, make sure it's an Administrator type and this will allow you to copy across and export all of your data files and settings from your old account into the new and hopefully much livelier one.

148. Here's a useful tip if you want to make sure your children switch the PC off at a particular time, or even limit your own usage to prompt you to go home/get to bed at a reasonable hour. XP has a built-in utility called Shutdown that can be programmed to switch the PC off after a predetermined delay. To use Shutdown go to Run on the Start menu and type 'cmd' (without the quotes) and this will bring up a DOS type window. Now type the following command: 'shutdown.exe -s -t xx', where -s is the shutdown 'switch', -t is the time switch and xx is the delay in seconds. So, if you want the PC to shutdown in 15 minutes, say, the command would be: 'shutdown.exe-s-t 900'. When Enter is pressed the countdown begins, with a dialogue box on the screen showing the time left and warning the user to save their work. For a full list of the switches available for this utility just type shutdown.exe at the command prompt.

149. Here's how to switch on the built-in Internet Firewall in Windows XP. This very useful feature protects your PC from snoopers but for some reason it's not enabled by default, or easily found, unless you know where to look. The procedure is Start > Control Panel > Network Connections, highlight your Internet or Network connection then click Change Settings in the Network Tasks Window. Select the Advanced tab and check the item 'Internet Connection Firewall' and it's done.

150. The internal clocks in most PCs are usually fairly accurate but they can drift by a few seconds a week. XP has a useful facility that allows you to synchronise your PC to an atomic clock when you are connected to the Internet. The next time you are on-line double click on the time display on the taskbar and select the Internet Time tab, check the item 'Automatically Synchronise…' and click the Update Now button. If the time-server website selected by default is slow to respond or busy you can find a list of alternative servers at http://www.eecis.udel.edu/%7Emills/ntp/clock2.htm

Glossary

8mm

Video and data recording system using 8mm wide magnetic tape; cassettes are roughly the size of an audio cassette.

286, 386, 486

Families of Intel microprocessor chips developed during the 1980s and early 1990s, forerunners of the Pentium chips used in the latest PCs.

ACTIVE-X

Powerful programming tools used to add multimedia components and features to Internet web pages.

ADMIN TEMPLATES

Poledit options that cover a range of Windows features, including how it looks and works, restrictions on Internet and email access, network configuration, etc.

ADSL

Asymmetric Digital Subscriber Line – high-speed digital connection using existing telephone lines. ADSL has the facility to be 'always on', so there is no need to dial up a connection.

ALGORITHM

A program or piece of software that processes data in a carefully ordered sequence of steps or according to a precise set of rules.

ASCII

American Standard Code for Information Interchange – a universal data code for text and alphanumeric characters, understood by virtually all computers.

ASPECT RATIO

The shape of an image, defined by the relationship between its height and width.

AT

ATtention – the prefix to a modem command, to tell the modem to expect an instruction.

ATAPI

AT Attachment Packet Interface – industry standard disk drive connection system and data communications protocols, used on the most CD-rewriters, suitable for use with most Windows PCs.

ATRAC

Adaptive Transform Acoustic Coding – digital audio compression system used by the MiniDisk format.

ATTACHMENT

Data file – usually containing a photograph or text document – sent with an email message.

AUTOCORRECT

Word feature that automatically corrects spelling mistakes as you type.

AUTOTEXT

A frequently used block of text – an address, salutation, etc., – that can be inserted into a document.

AVERY LABELS

A range of standardised label styles and formats, developed by the office equipment company of the same name.

.avi

Audio-Video Interleaved, standard format for PC video files.

BAD SECTORS

Parts of the hard disk drive which the test utility Scandisk marks as being faulty and incapable of reliably storing data. A sudden increase in the number of bad sectors is often a sign that the drive is damaged or starting to deteriorate.

BANNER ADVERTISING

Advertising graphic on a web page that when clicked will take you to the company's website.

BCC
Blind Carbon Copy sends a copy of a message to several recipients but without showing details of the other recipients on the email.

BETA
Beta software is usually a near final version of a program or application, made available to testers and volunteers on an at-their-own-risk basis, to help identify any last remaining bugs, glitches and conflicts.

BIOS
Basic Input Output System, a program stored in a microchip memory on the PC motherboard that checks and configures the hardware, memory and disk drives, before the operating system is loaded.

BINARY
Numbering system with a base of 2, where values are represented by zeros and ones.

BITMAP
Type of image file format (extension *.bmp) used by Windows and many other programs. Quality is high because no compression is used, however, bitmap files can be very large and are unsuitable for sending via email.

BITRATE
A measure of the amount of digital data a system can process, measured in bits per second or 'bps'. In the context of MP3 faster bit rates mean lower compression and higher sound quality.

BITS PER SECOND (bps)
The number of bits per second a serial communications system can handle determines how fast information can be conveyed from one point to another.

BOOLEAN
A branch of algebra named after nineteenth-century British mathematician George Boole.

BROWNOUT
A large reduction in the mains supply voltage, causing lights to dim and electronic devices like PCs to stop working.

BROWSER
An Internet access program, such as Microsoft Internet Explorer or Netscape Navigator/Communicator.

BURNING
The process of recording a CD-R or CD-RW disk in a CD writer drive.

BUTT
American slang for posterior.

CACHE
Part of a computer's memory set aside for storing frequently used data from a disk drive thus speeding up the transfer of information.

CAD/CAM
Computer aided design/manufacture – applications that require a high-performance visual display.

CARTRIDGE/TANK
Replaceable ink container, sometimes one colour or black but occasionally three or four or more colours, which may or may not be integrated with the print head.

CCD
Charge Coupled Device, type of microchip used in digital cameras, web cams, camcorders and video cameras, containing thousands, sometimes millions of light-sensitive picture elements or 'pixels'.

CD-R/RW
Recordable CD-ROM systems; CD-R uses disks that can be written to just once whilst CD-RW (read-write) disks can be recorded on and erased many times.

CHAT
When in a NetMeeting call you can communicate by typing text into a message window, which appears almost instantly on the recipient's screen.

CHIPSET

Whilst there are hundreds of modem manufacturers only a relatively small number of companies make the key microchips, which determine how they work and communicate with the PC.

CHIP SOCKETS

Most of the microchips used in a PC are soldered directly to the circuit boards but some, including the main processor and some memory components are mounted in sockets, so they can be easily replaced or upgraded.

CLEANER WIPES

Fabric cloths moistened with specially formulated cleaning and anti-static fluid, available from most office supply companies.

CLIENT

A PC or program used to access files on another PC on a network.

CLIP ART

Copyright-free pictures, icons, cartoons and graphics supplied with word processor programs, or available separately on disk or from thousands of websites on the Internet.

CLIPBOARD

Windows utility used to temporarily copy chunks of text, data, graphics or pictures. Once on the clipboard the item can be pasted into another part of the document, or transferred to any other Windows application with a copy and paste facility.

CMOS

Complimentary metal oxide semiconductor – family of low-power microchips used to store and process the BIOS program.

COBOL

Common Business Oriented Language – programming language used in data processing and business applications.

COLOUR DEPTH

The amount of data used to describe a colour, which determines the range and accuracy of colours in an image.

COLOUR MATCHING

Technique to ensure that the colours displayed on a PC monitor are as close as possible to the finished printed picture.

COLOUR SCHEME

Colouration of Windows desktop and screen elements, such as task, tool and menu bars, active and inactive windows and drop-down menus.

COLOUR TEMPERATURE

Means of describing the distribution of colours in a light source, measured in degrees Kelvin. (Typical values: tungsten lamp 2700k, fluorescent tubes 2700 to 6500k, noonday sun 5500k, blue sky 10000k.)

COMMAND PROMPT

DOS type operating mode that allows access to the PC's disk drives and files, without having to load Windows.

COMPATIBILITY MODE

Configures XP to run in a special Windows 95 or 98 emulation mode allowing older applications to be used.

COMPOSITE & S-VIDEO

Video signal formats. Composite video contains picture brightness, colour and synchronisation information mixed together whilst S-Video 'separates' the brightness and colour components, preventing them from interacting resulting in a sharper picture.

COMPRESSION

A technique used to reduce the size of a file, making it smaller, more manageable and quicker to send over the Internet.

CONSUMABLES

Components in a printer, such as the ink cartridge or ribbon, that need to be replaced when they run out or exceed their life expectancy.

CONTEXT MENU
A menu containing commands or actions relevant to an object or element on a program's desktop or dialogue box.

COOKIES
Small test files, stored on your PC by websites you've visited, that can contain a wide range of data including personal details and preferences and information about websites you have visited.

CORE FONTS
The basic set of fonts or typefaces that are installed and used by Windows 95/98.

COUNTER
Web page component that logs the number of visitors to a site.

COVER SHEET
Fax page that is sent before the fax message, giving details of the sender, recipient, date and time.

CPU
Central Processor Unit – the main microprocessor chip in a PC.

CRT
Cathode Ray Tube – basically a big glass bottle with all the air sucked out. The image is formed on a layer of phosphor coating the side of the glass faceplate that glows when struck by a stream of fast-moving electrons.

DAISY-CHAIN
USB devices have two sockets so they can be connected together, one to the other, like a chain.

DATA CARTRIDGE
A cassette, similar to audio or video tape (some tape backup systems use DAT and 8mm audio and video cassettes).

DATA FIELD
In the context of an address book a single item of information, i.e., a forename or surname, house number and street name, postcode, etc.

DATA SOURCE

A file used to store a particular type of information, such as names and addresses.

DAT

Digital Audio Tape, high-quality recording system using even smaller matchbox-sized tape cassettes spooled with 4mm wide magnetic tape.

DCC

Direct Cable Connection, a Windows utility for connecting two PCs together so they can exchange files.

DECOMPRESS

Files sent over the Internet are often 'compressed' to make them smaller and faster to send. However, in order to use the files they have to be decompressed or extracted on the host PC. Some compressed files come with their own automatic extraction utility, others – usually with the extension *.zip – depend on a separate program on the PC to 'unzip' the files.

DEFRAG

Over time the files on a PC's hard disk drive become disorganised – 'defragging' the drive restores order and speeds up reading and writing data. To defrag your PC click on Start then Programs > Accessories >System Tools.

DEGAUSS

Literally de-magnetise. A coil around the outside of the picture tube induces a collapsing magnetic field that eradicates any magnetic build up on metal components inside the tube.

DIAL-UP CONNECTION

Utility in Windows responsible for connecting a PC, via a modem, to the Internet.

DIGITAL ARTEFACTS

Processing errors in digital video recordings, typically the picture freezes momentarily or breaks up into large 'pixellated' blocks.

DIGITAL CAMCORDER
Camcorder that uses the 'DVC' (Digital Video Cassette) recording system. Pocket-sized models are capable of very high picture and sound quality.

DIMM
Dual in-line memory module, usually with 168 connecting pins.

DISK CONTROLLER
Microchip that identifies a disk drive or storage device to a computer and helps speed up the transfer of data.

DISPLAY CARD
A plug-in adaptor card or circuitry incorporated into the motherboard that converts digital information into an analogue video signal that is fed to the monitor.

DLL
Dynamic Link Library, a data file containing data or information needed by a program. DLLs may be shared by a number of applications, in which case they are stored in a central location, such as the System folder in Windows.

DMA
Direct Memory Access – a means of transferring data quickly between the hard disk and the PC's memory.

DNS
Domain Name System – used to identify computers connected to the Internet and networks.

DOMAIN
A group of computers, sharing a common address or identity, connected together by a network. Thus a desktop PC connected to the Internet via an Internet Service Provider is part of that ISP's domain.

DOMAIN NAMES (TOP LEVEL)
.ac.uk
UK academic organisation.

.com

World-wide 'commercial' entities, individuals or companies.

.co.uk

UK-based commercial entity, individual or company.

.edu

Assigned to higher-level educational establishments, colleges, universities, etc.

.gov/.gov.uk

Reserved for US government agencies and organisations and similar bodies in other countries when preceded by the relevant country code.

.mod.uk

UK Ministry of Defence establishment websites.

.net

Organisations that are part of the Internet infrastructure, i.e., Internet Service Providers, etc.

.nhs.uk

UK national health service website.

.org/org.uk

Originally reserved for non-profit-making organisations (charities, political bodies, professional institutions, trades unions, etc.) but now issued to some commercial enterprises.

.sch.uk

UK schools domain.

DOS/MS-DOS

Disk Operating System, a program that runs independently of Windows responsible for controlling disk drives, organising data and memory resources.

DOS MODE

The PC is 'booted' without Windows with DOS as the primary operating system.

DOT PITCH

A measure of the size and spacing of the coloured light-emitting phosphor dots or stripes that coat the inside of the screen. The current norm is around 0.28mm, higher performance CRTs have dot pitches of between 0.23 and 0.25mm transferred from the hard disk to the RAM memory chips.

DRIVER

Drivers are small programs that tell Windows 95 how to communicate with a particular piece of hardware, like a mouse, joystick or printer.

DTP

Desktop publishing – makeup and layout programs used to design pages in printed documents, magazines, newspapers, books and Internet websites.

DUPLEX PRINTING

Printing on both sides of a sheet of paper. A few printers can do this automatically, however, in most cases it is necessary for the user to re-load the paper or papers manually, facing the other way and in the right order.

DVD

Digital Versatile Disk – new high-capacity optical disk system with a capacity of up to 5.2Gb per disk (at the moment), DVD drives can also read CD-ROMs. DVD recordable or 'RAM' drives are now available.

ECP/EPP

Extended Capabilities Port/Enhanced Parallel Port; printer port settings that allow faster data transfer rates.

EDIT CONTROLLER

Stand-alone device (or PC) that controls the playback of a camcorder or video tape recorder, so that selected scenes can be joined together.

EDO RAM

Extended data out, random access memory, high-speed RAM chips used on recent PCs with specialised memory controllers.

EIDE

Enhanced Integrated Drive Electronics, disk drive interface and control system used on most recent PCs.

EISA/ISA EXPANSION SLOT

Extended Industry Standard Architecture, type of connector on a PC motherboard, used for expansion or adapter cards.

EMAIL ATTACHMENT

An attachment is a file – other than plain text – sent with or as an email message.

EMBEDDED COMMANDS

Cells in a spreadsheet or table can contain hidden instructions to perform calculations or carry out specific actions when data is entered.

EMBEDDED FONTS

Typeface information included in a file that allows fonts and character sets to be displayed that may not be on the host PC.

EMERGENCY RECOVERY DISK

A floppy disk created by Windows containing files that will allow your PC to boot up in DOS mode, plus various tools and utilities to assist recovery following a crash.

ENCRYPTION

Encryption or scrambling renders files unreadable by any conventional means without the correct decryption software and a unique 'key' code, which is needed to unlock the data.

ENGINE

A self-contained program designed to do a specific task that operates within a larger application.

10/100MBS ETHERNET

Industry standard networking system. The standard operating speed is 10 megabits per second (Mbps), however the faster 100Mbs format is increasingly used and costs only slightly more.

EXE

Files ending in .exe are 'executable' which basically means they contain a program that will start when the .exe file is opened.

EXPANSION CARDS

Most PCs contain a set of small circuit boards, plugged into the main motherboard for controlling the video output, processing sounds or communicating with the outside world (modems and network cards).

FAQs

Frequently asked questions, a simple guide to a particular topic or subject area.

FAST CHARGING

Rapidly charging a battery pack, typically in an hour or so, however, unless the charging current is very carefully controlled this can result in a shortened life and/or reduce capacity. Normal charge times for nicad and NiMh batteries/cells is in the order of 14 hours, the so-called 'overnight' rate.

FAT 32

File Allocation Table – the indexing system used by the PC to control where and how data is stored on the hard disk. The FAT 32 system makes more efficient use of the storage space available and allows drives larger than 2Gb to function as a single drive.

FIELD

An area on a document that acts as a container for text or data that needs to be entered or might change, without affecting the rest of the document.

FILE EXTENSIONS (WINDOWS AND POPULAR APPLICATIONS)
.avi
Audio-Video Interleaved, Microsoft standard movie files.

.bak
Backup or archive file, usually created automatically by a program.

.bmp
Bitmap, standard Windows image or graphics file.

.cab
Cabinet, compressed data file used on Microsoft software installation disks.

.dll

Dynamic Link Library, contains information or data that may be shared by several programs.

.doc

Microsoft Word document.

.exe

Executable, a file containing a program or instructions to start a program.

.gif

Graphics Interchange Format, a graphics file, mainly used on Internet web pages.

.hlp

Help file.

.htm/html

HyperText Markup Language, Internet web page files.

.ico

Windows icon files.

.ini

Initialisation file containing information needed to start and configure Windows.

.jpg/.jpeg

Joint Photographic Experts Group, compressed image file.

.lwp

Lotus Word Pro document.

.mdb

Microsoft Access database file.

.mid

Musical Instrument Digital interface, music file.

.mov

QuickTime Movie file.

.mp3

Moving Picture Expert Group 3, CD-quality sound file used for music on the Internet.

.mpg/mpeg

Moving Picture Experts Group, video movie file.

.old

Convention for renaming old or disused files that may be needed at some time in the future.

.pdf

Portable Document Format, interactive text file with web-like links.

.rtf

Rich Text Format, industry standard text file, can be read by most word processors.

.scr

Screensaver file.

.sys

System file, containing information needed to load and configure Windows.

.tif/.tiff

Tagged Image Format File, graphics file.

.tmp

Temporary file, generated by Windows and various applications, normally deleted when the program or Windows is closed.

.ttf
True Type Font, file containing typeface information.

.txt
File containing plain or unformatted text.

.uue
Text file format used to send program files containing binary information by email.

.wav
Waveform, Windows sound file.

.wpd
Word Perfect document file.

.xls
Microsoft Excel worksheet.

.zip
File containing compressed binary data, used for sending programs or information on the Internet.

FILE FRAGMENTS
Files or bits of files left behind on the hard disk when a program is deleted.

FILE AND PRINTER SHARING
Allows PCs in a network to access files and resources on other computers, clicking the Network icon in Control Panel enables it.

FIREWALL
Program that monitors an Internet connection, preventing unauthorised access to files on your PC whilst on-line.

FIREWIRE
(aka IEEE 1394) High-speed serial data connection system used on some

high-end PCs and laptops used for demanding video and graphics applications.

FLAG
Red flag icon, next to an email message, used to identify or draw the user's attention.

FLAME
Offensive or abusive emails, usually sent in response to someone infringing basic newsgroup netiquette.

FLATBED
Desktop scanner with horizontal (flat) picture/document holder, usually covered by a hinged top.

FLIP & ROTATE
An option in most graphics programs and word processors to rotate a text or graphics object on the page.

FLOAT
A drawing tool or option that lets you copy and move a defined area of an image to another part of the picture.

FOLLOW-UPS
A response to a newsgroup message or posting, which will form part of a 'thread' for others to read and reply to.

FONT/TYPEFACE
Text style and size. Virtually all word processors have a 'wizzywig' display (actually WYSIWYG, or what you see is what you get) so what appears on the screen is what ends up on the printed page.

FORMAT
Process of preparing a disk drive to store data by organising a file structure so that information can be systematically written and retrieved by the PC's operating system.

FORMATTING

Process that prepares a disk for use by effectively deleting all the data on it by creating a new filing structure.

FORMULAE

Mathematical expressions, such as add, subtract, multiply and divide, used to create an instruction that tells a cell how to behave or process a piece of information.

FREEHAND SELECTION TOOL

Drawing tool that lets you define irregular shapes by moving the mouse cursor – usually displayed as a set of crosshairs – around an object whilst holding down the left mouse button.

FREEWARE

Shareware programs that are free to use, but the author retains control and copyright over the original programming code.

FTP

File Transfer Protocol, Internet system used to move data files from one computer to another.

FUNCTION KEYS

The row of keys along the top of the keyboard, which can be assigned to various functions in an open application (F1 traditionally calls up Help).

GAMEPORT

A 15-pin female connector socket designed exclusively for joysticks and other control devices.

GENERATIONS

In linear editing selected scenes are copied from one video recorder to another, creating a second-generation recording. The copying process degrades the picture and if subsequent copies of the edit 'master' are made – a third-generation copy – the imperfections can become very noticeable.

GEOMETRY

The size and shape of the display on a monitor screen. Most monitors have controls to alter the vertical and horizontal position and the linearity of the top and sides (sometimes called trapezoid adjustment). Some models also have a tilt control, to ensure the display aligns with the edges of the screen, to compensate for the Earth's magnetic field and local influences.

GIF

Graphics Interchange Format – standard file format for images and graphics used on Internet web pages.

GPF

General Protection Fault – a 'fatal' software error, causing a running program to stop working because it fights (and loses) over the amount of memory resources it and other programs have been allocated by Windows.

GPS

Global Positioning by Satellite – fleet of low earth-orbit satellites that broadcast highly accurate timing signals that can be picked up by small hand-held receivers, giving the user's location anywhere on the planet to within a few metres.

GRAPHIC EQUALISER

Sophisticated tone control for precisely setting bass, mid-range and treble frequencies during playback on an audio system.

GREYSCALE

The number of shades of grey, between white and black – typically 256 – that a PC imaging system can handle.

gsm

Grams per square metre, measurement of paper weight and consequently thickness. Standard copier paper is usually 80 to 100 gsm, thin card starts at around 120gsm.

GSM

Global System for Mobile communications – digital cellular telephone system used by the Cellnet and Vodaphone networks in the UK and in more than 100 other countries.

GUID

Global Unique IDentifier – long string of letters and numbers (e.g. '{1345E 5E0-40HH-1D41-K189-F89D946S AD6B}') that Windows uses to identify files specific to a particular PC or user.

GUTTER

The blank space between the inner margins of two facing pages in a magazine, newspaper or book.

HELICAL SCAN

System of recording information on to magnetic tape where the recording head (or heads) are mounted on a rotating head drum, around which the tape is wrapped.

HEXADECIMAL

Numbering system used by computers, with a base of 16, represented by the numbers 0 to 9 and the letters A to F.

HIBERNATION MODE

The PC is 'asleep', with the disk drives dormant and Windows and running programs suspended but the processor is still active and the system can be revived in just a few seconds by pre-determined actions (mouse or keyboard activity, modem ring, etc.).

HIGH SPEED GRAPHICS

Multimedia computers are great for fast-action games but they can actually be too quick for applications like word processors. When scrolling through a document the display can move so fast that it's almost impossible to read the text.

HITS

Search results, usually a brief summary of a website's contents, the site address, a relevance rating and an underlined link to click on, to take you to the site.

HOME PAGE

The Internet page or website that your browser goes to automatically as soon as you go on-line.

HOST

An Internet company providing storage space for websites on their server computer.

HOST COMPUTER

A computer – usually part of a wider network, like the Internet – that is accessed by one or more users at remote terminals.

HOT KEYS

A combination of two or three keys strokes that activates a command or a program.

HOT PLUG/SWAP

Connecting a device or peripheral to a PC (using a USB or Firewire connection) whilst one or both are switched on.

HTML

Hypertext Mark-up Language – hidden codes in text documents, web pages and emails that allow the reader to move about the document quickly or jump to another by clicking on underlined 'links' which appear as coloured highlighted words or phrases.

HTTP

HyperText Transfer Protocol – a set of rules used that governs how text is displayed on Internet documents plus a means of moving around inside documents and accessing other web pages by clicking on highlighted or underlined links.

HUB

A multi-way connector with one input and several outputs.

HYPERLINK

Highlighted and underlined text or icon on a web page, clicking on the 'link' takes you to another part of the document or another web page.

ILS

Internet Locator Server – an Internet site or server that allows users logged on to that site to communicate with one another, either individually or in groups.

IMAGESETTER

Device used to convert image data produced on a PC into photographic film used for making lithographic printing plates.

IMAGE STABILISER

Feature on many recent camcorders that eliminates camera shake; two systems are in use. 'Electronic' stabilisers compensate for movement by shifting the target area of the image sensor in response to signals from motion sensors. This involves some loss of picture quality but is good at compensating for rapid motion, such as shooting from a moving vehicle. 'Optical' image stabilisation employs a flexible variable geometry optical element in front of the lens that changes shape according to information from motion sensors, ensuring the scene is always centred on the image sensor. Optical stabilisers cope best with relatively slow movements, such as shooting whilst walking.

IMPEDANCE

Measurement of resistance in relation to an alternating current.

INBOX

A folder created by Outlook Express where all your incoming email messages are stored.

INCREMENTAL BACKUP

A backup strategy that records only the changes made to the chosen files.

INFRA-RED WAND

Device, attached to an edit controller or PC, that emits the same sort of infra-red signals as a remote-control handset, to operate a VCR.

INTERNAL STORAGE

Many non-PC email devices cannot store email messages as they have limited memory capacity. Instead, messages are kept on the server computer though there may be a limit on the number of messages and the space they occupy and in some cases old messages will be deleted to make way for new ones.

IP ADDRESS

Internet Protocol Address – unique 32-bit code, represented by four groups of digits, used to identify websites and Internet users.

IR

Infra-red, cordless serial data communications systems used on many laptops and peripherals and a number of cellphones. The common standard is known as IrDA (Infra-red Data Association).

IrDA

Infra-red Data Association, the organisation responsible for setting and maintaining technical standards for IR wireless communications systems used on PCs and peripherals.

IRQ

Interrupt Request – a set of instructions that enable the processor to manage a succession of tasks in sequence.

ISA

Industry Standard Architecture – connection system used on IBM PCs and compatibles, for plug-in 'daughter boards' such as sound and video cards and modems, etc.

ISDN

Integrated Services Digital Network – high-speed data connection over a specially installed telephone line.

ISP

Internet Service Provider – a company providing Internet access, an email address and a mailbox where messages sent to you are stored before they're downloaded onto your PC.

JAVA

A versatile Internet programming language used in a wide range of applications, including creating animation and web page forms.

JPEG

Joint Photographic Experts Group – part of the International Standards Organisation, responsible for devising software compression systems. A 'lossy' or compressed image file format.

KERNEL

The core computer code in an application or operating system that controls how it looks and works.

KEYBOARD MAP

Keyboard character and function assignments, controlled by small driver program, accessed from the Keyboard icon (Language tab) in Control Panel.

KEYBOARD SHORTCUT

A simple and ideally memorable sequence of two or three keystrokes, used to invoke a frequently used action or activity within a program or application.

KEY CAPS

Press-fit embossed key tops on a PC keyboard.

KEYS

Data held in the Registry containing values, settings and preferences for the various programs stored on a PC.

KEYWORDS

Words or phrases that elicit a programmed response from a software application.

LAN

Local Area Network – a computer network where all the PCs are physically close to one another in the same room, office or building.

LAPLINK

Easy-to-use program that enables the transfer of large files between desktop PCs and PCs and laptops, via a simple cable link see: http://www.laplink.com/

LASERDISK

Now virtually obsolete, the limited storage capacity of the LP-sized disks meant films had to be recorded on both sides of the disk or on two disks.

LCD

Liquid crystal display – flat panel display used on laptop and portable PCs and now available for desktop machines. LCD monitors consume far less power than CRTs and generate no harmful emissions. The image is made up of tens of thousands of picture elements or 'pixels' that can be switched on and off to control the passage of light.

LINE INPUT

Low impedance analogue audio input connection on a PC – usually a 3.5mm stereo minijack socket – suitable for connection to audio devices like tape recorders and hi-fi systems.

LOG FILE

A record of the name and location of all the files stored on the hard disk, and any alterations made to other files during software installation.

MACHINE CODE

The basic language of computers, usually a form of binary code, where instructions are represented by groups of 'ones' and 'zeros'.

MACRO

Simple programming function in Word (and many other programs) used to automate frequently used commands and functions.

MAILBOX

Storage space on an ISP's server computer where incoming email messages are stored prior to them being downloaded and read on your PC.

MAIL MERGE

Word facility to help automate the process of printing form letters, envelopes and address labels.

MAINFRAME

Large and powerful computer, the earliest machines often occupied several air-conditioned rooms and had to be tended by teams of technicians.

MARK AS UNREAD

Unread messages in Outlook Express are marked in bold type, read messages can be marked as unread using the right click context menu.

MEASUREMENT UNITS

The ruler at the top of the Word page can be configured in inches, centimetres, points or picas. From Options on the Tools menu, select the General tab.

MEGAPIXEL

As near as makes no difference one million pixels or picture elements.

MEMORY CARD

Removable non-volatile (i.e., information is retained when power is removed) memory module used to store data – typically images and sounds – in portable devices like digital cameras and MP3 music players.

MESSAGE COMPACTING

Facility in Outlook Express to reduce the amount of disk space wasted by email messages.

MESSAGE RULES

A facility in Outlook Express that automatically ignores or disposes of email messages from nominated addresses/senders.

MIME

Multipurpose Internet Mail Extensions, a widely used system for converting non-text files and information – images, HTML commands, etc. – to and from plain text so it can be sent as email.

MIRROR SITE

A website containing a duplicate set of archives or data – usually geographically distant to the parent site – to help relieve strain on busy sites and net infrastructure.

MMC

MultiMedia Card, postage-stamp sized memory card used in digital cameras and MP3 music players.

MODEM

MOdulator/DEModulator, a device that converts digital signals coming from your PC into audible tones that can be sent via a conventional telephone line.

MODEM COMMANDS
Instructions issued by the PC to tell the modem to do things like open the line and dial a number.

MOTHERBOARD
The main printed circuit board inside a PC, containing the main processor chip (Pentium, etc.) memory chips (RAM) and plug-in expansion cards or 'daughter' boards.

MOVIE CLIPS
Short low-resolution video sequences can be 'attached' to an email message, however, the image is generally small, jerky and of relatively poor quality.

MP3
Motion Picture Experts Group audio layer 3 – digital audio compression system commonly used to send files containing audio and music over the Internet.

MPEG-2
Moving Pictures Expert Group – MPEG-2 is one of a set of technical standards for compressing video into digital data; picture quality is at least as good as normal broadcast TV.

MS-DOS
Microsoft Disk Operating System, a program, using text-based commands that works beside Windows to control the way disk drives handle and process information.

MULTI-GIGABYTE DRIVE
Very large hard disk drives are needed to store digital video information. Footage shot on a typical digital camcorder typically consumes around 3.6 megabytes of disk space per second!

NAG SCREEN
A window or display that appears when a program has started to remind the user to pay a registration fee or indicate how many days of the trial period remain.

NEWSGROUP

Public notice boards on the Internet where like-minded net users can post email messages, articles or announcements for others to read and respond to.

NICAM

Near Instantaneously Companded Audio Multiplexing, since you ask. The digital stereo TV sound system used by UK TV broadcasters.

NODE

A 'location' in a network, either a computer or a peripheral device, with its own unique address.

NON-VOLATILE MEMORY

A memory chip that retains data when the power supply is removed.

NULL MODEM

Type of serial communications cable, configured for two-way data transfer between a PC and a modem, or two PCs. A spreadsheet table is divided into boxes or cells, each of which is assigned a unique identity code. A cell can contain a mixture of text, numbers and mathematical formulae.

NUMBER FORMAT

A set of styles that decide how numbers, symbols and mathematical expressions are presented.

OCR

Optical Character Recognition – converting the scanned image of a document into a text file that can be read by a word processor.

OFFICE ASSISTANT

Help feature in Word where a 'friendly' cartoon character pops up and tells you how to do things. For example typing 'Dear Sir' will bring up advice on how to write a letter.

OHM

Unit of electrical resistance.

ON-SCREEN KEYBOARD

A virtual keyboard where characters are selected using a mouse pointer or other means, such as voice control or movement.

OPERATING SYSTEM

A collection of programs, such as Windows 95, 98 and DOS (disk operating system) which manage all your PC's resources – RAM memory, disk-drive, display screen, etc. – and controls how files are stored and retrieved.

ORDINAL

The subscript or superscript 'st', 'nd', 'rd', etc., after a number, i.e., 1st, 2nd, 3rd, and so on.

OSR2

Original equipment manufacturer Service Release 2, the later version of Windows 95 supplied to PC manufacturers, incorporating many of the features of Windows 98 (including FAT 32). This was not sold separately by Microsoft but it is widely available from 'friendly' dealers and through ads in computer magazines.

OVERTYPE

Typing a letter or character replaces the character or space next to it.

PACKET

Data travelling around the Internet is chopped up by the server computers and sent in brief bursts or packets, to be reassembled by the software on the end-user's PC.

PAPER PATH

The rollers and guides inside a printer through which sheets of paper pass.

PAPER WEIGHT

Paper weight and thickness of paper is measured in grams per square metre (gsm). Ordinary copier/printing paper is normally between 80 and 85gsm; lightweight card is in the range 200 to 300gsm.

PARALLEL PORT

One of the rear panel connections on your PC (or laptop) usually used by printers and scanners. Data is transferred relatively quickly 4 or 8 bits at a time.

PARTITION

Dividing a large disk drive up into partitions or virtual drives gets around capacity limitations imposed by an operating system or the drive's own control system.

PATCH

A program or file intended to fix or work around a problem in a software application.

PATH

The location of a file or program on a hard disk, e.g., to specify the file that starts Microsoft Word the path might be: C:\Program Files\Microsoft Office\Office\Winword.exe

PC-CARD ADAPTOR

Credit card sized modules (but a little thicker) used in laptops for modems, memory expansion and other peripherals. Adaptor modules have slots for memory cards.

PCI

Peripheral Component Interconnect – high-speed connector and control system, used on most recent PCs, also used for sound, video, adaptor cards.

PCMCIA

Personal Computer Memory Card International Association. Body responsible for PC card standards. PC cards are credit card sized modules (but a little thicker) used in laptops for modems, memory expansion and other peripherals.

PCN

Personal Communications Network (aka GSM 1800) digital cellular telephone system used by Orange, T-Mobile and Virgin in the UK and more than 100 other countries.

PERSONAL PASSWORD

The password chosen by you, or issued to you when you opened your Internet and email account.

PHOTOREALISTIC

Printing technology that produces high-quality prints on specially coated paper that in some cases are almost impossible to distinguish from normal photographic prints.

PHOTO VIEWER

Program that allows you to view the contents of folders containing image files, usually as small 'thumbnails', which can then be displayed full size.

PIXEL

Picture-Element, a single dot in a digitally generated image or display. The greater the number of pixels the greater the amount of detail.

PLATEN

The glass plate on a flatbed scanner on to which documents are placed.

PLUG-IN

A data file that extends the capability or adds extra features to a program or application.

POP3 & SMTP ADDRESSES

Post Office Protocol & Simple Mail Transfer Protocol, systems used to move email messages around the Internet and inside your PC. ISPs assign separate email addresses to handle incoming (POP3) and outgoing (SMTP) mail messages.

POWER DENSITY

The amount of energy a battery can store in relation to its physical size and weight.

POWER MANAGEMENT

Windows utilities that help to reduce power consumption by switching off components when they are not being used. It can be disabled by clicking on the Power Management icon in Control Panel (Start > Settings, or Control Panel icon in My Computer).

POWER PROFILE

Power management settings for your PC, accessed via the Power icon in Control Panel.

POWER SUPPLY MODULE

The power supply module converts mains electricity into low-voltage DC, needed by the motherboard and disk drives. It's normally housed inside a metal box, fitted with a cooling fan, attached to the back of the case or system unit.

PREVIEW PANE

Facility in Outlook Express to open and display automatically the contents of an email message, which can be dangerous if the message contains a virus.

PRINT HEAD

Device that squirts microscopic droplets of ink onto the paper as the print head passes over the paper.

PROFILE

Windows facility (see Passwords in Control Panel) that allows several users to share a PC, setting up their own custom preferences and desktop settings.

PROTOCOL

A set of rules for controlling the way data is sent over PC networks and the Internet.

PROXY

A program that acts as a go-between, allowing PCs connected to a network to send and receive data from the Internet.

QIC

Quarter Inch Committee; standards organisation responsible for devising data.

RAM

Random Access Memory, a computer's working memory, where programs store data and information when they are running.

RED-EYE

Demonic effect, giving people (and animals) bright red (or green) pupils, caused by camera flash reflecting back from the subject's retina.

REFRESH RATE

Like a TV picture, the display on a PC monitor is 'redrawn' many times each second but our eyes and brain perceive it as a single continuous image. If the image is redrawn less than 75 times a second some people may perceive a slight flicker.

REGISTRY

A large, constantly changing file in Windows 95/98 and ME containing details of how your PC is set up and configuration information for all the programs stored on the hard disk.

REN

Ringer Equivalence Number – all devices (modems, fax machines, answering machines, etc.) that can be connected to the public switched telephone network (PSTN) are required to have a REN number. This determines how many other devices can be connected to the same line. Most phone lines can support a REN of 4. If it is any higher some devices may not function correctly.

RENDER

Process in desktop video editing where effects and transitions are generated by the editing software and added to clips.

RESOLUTION

A measure of how much fine detail a video screen can display. To change the setting on a Windows PC go to Start > Settings > Control Panel, select the Display icon and the Settings tab.

RESPONSE BOX

A blank area or box on a form for text or data entry.

RIBBON CABLE

Flat multi-way cable, used inside a PC to connect disk drives to the main motherboard or plug-in controller cards.

RIP

Extract tracks from an audio CD, so they can be re-recorded or converted to other audio formats, like MP3.

ROM/PROM/EPROM

Read Only Memory/Programmable Read only Memory/Erasable Programmable Read only Memory; a 'non-volatile' memory chip that retains information when the power is removed. Information in ROMs and PROMs is fixed whilst an EPROM can be re-programmed with new data.

RTFM

Read The Flipping Manual (or something very similar...)

RULES

A set of conditions, decided on by the user that state how email messages are processed. Emails from a particular person or address might be routed to a separate folder or 'flagged' with an on-screen indicator. Junk email from a nominated address or containing a specified keyword can be sent straight to the waste bin.

SAFE MODE

Special Windows diagnostic mode used to help trace faults by loading a minimum configuration, avoiding sometimes-troublesome start-up files and drivers.

SCANDISK

Windows utility that checks the integrity of data stored on a hard disk drive, identifies problems, and where possible, puts them right. (Click Start > Programs > Accessories >System Tools).

SCANNER

Device attached to a computer that converts a photograph or image into digital data, stored on the PC as an image file.

SCREEN GRAB

A snapshot of the PC's video display, copied to the Windows Clipboard as a bitmap file. Pressing PrintScreen captures the whole screen, Alt + PrintScreen grabs just the active window.

SCROLL BAR FOCUS

The moving slider or box in a horizontal or vertical scroll bar that shows which part of a long list or large document or page is currently in view.

SDRAM

Synchronous dynamic random access memory, another family of memory chips that allows data to be accessed at higher speeds.

SEARCH ENGINE

Internet sites that seek out information, by topic, keyword or name. Good places to start a name search are: www.google.com, www.yahoo.com, www.lycos.com and www.altavista.com.

SEARCH FIELD

The space in a search engine where you type in keywords, a short phrase or question.

SELF-EXTRACTING

A compressed program or file that contains its own 'unzip' utility.

SERIAL PORT

Most PCs have two serial ports. One may be used by the mouse, the other by an external modem and other peripherals. Data is transferred relatively slowly, one bit at a time.

SERVER

Fast, powerful computers with vast storage capacity, used to communicate and share data with other computers connected to local or large-scale networks.

SHAREWARE

Software programs that you can try, before you buy. If you decide to use it you are obliged to send a payment to the author or publisher. Some programs are automatically disabled when the trial period has expired.

SHRED

Simply deleting files in Windows doesn't remove them from the hard disk, the space they occupy is simply marked as available and they can still be retrieved. Shredding removes all traces of deleted files by overwriting them with random or meaningless data.

SIMM

Single in-line memory module, with 30 or 72 connecting pins.

SIZING HANDLES

Highlights – usually small black squares around the edge of a graphic object or picture – that can be used to change its size and shape by clicking and dragging the mouse pointer.

SKIN

Essentially, the visual appearance of a computer program – the cosmetics, colour, shape and layout of graphical elements like buttons, menus and dialogue boxes, etc. A growing number of programs allow the skin to be changed – like the cover of a mobile phone – to reflect the user's mood or personality.

SMTP

Simple Mail Transfer Protocol – system used to move email messages around the Internet.

SNAPSHOT

A compilation of data and statistics about your PC including details of the operating system, memory resources and status and running programs.

SOCKET TESTER

Device that plugs into a normal mains socket and checks the status of the wiring.

SOHO

Small Office, Home Office, a category of PC peripherals and office equipment designed for light to medium workloads.

SOUND CARD

A more or less standard fitment on modern desktop PCs, generating the sounds and music heard through the PC's speakers. Most sound cards also have a microphone input, necessary for voice recognition.

SPIKES, SURGES AND TRANSIENTS

Brief increases in mains voltage, varying from a few volts to several thousand volts.

SPLASH SCREEN

An image or logo that appears on a PC screen whilst a program is loading.

SPOOL

Simultaneous Peripheral Operations On-Line; a way of maximising PC and printer efficiency. Information to be printed is transferred to a temporary file, enabling the PC to get on with other jobs and carry on printing when it has a moment to spare.

SPYWARE

Program, usually put onto your PC after visiting a website, that makes use of your Internet connection without your knowledge or permission to send data back to its parent site.

SSL

Secure Sockets Layer, a powerful encryption system used to send data and information, like credit card details, over the Internet.

STANDBY

PCs with motherboards that support the Standby function, switch to a low power mode when the standby function is engaged. A variety of actions, including mouse clicks, key presses, or signals from the modem wakes up the PC.

STARTUP FOLDER

Folder containing programs that load automatically after Windows.

STREAMING

Technique used to send sound and pictures over the Internet. Data is 'buffered' or stored in a temporary memory by player software on the PC to minimise the interruptions that would otherwise occur as data on the net is sent in chunks or 'packets'.

SURGES AND SPIKES

Potentially damaging high-voltage transients carried on the mains supply and on telephone lines.

SWITCH

An extra instruction (or instructions) added to the end of a DOS command.

SYSTEM FILES

Important files that configure Windows during boot up, telling the operating system what settings to use, what software is loaded and the hardware or peripherals attached to the PC.

SYSTEM FONTS

Fonts used by Windows and other core programs found on most PCs.

SYSTEM TRAY

Area on the far right of the Windows Taskbar reserved for running applications, frequently used utilities and the desktop clock.

TAPE DRIVE

Data backup systems that store huge amounts of data on magnetic tape, stored in small cassettes.

TCP/IP

Transmission Control Protocol/Internet Protocol, the common language of the Internet that allows computer networks – even if they are technically very different – to communicate with one another.

TEMP FILES

Temporary files, ending in .tmp are created by Windows and other programs and normally deleted automatically though some will remain if Windows crashes or is not shut down properly.

TEMPLATE

A ready-prepared document or layout that can be easily modified or personalised by changing sample text and graphics.

THREAD

Messages in a newsgroup, forum or on a bulletin board linked by a common theme.

THUMBNAIL PREVIEW

Reduced-sized image, quicker to load and display and cuts down on memory resources.

TIFF
Tagged Image Format File – lossless 'bitmapped' picture file format that describes in detail the attributes of each pixel in a digital image.

TIMECODE
Unique code assigned to each frame of a video movie, enabling edit controllers to make 'frame-accurate' cuts and joins between scenes.

TIME-LIMITED
Programs with a built-in time switch, which will stop it functioning after a pre-set period – usually 30 days – after it was installed.

TLD
Top Level Domain – the part of a website address, after the second or third 'dot', that denotes the site owner's status (i.e., .com for commercial entity, .org for non-profit-making organisations like charities, etc.) or country where the site is based (.uk for UK, .fr for France, etc.).

TOOLBARS
The menus and icons at the top of the Word desktop.

TOOLS
Small programs or applications that modify or change the way things work or happen on a PC.

TOP-UP CHARGING
Charging a rechargeable battery before it has been completely drained. Some battery types (i.e., nicads), develop a 'memory' or 'cell imbalance' that over time prevents them from retaining a full charge.

TRACKBALL
A kind of upside-down mouse, where screen pointer movement is controlled by moving a large ball.

TRACKPAD
Pressure-sensitive pad that moves the mouse pointer around the screen with light finger movements.

TRANSCEIVER
Combined transmitter-receiver.

TRANSITION
The changeover point in an edited video recording or movie from one scene to the next, i.e., 'cut', 'wipe', 'mix' or 'fade'.

TRIAL/DEMO PROGRAMS
Programs distributed by software manufacturers that allow potential users to try before they buy. Some key functions may be disabled or the program is time-limited and will stop working after the trial period. Trial programs can usually be unlocked with a 'key' issued by the manufacturer, who will also provide support and updates, when the program has been purchased.

TROJAN
Hidden program on a PC, usually installed surreptitiously or by an email attachment that allows an external 'client' PC to access files stored on the hard disk drive when it is connected to the Internet or a network.

TWEAK UI
Unsupported Microsoft utility program for making detailed changes to the way Windows looks and behaves by editing the Registry.

UNINSTALLER
A program removal utility included with a lot of Windows software; programs with uninstallers are usually (but not always) listed in Add/Remove Programs in Control Panel.

UNLOCK CODE
Shareware that is time-limited or has restricted functionality can be fully enabled with an unlock code, sent to the user by email from the author or publisher once they have received the appropriate fee – usually by on-line credit card payment.

UPS
Uninterruptible Power Supply – battery power unit, designed to keep your PC working during a power cut, to prevent data loss and to enable it to be safely shut down.

URL

Uniform Resource Locator – a standard Internet address e.g.: http://www.telegraph.co.uk

USB

Universal Serial Bus, high-speed industry standard connection system for peripherals including monitors, modems, joysticks, printers, etc., that does away with confusing technicalities and allows 'hot swaps', allowing connection and disconnection with the PC switched on.

USENET

A network of server computers used to distribute the 'official' Newsgroups on the Internet.

VA

Volt-Ampere, a measure of electricity supply and generation. You can work out the required capacity of a UPS by adding up the power consumption figures (RMS values measured in watts) of your PC monitor, etc., into a VA figure by multiplying it by 1.414.

VDU

Visual display unit – old name for a computer monitor.

VGA

Video Graphics Array – standard display format used on PCs, typically made up of 640 x 400 pixels and 256 colours. Small programs that tell Windows how to communicate with internal hardware – such as disk drives – and peripherals like printers, scanners, etc.

VIDEO CAPTURE CARD

PC expansion card that converts analogue video – from a camcorder, TV tuner, VCR, etc. – into digital data that can be processed on a PC. Some cards also convert PC video back to analogue, for recording on a VCR or display on a TV. Digital video capture cards are also available for digital camcorders with FireWire digital video connections.

VIEWER

A program that allows a file to be read or displayed though not changed.

VIRUS SIGNATURE

A distinctive section of code within a virus program that scanner software uses to identify them.

VISUALBASIC AND WORDBASIC

Text-based programming languages used to create macros.

VOICE SYNTHESISER

Software that converts text – including menu options and commands – appearing on the PC screen into speech.

WAP

Wireless Application Protocol – new generation of Internet compatible digital mobile phones capable of sending and receiving email messages.

WAV

Short for waveform; the file extension .wav denotes digital sound files used by Windows and most Windows games and applications.

WEB CAM

A small video camera that plugs into your PC. Most budget models use the universal serial bus (USB) port.

WEB HOST

Company providing disk space on its server computer for a website, most Internet Service Providers allocate a small amount of free web space for their subscribers (typically 10 to 20Mb) larger amounts of space generally have to be paid for.

WEB MAIL

Email messages can be sent to and from websites, bypassing the need for special software.

WET CLEANERS

Disk drive cleaners that use a liquid agent (usually isopropyl alcohol) to remove dirt and dust from the read/write heads or laser pickups.

WHITE BALANCE

Colour correction system used in electronic cameras to compensate for different types of lighting conditions.

WHITEBOARD

Facility in NetMeeting that opens a blank page that you can write or sketch on and is immediately seen on your contact's screen.

WILDCARD

A wildcard is an asterisk '*' which in PC language means literally anything. In this context a wildcard in place of the first part of an Internet address – i.e., *.com – signifies all addresses ending in .com

WINDOWS NT

Windows New Technology, highly stable but less well featured version of the Windows operating system, designed for critical business and network applications.

WIND ROAR

Literally a loud roaring sound, caused by wind blowing against the microphone.

WIRELESS NETWORK

Short-range two-way communications systems for PC, providing the same kind of speed and functionality as a cabled network, but without the wires.

WIRELESS SUPPORT

Automatic configuration for wireless networking systems.

WIZARD

Simple helper program that automatically starts when you begin a task.

WORDBASIC

Simple text-based programming language used by Word to control various behind-the-scenes functions and features. (BASIC = beginners all-purpose symbolic Instruction code.)

WORM

A type of virus, usually hidden inside another program, designed to penetrate a computer's operating system. Once activated it is programmed to replicate and attach itself to other programs or emails.

WRITE PROTECTION SWITCH

Mechanical device – usually a simple slide switch – that indicates that the data on the card is protected and cannot be over-written.

WRITING SPEED

Current norms are 300 and 600 kilobits/second or ×2 and ×4 'normal' speed. Faster (and dearer) drives can achieve speeds of ×8 and ×12.

ZIP

Type of compressed file, requires special program (Pkunzip, WinZip, etc.) to expand or decompress the file.

Index